The Power of Large Numbers

THE POWER OF LARGE NUMBERS

POPULATION, POLITICS, AND GENDER IN NINETEENTH-CENTURY FRANCE

JOSHUA COLE

CORNELL UNIVERSITY PRESS

ITHACA AND LONDON

Copyright © 2000 by Cornell University

First published 2000 by Cornell University Press

Printed in the United States of America

Library of Congress Cataloging-in-Publication Data

Cole, Joshua, 1961–
    The power of large numbers : population, politics, and gender in nineteenth-century France / Joshua Cole.
        p.   cm.
    Includes bibliographical references and index.
    ISBN 0-8014-3701-6 (cloth)
        1. France—Population policy—History—19th century.   2. France—Population—History—19th century.   3. Statistics—France—History—19th century.   I. Title.
    HB3593.C614 2000
    304.6'0944'09034—dc21   99-046229

Cornell University Press strives to use environmentally responsible suppliers and materials to the fullest extent possible in the publishing of its books. Such materials include vegetable-based, low-VOC inks and acid-free papers that are recycled, totally chlorine-free, or partly composed of nonwood fibers. Books that bear the logo of the FSC (Forest Stewardship Council) use paper taken from forests that have been inspected and certified as meeting the highest standard for environmental and social responsibility.
For further information, visit our website at www.cornellpress.cornell.edu.

Cloth printing   10 9 8 7 6 5 4 3 2 1

CONTENTS

ACKNOWLEDGMENTS

Grants and fellowships from the Council for European Studies, the French government's Chateaubriand program, the Mellon Foundation, the Social Science Research Council, the National Endowment for the Humanities, and the University of Georgia made the research for this book possible. I am grateful for the support given by these institutions. I thank the editors and anonymous readers of Cornell University Press for their help in bringing the manuscript to the light of day. Chapter 5 appeared in *The Journal of Family History* vol. 21, no. 4 (1996) and is reprinted by permission of Sage Publications Inc. Chapter 6 appeared in *French Historical Studies* vol. 19 no. 3 (Spring 1996) copyright © 1996 Society for French Historical Studies.

I owe a tremendous debt to Susanna Barrows at the University of California, Berkeley, who first encouraged me to think about the depopulation debates in France and who patiently guided my work in this area. Susanna's seminar was my introduction to nineteenth-century France, and ever since leaving Berkeley I have been trying to reestablish in my own classes that combination of rigorous questioning and community endeavor that characterized our discussions with her. At Berkeley, I also learned a great deal from Lynn Hunt and Thomas Laqueur, whose work and teachings are still models for me today. Perhaps the best part of my graduate education was association with a marvelous cohort of scholars-in-the-making, both in Berkeley and in Paris, who offered their help: Andrew Aisenberg, David Barnes, Marjorie Beale, Ian Burney, Sarah Farmer, Paul Friedland, Jennifer Jones, Sheryl Kroen, Catherine Kudlick, Rene Marion, Thomas Pepper, Tip Ragan, Jeffrey Ravel, Dan Sherman,

Regina Sweeney, Vanessa Schwartz, Matthew Truesdell, Jeffrey Verhey, and Susan Whitney. I owe special debts to Sylvia Schafer and Lou Roberts, who generously shared their ideas and research with me on many occasions.

While working on another project, Jay Winter, Jean-Louis Robert, and Catherine Rollet taught me a great deal about demographic research, and the book has benefited from their influence. Rachel Fuchs helped me navigate the Archives de Paris and later encouraged me to develop Chapter 6 into an article. Alain Corbin read and commented on my initial proposal, and Paul-André Rosental guided me through the sources available in France for research into the history of population questions. Libby Schweber gave me the benefit of her tremendous knowledge of French population research, Catherine Rollet shared with me her remarkable thesis on infant welfare policies in the Third Republic, and Elinor Accampo drew my attention to her important work on Nelly Roussel, Paul Robin, and Manuel Devaldès. Kirstie McClure, Patricia O'Brien, and Ann-Louise Shapiro commented constructively on papers arising from this work at the Society for French Historical Studies and the History of Science Association meetings. Oto Luthar invited me to Slovenia to present Chapter 5 to the Historical Seminar at the University of Ljubljana, and he and his wife, Breda, were marvelous hosts.

I finished the book at the University of Georgia, where I have enjoyed the company of an exceptionally generous community of scholars and friends. Monica Chojnacka, Michael Kwass, Laura Mason, Miranda Pollard, Chris Rassmussen, David Schoenbrun, Bryant Simon, and Eve Troutt Powell have all read parts of the manuscript and offered their criticisms and encouragement. Ann Marie Reardon has not read the manuscript, but she has listened to me talk about it so much on our runs through Athens that I'm sure she feels as though she has.

In the last year, Judith Coffin, Peter Hoffer, Lynn Hunt, Joan Scott, and Simon Szreter read the entire manuscript, and I thank them for their comments, which both saved me from several embarrassing errors of fact and helped clarify my argument in several key sections. Of all of my teachers, Joan Scott has shaped my scholarship the most, and this book owes its greatest material and intellectual debts to her. Ever since she directed my undergraduate thesis in 1983 she has been a constant support of my work, offering advice, criticism, and, most generously, her time.

I dedicate this book to my family. My mother, Susan Cole, has always been my role model as a historian and as a teacher. Her scholarly obsessions and cheerful curiosity about the world are matched only by her indignation at what's wrong with it. My father, Brock Cole, taught me to take writing seriously and when and how to take naps. My brother, Toby, has shared more of this project than most siblings would or should tolerate. Finally, Kate Tremel married me as I was finishing this book. I can't think of a better ending than that.

JOSHUA COLE

Athens, Georgia

ABBREVIATIONS

AAP   Archives de l'Assistance Publique
AdP   Archives de Paris
AN   Archives Nationales
APP   Archives de la Préfecture de Police
BARM   *Bulletin de l'Académie royale de médecine,* v. 1 (1836–37)
RSVP   *Recherches statistiques sur la ville de Paris et le département de la Seine*

The Power of Large Numbers

INTRODUCTION

The Power Of Large Numbers

The belief that a strong and vigorous nation requires a large population has a peculiar history in modern France. Before the Revolution of 1789, royal administrators justified population growth, territorial expansion, and colonial conquest by equating numbers of people with wealth. This assumption became more difficult to maintain during the turbulent first half of the nineteenth century. Between 1800 and 1850, Paris doubled in size from half a million to a million people, and this growth was accompanied by violent revolutions in 1830 and 1848. Influential political economists looked at the poor, illiterate, and often angry crowds filling French cities and reconsidered their enthusiasm for population growth. The tide of opinion shifted again in the 1860s, when some of these same economists noted population declines in rural areas, and the Malthusian warnings of overpopulation that had been so common in the 1840s were heard less frequently. After the French defeat in the Franco-Prussian War of 1870, widespread fears of cultural and national degeneration led many public figures to call once more for increases in the number of births.

These changes in attitudes toward population growth in France took place against the background of another development: the emergence of statistics as a new language for describing the population, its composition, behavior, and vital characteristics. Compiled for the first time in regularly published official tables, population statistics revealed unsuspected patterns and consistencies in the apparently chaotic complexity of social life. Inevitably, this new knowledge about the dynamics of population transformed the nature of political, social, and economic debate in the nineteenth century. The most pressing concerns of the French nation—the benefits of economic development, the causes of revolution, the need for social reform, the nature of citizenship, and the proper relationship between state and society—all were more or less recast by the language of number. This power of numbers to represent the life and death of the French and, in so doing, to transform the process by which social reformers justified their proposals in nineteenth-century France is the subject of this book.

The French preoccupation with population is both comparable to and different from parallel developments in other European countries. The most significant difference arises from the unique position occupied by the French in what historians have come to call "the demographic transition."[1] This transformation, which began in Europe in the late eighteenth century and continued through the first half of the twentieth, was characterized by substantial declines in mortality and fertility rates, as people began to live longer and restrict their family size. No single pattern or sequence of factors seems to explain this transition in all areas where it has been recorded, but it was usually accompanied by industrial development, immigration from rural areas to cities, and widespread changes both in family organization and in attitudes toward marriage and sexuality. For reasons that demographers have yet to explain completely, the French experience differed markedly from that of their European neighbors. In other countries, the decline in mortality preceded the decline in fertility by several generations. A period of rapid population growth followed throughout much of Europe until fertility declines began to slow the rate of expansion in the twentieth century. In France, however, the mortality and fertility declines began almost simultaneously at the end of the eighteenth century, so that for the next hundred years French population growth was very slow.

These trends were not immediately apparent in the first half of the nineteenth century, but even if they had been, most social observers would probably have welcomed any evidence of slow population growth. During these years, French attitudes toward such questions were heavily influenced by Thomas Malthus's *Essay on the Principle of Population* (1798), first translated into French in 1809. Malthus drew a much more somber picture than that traced by his more optimistic eighteenth-century pre-

---

1. On the demographic transition see Ansley J. Coale and Susan Watkins, *The Decline of Fertility in Europe* (Princeton, 1986); Etienne Van de Walle, "La Fécondité française au XIXe siècle," *Communications* 44 (1986): 35–45; and Jacques Dupâquier, ed., *Histoire de la population française*, vol. 3, *De 1789 à 1914* (Paris, 1988), esp. pp. 351–78. Two indispensable sources on French reactions to these trends are Joseph J. Spengler, *France Faces Depopulation* (Durham, 1979), and Yves Charbit, *Du malthusianisme au populationisme* (Paris, 1981). For an excellent treatment of the historical literature on the demographic transition, see Simon Szreter, *Fertility, Class and Gender in Britain, 1860–1940* (Cambridge, 1996), esp. Part I, "Historiographical Introduction: A Genealogy of Approaches," pp. 7–66.

decessors. Rejecting the liberals' facile faith in progress, Malthus claimed that populations always increased faster than the food supply. If individuals did not limit the size of their families, he argued, the poor paid the price of continued expansion in increased misery, hunger, and death. Convinced by Malthus's work, the first generation of postrevolutionary liberal political economists in France looked for signs of restraint among the working populations and waxed indignant at any evidence of sexual promiscuity.

The political economist's conclusions on the destabilizing tendencies of population growth were reinforced by the expanding mass of empirical information available to social observers in the early decades of the nineteenth century. In 1802 the prefect of police in Paris established both the Conseil de salubrité and the Conseil permanente chargé d'hygiène publique. These committees published an average of five hundred reports a year between 1802 and 1848 on such diverse topics as drinking water, factories, epidemics, cemeteries, slaughterhouses, and dissection rooms.[2] Much of these data documented in alarming detail the material hardship, the economic dislocation, and, by modern standards, the appalling physical state of the French population. Awareness of these facts became widespread in the 1820s, when the prefect of the Seine, Chabrol de Volvic, published the first extensive collection of Parisian population and economic statistics, a series that was continued intermittently until 1860.[3] In 1829 the first volume of the *Annales d'hygiène publique et de médecine légale* appeared, followed in the 1830s and 1840s by monumental works of sociological research by Adolphe d'Angeville, Louis-René Villermé, H. A. Frégier, and Alexandre Parent-Duchâtelet. These volumes, appearing against the background of revolution in 1830 and 1848 and serious cholera epidemics in 1832, 1849 and 1854, focused public attention on the population, emphasizing above all the sordid conditions of working-class life, public health, and problems of criminality.[4]

2. Bernard-Pierre Lécuyer and Jean-Noël Biraben, "L'Hygiène publique et la révolution pastorienne," in *Histoire de la population française*, ed. Jacques Dupâquier, vol. 3 (Paris, 1988), p. 324. See also D. B. Weiner, "Public Health under Napoleon: The Conseil de Salubrité de Paris, 1802–1815," *Clio Medica* 9 (1974): 3–30.
3. *RSVP*, 1821, 1823, 1826, 1829, 1844, 1860.
4. Adolphe d'Angeville, *Essai sur la statistique de la population française* (Bourg, 1836); Louis-René Villermé, *Tableau de l'état physique et morale des ouvriers employés dans les manufactures de coton, de laine, et de soie*, 2 vols. (Paris, 1840); H. A. Frégier, *Des classes dangereuses de la population dans les grandes villes et des moyens de les rendre meillures*, 2 vols. (Paris, 1840); Alexandre Parent-Duchâtelet, *Hygiène publique, ou Mémoires sur les questions les plus importantes de l'hygiène appliquée aux professions et aux travaux d'utilité publique* (Paris, 1836), and *De la prostitution dans la ville de Paris, considérée sous le rapport de l'hygiène publique, de la morale et de l'administration* (Paris, 1836). On the

Aware of this rapidly growing body of empirical research, many economists and population researchers actually welcomed the initial indications of fertility decline in the first half of the nineteenth century. Prominent French Malthusians such as Alfred Legoyt, director of the Statistique Générale de France (SGF) from 1852 to 1870, greeted the news with aplomb, even going so far as to congratulate the French for their foresight in spontaneously establishing an equilibrium between population and resources. Noting that this equilibrium was being imposed much more brutally by famine in Ireland and by emigration in parts of eastern Germany, Legoyt commented with satisfaction upon the evident restraint and prudence of the French working classes.[5]

The defeat of the French by the Prussians in 1870 caused Legoyt to lose his job as France's premier statistician, and this military humiliation famously brought the French to a different awareness of the costs of declining fertility. The specter of underpopulation, which had not aroused much concern since Montesquieu first warned of its effects in the eighteenth century, rose once more to the forefront of public consciousness. After 1870, senators and members of the Third Republic's National Assembly were nearly unanimous in their horror of depopulation, and politicians and publicists endlessly discussed measures to increase the birthrate in the decades leading up to World War I. Unlike the eighteenth century, however, when royal administrators encouraged population growth in any form, including foreign immigration and annexation of territory, late nineteenth-century natalists focused above all on increasing native fertility.[6] Put simply, *French* women were not having enough *French* babies. Although nationalist fears certainly played a part in this resurgent natalism during the first half of the Third Republic, other concerns are also evident in the literature on depopulation between 1870 and 1914. Above all, fin de siècle natalism expressed widely shared anxieties about women who chose not to conform to conventional standards of domestic care and motherhood. Like the Malthusians earlier in the century, natalists believed in an important link between the private realm of sexuality and childbirth and national well-being, but they drew the opposite conclusion from this linkage. The natalists called for larger families, not prudential restraint, but they nevertheless shared with their Malthusian

---

establishment of the *Annales d'hygiène publique*, see Bernard-Pierre Lécuyer, "Démographie, statistique et hygiène publique sous la monarchie censitaire," *Annales de démographie historique* (1977): 215–45.

5. Alfred Legoyt, "Du mouvement de la population en France d'après les dénombrements," *Journal des économistes* ser. 2, 13 (1857); see also Charbit, *Du malthusianisme au populationisme*, p. 28.

6. Hervé Le Bras, *Marianne et les lapins* (Paris, 1991), pp. 170–71.

predecessors a belief that a well-regulated family life was essential for a healthy France.

This book is about the relationship between the human sciences that first made these demographic transformations visible and parallel debates about the state's responsibility to understand, protect, and ensure the well-being of the population. These discussions, in which doctors, municipal officials, hygienists, and political economists participated, played an important role in shaping the institutions of what was to become the modern welfare state. Within this larger set of issues, I have chosen to concentrate on one particular theme: the connection between the new vision of population that emerged in the early years of the nineteenth century and the reconceptualization of the family and its place in the social order that took place in the decades leading up to World War I. I am interested in the shifting logic of population research across this period and the effects of these shifts on public attitudes toward families and the place of men and women in them. Such an approach demands a long view because the statistical portrait of population that became so ubiquitous in the nineteenth century had arisen first from the fertile imagination of the eighteenth-century Enlightenment.

THE ONE AND THE MANY

French thinkers were among the first to create an awareness of population as an object of study in the eighteenth century. Even before the Revolution of 1789 the centralized administration of the old regime provided an institutional framework for early experiments in census-taking and population research. Jean-Jacques Rousseau had put the matter most succinctly in *The Social Contract*, when he asked:

> What is the goal of political association? The preservation and the prosperity of its members. And what is the most certain sign that they preserve themselves and prosper? Their number and their population. No need to look elsewhere for this much disputed sign. All other things being equal, that government under which the citizens reproduce and multiply the most, without foreign means, without naturalizations, and without colonies, is infallibly the best: that [government] under which a people diminishes and perishes is the worst. Calculators, it is up to you: count, measure, compare.[7]

7. Jean-Jacques Rousseau, *Oeuvres complètes* (Paris, 1964), 3:419–20.

In many respects, of course, Rousseau was a most untypical Enlightenment thinker, but his ideas on population mirrored those of many innovative royal administrators in the decades before the Revolution of 1789.
The Revolution itself did little to interrupt the development of a regular
official accounting of population statistics in France. If anything, the experience of cataclysmic social unrest served to intensify official interest in
matters pertaining to the population. In 1801, the director of the newly
established Bureau de statistique at the French Ministry of the Interior
wrote to the nation's prefects: "Delve deeply and with care into all that
pertains to the population, no material is more deserving to fix the gaze
of an administrator."[8] Under Napoleon's system of prefectural government, officials made the first attempts to regularize the gathering of information about the population, and their practice of taking a census at
five-year intervals, begun in 1801, continued after the Restoration in 1814.
After 1820, so many statistics were published in Europe that the philosopher of science Ian Hacking has referred to the period as "the avalanche of printed numbers."[9] From the monarchy of the late eighteenth
century, through the revolutionary years of the 1790s and the first decades of the nineteenth century, population emerged as a central problem
for government.

Developments in the study of population and the growth of the French
state thus went hand in hand. Administrators in government service and
population researchers both sought for ways to make generalizations
based on the smallest of particulars, and both shared the desire to turn a
microscopic gaze toward the lives of individuals in the hopes of finding a
key to understanding (and controlling) the largest of agglomerations.
The population sciences were thus implicated in the classic problem of
political rule: the problem of the one and the many, or how effectively to
build a society that served collective interests while simultaneously granting room for individuals to pursue their own needs and desires. Solving
this dilemma in political terms was a major preoccupation of Enlightenment thought, and by the end of the eighteenth century the proponents
of empirical research into population questions believed that their work

8. Archives Nationales: F20 1, p. 19, letter from the Bureau de statistique to the prefect of Pas-
de-Calais, dated 12 frimaire, year IX (3 December 1800). For discussions of this early example of a
centralized statistical bureau, see Bertrand Gille, *Les Sources statistiques de l'histoire de France, les enquêtes du 17e siècle à 1870* (Paris, 1964), p. 121; Stuart Woolf, "Towards the History of the Origins
of Statistics: France, 1789–1815" in *State and Statistics in France, 1789–1815*, ed. Jean-Claude Perrot
and Stuart Woolf (Paris, 1984), pp. 113–23; Marie-Noëlle Bourguet, *Déchiffrer la France: La statistique départementale à l'époque napoléonienne* (Paris, 1989), pp. 53–87.
9. Ian Hacking, "Biopower and the Avalanche of Printed Numbers," *Humanities in Society* 5 (1982):
279. See also Hacking, *The Taming of Chance* (Cambridge, 1990), pp. 2–3.

would succeed in placing the exercise of political authority on a scientific footing.

One should not separate the history of population research into a scientific kernel and a political context, however; no clear distinction can be made between breakthroughs in a scientific domain and subsequent political applications of the resulting knowledge. In fact, this distinction between a pure population science and pure politics was a product of the historical developments that are the subject of this book. As administrators, statisticians, and population researchers searched for ways to legitimate their activities within the newly emergent institutional structures of the modern state, they negotiated a careful path between the twin goals of truth and raison d'état.

Michel Foucault laid out the grounds for analyzing this close connection between rationality and politics in his distinction between the totalizing and the individualizing tendencies of the human sciences after the eighteenth century. Foucault argued that the medical and statistical sciences of population, public health, and demography constituted a "great bipolar technology," divided between a "bio-politics of population" and an "anatamo-politics of the human body." [10] The latter focused on the individual body's mechanical functions, its organizational structures, and the principles of their preservation. The "bio-politics of population," in contrast, was a system for understanding and investigating a collective entity, the "species body." This new form of knowledge sought patterns within larger populations, such as mortality and fertility rates or the relationship between the number of inhabitants and the food supply. Foucault argued that these technologies together constituted a form of "pastoral" power which differed in fundamental ways from the political power traditionally ascribed to the state. Whereas political power functioned through legal categories and institutions that determined the status and rights of citizens in the polity, "pastoral" power made its presence known through a diverse range of discursive "practices" that focused on individuals and defined their existence in normative terms. Its role was to "constantly ensure, sustain, and improve the lives of each and every one." [11] In an effort to explore the various manifestations of this pastoral power, Foucault examined the many institutions, sciences, and practices that brought a specialized knowledge to bear on individual subjects: medicine and the

10. Michel Foucault, *The History of Sexuality* (New York, 1980), 1:139. See also his comments on the emergence of population as an economic and political problem, p. 25.
11. Michel Foucault, "Omnes et Singulatum: Towards a Criticism of 'Political Reason,'" in *The Tanner Lectures on Human Values*, ed. Sterling M. McMurrin (Salt Lake City, 1981), 2:235.

clinic, punishment and the prison, psychology and the asylum, pedagogy and the school.

As an analytic tool of the historian, Foucault's conception of "pastoral" power is simultaneously seductive, useful, and potentially misleading. Seductive, because it allows us to step outside the self-legitimating vocabulary of a liberal tradition in social science and political thought that has been inattentive to its own participation in the ideological defense of rigid and normative social hierarchies. Useful, because it allows us to make connections between parallel developments in a wide variety of fields, each of which contributed in some way to the elaborate process of describing populations, their composition, their development, and their history. Potentially misleading, however, because the resulting analysis can slip quickly into reductive or excessively monolithic characterizations of an extremely complex and at times even contradictory history. As I will show in subsequent chapters, the application of statistical methods to the study of population often became the subject of intense controversy, and these debates, far from being incidental to the construction of normative categories, shaped subsequent work on the population in important ways.

A fundamental debate revolved around the question of representation: what did statistics actually mean and could the significance attributed to them by their users be trusted? The defenders of statistics argued that only numbers could render the new social realm visible because only the language of figures, frequency, and average could hope to impose order on the apparently limitless complexity of human activities.[12] By their very nature, however, statistics challenged other forms of social description, especially those that relied on textual representations. The remarkable *Recherches statistiques sur la ville de Paris*, produced in the 1820s under the authority of the prefect of the Seine, the comte Chabrol de Volvic, are a case in point. These immense volumes contained hardly any conventional text aside from the introductory essays written by the mathematician Jean-Baptiste Fourier. Instead, Chabrol, Fourier, and their collaborators chose to present the statistical information with little explanation. The prefecture's archivist, Frédéric Villot, wrote nothing for the series, although it was his painstaking work, more than that of anybody else, that made possible the wide breadth of the first four volumes of the *Recherches*. In his introduction, Fourier made clear that this was a con-

12. As the historian William Coleman argued, "The logical progression from a commitment to social amelioration to the acceptance and exploitation of the numerical method was direct" (*Death Is a Social Disease: Public Health and Political Economy in Early Industrial France* [Madison, 1982], p. 125).

scious decision: "We have chosen the [numerical] table," he wrote, "because it is the most concise form of expression and because it is the best way to render easy comparisons.... The composition of tables has the advantage of excluding useless discussions; it reestablishes the principal goal of all research, which is the methodical enumeration of facts." [13] From the point of view of the administrator, then, the advantages of statistics lay in their ability to restrict the possible field of debate and to prevent any potentially distracting proliferation of opinions, speculations, counterexamples, or alternative views. Numbers allowed the administrator to have, quite literally, the last word.

Of course, the statistical table did not do away with a verbal language altogether. It merely subjected words to the regimented columnar discipline of the two-dimensional grid. Chabrol's *Recherches statistiques sur la ville de Paris* had no lack of words, but they appeared in the form of labels and lists, arranged along the top rows of each table and descending vertically along the left-hand side of every page. In Villot's tables from the nominative census of 1 March 1817, for example, the old medieval names of Parisian neighborhoods, with their colorful associations—Marais, Bonne-Nouvelle, Quartier du Roule, Quinze-Vingts—appeared in ascending numerical order according to *quartier* and arrondissement, as one column among twenty-four. The fashionable neighborhood of Saint-Germain found itself brushing up against such revolutionary hotbeds as the Faubourg Sainte-Antoine. Each district surrendered peacefully to the concerted gaze of the municipal statisticians, revealing its own proportions of inhabitants per household, age structure, number of invalids in the hospital, and causes of mortality.[14] In this new world of interchangeable juxtapositions, every comparison was potentially of interest, and distinctions that had previously been seen as purely qualitative—between noble and peasant, rich and poor, urban and rural, male and female— were shown to exhibit meaningful relationships that could be measured quantitatively.

This new knowledge demanded new institutions for managing information. As these institutions developed, the state gradually took on a new role, the collection and maintenance of a new kind of national memory. Armed with a statistical portrait of the nation, legislators and reformers looked for ways to influence the outcome of events while simultaneously avoiding the appearance of active intervention in the lives of individuals. Their task was to provide the nation with an objective tally sheet of its

13. *RSVP*, 1821, pp. iv–v.
14. *RSVP*, 1821, Table 3, "Etat de la population au 1er Mars 1817, *intra muros*," no page number.

progress and its setbacks. During the July Monarchy, the political economist F. F. de La Farelle asked, "What is the task of political economy and
what does it have to do with government? [We] must study the *facts*, examine the requirements of the situation, and protect or counter the movement of the population according to the necessity of *time* and *place*; [we]
must . . . make legislation and administration symptomatic." [15] In 1889,
the prominent geographer, demographer, and economist Emile Levasseur pointed to the same political function for this new science. "The
knowledge of social facts," wrote Levasseur, "is as necessary for the governing of society and for the study of science . . . as is the knowledge of a
commercial house's operations for the office of the director." [16] With the
end of the ancien régime, the metaphors of capitalist enterprise gradually
replaced the language of kingly rule. The measure of good government
became its ability to analyze risk and reduce the uncertainty and dangers
of daily existence at home, in the workplace, and in the public spaces of
the city and countryside.

The Emergence of the Social

The modern idea of "population" came into being as a part of an emergent epistemological domain: the universe of the "social." [17] Taken abstractly, the social domain can be seen as a discursive site for the elaboration of more or less coherent explanations of how societies are structured,
the place of individuals in them, and their development across time. Insisting on seeing the social domain as an element of discourse about society is simply a way of emphasizing that representations of populations—
whether in statistical publications or administrative reports—were much
more than transparent reflections of the complex ebb and flow of human
existence. They were powerful constructions of social realities that influenced the way officials and legislators interpreted the lives of the French
people.

Most important, the social realm emerged as the arena for exploring
the causal relationships that operated within populations. Such causal re-

15. F. F. de La Farelle, *Du progrès social au profit des classes populaires non indigentes* (Paris, 1847),
p. 103. Emphasis in the original.
16. Emile Levasseur, *La Population française*, 3 vols. (Paris, 1889), 1:5.
17. On the concept of the "social," see Jacques Donzelot, *L'Invention du social, essai sur le déclin des
passions politiques* (Paris, 1984); François Ewald, *L'Etat providence* (Paris, 1986); Mitchell Dean, *The
Constitution of Poverty: Toward a Genealogy of Liberal Governance* (London, 1991); and George
Steinmetz, *Regulating the Social: The Welfare State and Local Politics in Imperial Germany* (Princeton, 1993).

lationships could be internal, resulting from the activities of individual members of the population and their behavior toward one another; they could also be external, the result of environmental or historical influences. The idea that one could not only count inhabitants but measure the effects of both internal and external dynamics of population through quantitative analysis simply did not exist before the end of the seventeenth century in Europe. Early examples of such work in France included Antoine Déparcieux's *Essai sur les probabilités de la durée de la vie humaine* (1746), Louis Messance's *Recherches sur la population des généralités d'Auvergne, de Lyon, et de quelques provinces et villes du Royaume* (1766), and Jean-Baptiste Moheau's *Recherches et considérations sur la population de la France* (1778). Similar work from elsewhere in Europe included William Petty's *Political Arithmetick* (1690), Gottfried Achenwall's *Staatswissenschaft* (1749), and Johann Peter Süssmilch's *Die Göttliche Ordnung in den Veränderungen des menschlichen Geschlechts* (1741). Such investigations remained the province of a relatively small number of authors and readers until the end of the eighteenth century, however. Most eighteenth-century European states only intermittently attempted to gauge the size of their populations, and only after the beginning of the nineteenth century did population research become a regular activity of government.

After the Napoleonic wars ended in 1815, the combined effects of industrial development and political revolutions created wide public interest in population, leading to a veritable explosion of published works on the "social question." No issue did more to bring population research out of this relative obscurity than the poverty of the working classes. For liberals in the postrevolutionary period, poverty presented a paradoxical challenge. On the one hand, the very existence of large numbers of poor people confounded their argument that a free market would work to the benefit of all. On the other hand, liberalism's commitment to limited forms of government demanded that its supporters firmly oppose more radical demands for collective solutions to the problem of poverty. As Giovanna Procacci has argued, the notion of a "social" realm for official and philanthropic action emerged precisely as a result of this paradox: liberal reformers attempted to find ways of alleviating the inequalities of the emerging industrial economy without suggesting that the obligation to assist the poor should be inscribed in law or that such inequalities were a threat to the social order in themselves.[18]

Solving this political paradox required defining the parameters and logic of a new social domain in which philanthropic and official actions

---

18. Giovanna Procacci, *Gouverner la misère: La question sociale en France* (Paris, 1993), pp. 24–30.

would not be perceived as either coercive or intrusive. Instead, public and private reformers could present their activities as necessary measures to protect such "natural" national priorities as public health, the integrity of families, and the well-being of the working classes. Statistical analysis was essential to this process. Statistics provided the necessary portrait of coherent social aggregates whose collective lives were laid bare in the tables of the census. Within the tables themselves, the multiplication of social categories testified to the complexity of this process. Under the old regime, the realm had been divided into three estates, nobility, clergy, and the *troisième état*. Under the new regime of number, statistical tables exhibited a potentially infinite litany of aggregates: male workers, female workers, city dwellers, migrant laborers, the indigent, child laborers, abandoned children, and so forth. Statisticians had no sooner succeeded in unifying the three estates of the old regime into a coherent national population before they took to disassembling it once again according to the new rules of social reasoning.

The new tools of quantitative research also served to distinguish the "social" realm from older conceptions of the "political" or "economic." This process of epistemological *disaggregation* created a new vocabulary and terminology for describing the workings of society. In postrevolutionary France, the political domain was articulated in terms of the opposition between (male) citizens and the state, between a body politic and a sovereign power, which together formed a nation. The economic domain, in contrast, was constituted by relations of exchange between rational (male) individuals, whose public behavior followed a logic of calculation, competition, and enterprise oriented toward the acquisition of wealth. The "social" realm distinguished itself from the "political" and the "economic" by straddling many of the oppositions that distinguished one from the other, encompassing both public *and* private spaces, the activities of men *and* women, the effects of politics *and* commerce, the activities of both institutions *and* individuals. The social realm thus became a primary arena for examining the relationship between private decisions and public good, collective will and individual responsibility, and the various obligations that members of each aggregate group owed to the community as a whole.[19]

19. My argument here owes a great deal to the work of Mary Poovey on the social problem in Britain. Poovey wrote: "These two developments—the aggregation of distinct populations and the conceptual disaggregation of a social domain—were intimately connected, for identifying the problems that afflicted the nation involved isolating the offending populations, abstracting from individual cases the general problems they shared, and devising solutions that would not contradict the specific rationalities of those domains by which British social relations had traditionally been organized" (*Making a Social Body: British Cultural Formation, 1830–1864* [Chicago, 1995], p. 8).

In the early decades of the nineteenth century doctors, political economists, and government administrators undertook a broad range of scientific research into matters pertaining to the health and wealth of the population. The vast and heterogeneous body of work they produced was unified by a single theme: an impulse to assign rank and value to the vicissitudes of individual fortune, while simultaneously calculating the costs and responsibility for alleviating these uncertainties at the collective level. Consider the following statement from an 1836 report on the situation of indigent men and women in Paris, written by François Leuret, the secretary of a commission headed by several prominent doctors from the Ecole de médecine:

> If the poor were all men who had fallen from a superior position, and if by their work and their good conduct they were able to re-establish themselves . . . then it would be reasonable to regard their misfortune as the inevitable result of the hazards of commerce, the result of illness, or of fortuitous events that even the prudent could not have planned for, or of lack of planning, or dissipation, and laziness. But this is not the case. The majority are born in abject poverty, live amidst privation, and die before their time, and this perpetuates itself like the generations of kings, by the singular hazard of birth. This is a problem that must be resolved, because such a state of things cannot be inherent to society, since it is opposed to the perfection of man.[20]

Leuret's characterization of poverty accomplished several things. First, it established the "the singular hazard of birth" as the primal scene of the social order that imprinted the individual with both an origin and a destiny. His account made clear references to an *economic* realm of market forces—"the hazards of commerce." At the same time, his call for active intervention to remedy the problem situated poverty squarely within the realm of *politics*—and the linkage between the "generations of kings" and the "hazards of birth" was also an inescapable reference to the political hierarchies that had structured the ancien régime. The essence of his description, however, placed the poor in a larger *social* space whose inhabitants are subject to a worrying degree of chance and inconstancy. About some of these hazards, Leuret was a fatalist. It was acceptable that one might fail in a business enterprise, perhaps inevitable that one might be stricken with disease. But that one might be doomed to a short life

---

20. François Leuret, "Notice sur les indigens de la ville de Paris," *Annales d'hygiène publique et de médecine légale* 15 (1836): 308.

of misery and deprivation by the mere fact of birth he could not accept. These particular conclusions are less indicative of the social realm than the larger framework in which they were made, however, for it is this vision of an uncertain world, filled with variations that could be tabulated, measured, and compared, that constituted the essence of the "social."[21]

Leuret's focus on birth and risk also pointed to the importance of the family for the elaboration of the social realm. The family lay at the heart of Malthus's fears of overpopulation, Jean-Baptiste Say's conception of women's wages, the hygienist's description of urban dislocation, and the demographer's definition of fertility. But if the family stood at the intersection of much that occupied the social sciences, one member of that family received particular attention: woman. As Denise Riley argued, the social realm itself was defined in familial terms; here, one investigated and assessed the state of public hygiene, education, sexual mores, fertility, and health. Since women had traditionally been given responsibility for guaranteeing these values within families, their position took on new significance in the wider social world.[22] In Riley's provocative formulation, the invention of the social was not merely a neutral process of revaluation, which redefined the individual's relation to the collective. Rather, the social realm allowed traditional gender distinctions to resonate within a complex web of dependence, obligation, protection, and vulnerability that connected family activities such as mothering, the care of infants, and sexual behavior to the health of the population as a whole. It is crucial to recognize the result of this new social context for evaluating the contributions that men and women were expected to make to the collective body of the population. Familial reforms had already been publicly discussed in the eighteenth century, and measures such as Rousseau's advocacy of breast-feeding had even led to a fad for the practice among aristocratic women. Rousseau's arguments surfaced during the Revolution as justification for denying women the vote, but this exclusion still worked primarily to construct an image of the individual, masculine, citizen. By the late nineteenth century, however, such proposals resonated within a

21. On the changing attitudes toward probability and risk, see especially Hacking, *Taming of Chance*, and Gerd Gigerenzer, Zeno Switjink, Theodore Porter, Lorraine Daston, John Beatty, and Lorenz Krüger, *The Empire of Chance: How Probability Changed Science and Everyday Life* (Cambridge, 1989). On the socialization of risk, see Ewald, *L'Etat providence*, and Steinmetz, *Regulating the Social*.

22. Riley wrote: "In so far as the concerns of the social *are* familial standards—health, education, hygiene, fertility, demography, chastity and fecundity—and the heart of the family is inexorably the woman, then the woman is also solidly inside of that which has to some degree already been feminised. The 'social' does not merely admit women to it; something more constructive than a matter of entry or access is going on; it is as if 'women' become established as a new kind of sociological collectivity" (*Am I That Name? Feminism and the Category of 'Women' in History* [London, 1988], p. 50).

much wider collective realm, as entire populations of women became the targets of reformers' zeal in the name of a healthier population.[23]

As the family became an object of both intensified philanthropic activity and legislative reform, women increasingly found their contribution to society measured by their success or failure as mothers. Working women found themselves the object of a new benevolence as reformers and legislators extended state protection to their families through measures that regulated employment or gave them access to medical assistance. When feminists attempted to find alternative ways for women to exercise their membership in the larger community, however, their efforts met with almost universal condemnation. Women who sought the benefits of full citizenship faced an intractable dilemma, for claiming political rights as *women* only drew attention to the narrow web of sociological categories that the social realm had reserved for them. Feminists perceived this contradiction, and some attempted find a way out of the social roles reserved for individuals on the basis of sex. As early as 1833, the Saint-Simonian theorist Claire Démar argued: "The social individual is neither men only nor women only: the complete social individual is man and woman; however, as *mothers*, *sisters*, and *wives* we are slaves of men."[24] In fact, women in France were explicitly denied full citizenship rights by successive republican governments in 1792, 1848, and 1871. Not until 1944 did French women get the vote. Only a committed functionalist would argue that this enduring political exclusion was the whole purpose of the way gender worked to define the social realm, but it was certainly one of its most significant effects.

The scientific study of population thus served many purposes in nineteenth-century France. It created a vast epistemological space, to be filled with a new knowledge about society and the place of individuals within it. This knowledge was potentially limitless in complexity, but statistics could reduce this complexity to identifiable patterns of risk and uncertainty at the collective level. The newly conceived social realm created

23. The targeting of female populations or families by social reformers in nineteenth-century France has been studied by Elinor Accampo, *Industrialization, Family Life, and Class Relations: Saint Chamond, 1815–1914* (Berkeley, 1989); Rachel Fuchs, *Abandoned Children: Foundlings and Child Welfare in Nineteenth-Century France* (Albany, 1984) and *Poor and Pregnant in Paris: Strategies for Survival in the Nineteenth Century* (New Brunswick, 1992); Katherine Lynch, *Family, Class, and Ideology in Early Industrial France* (Madison, 1988); Sylvia Schafer, *Children in Moral Danger and the Problem of Government in Third Republic France* (Princeton, 1997); and Mary Lynn Stewart, *Women, Work, and the French State* (Montreal, 1989).
24. Claire Démar, "Appel d'une femme au peuple sur l'affranchissement de la femme," in *Textes sur l'affranchissement des femmes*, ed. Valentin Pelosse (Paris, 1976), p. 14. Démar first published this article in 1833. For an indispensable treatment of the contradiction posed by sexual difference for liberal thought in France during this period, see Joan Scott, *Only Paradoxes to Offer: French Feminism and the Rights of Man* (Cambridge, Mass., 1996).

the possibility of new meaning for individual lives by casting them on an interlocking network of personal, physical, political, and economic relationships. The sum total of these relationships defined the limits of individuals' existence, both in terms of what they could enjoy as members of civil society and what they owed as a condition of that membership. For men, these conditions were defined increasingly in terms of labor, productivity, and paternal authority; for women, the key terms became consumption, reproduction, and nurture.

THE ARGUMENT IN BRIEF

The first three chapters of this book examine the development of a statistical model of population in the late eighteenth and early nineteenth centuries. The new model replaced the old regime's traditional legal categories of estates and corporate bodies with quantitative measurements of newly conceived social aggregates: male and female populations, age cohorts, the single, the married, the rich, the poor, the indigent. As late as the Napoleonic period, many population researchers continued to believe that universal laws governed the behavior and destinies of these aggregates. To support this view, they cited the astonishing statistical regularities that emerged from their research—the fact that every year, given populations tended to produce relatively consistent figures for phenomena as diverse as births, deaths, marriages, murders, and undeliverable letters at the post office. Eventually, however, population researchers abandoned the search for universal laws and focused more on accounting for variations in mortality, fertility, and economic prosperity.

The stakes in this transition were significant. If universal laws governed the behavior and destiny of aggregate groups, then the role of the state would simply be to identify these limits and to ensure that the customs and laws of human society did not contradict the natural order. If populations were not subject to external laws, however, but simply subject to their own internal dynamic processes of flux and variation, then the role of government was less clear. Should the state actively intervene in the lives of individuals in an attempt to promote beneficial outcomes that could be measured for the population as a whole? What standards could the population researcher use to determine "normal" levels for births, deaths, the incidence of disease, or the number of indigent individuals in the capital? The answers to such questions depended on how one defined "individual" and how one conceived of the benefits that were observable at the aggregate level.

Important statistical research in the 1820s focused on the question of urban poverty and its effects on the population as a whole. In a path-breaking series of articles, the hygienist Louis-René Villermé used quantitative data to demonstrate that the poor in Paris were susceptible to higher rates of mortality than the general population. His work was confirmed in the 1830s by research on the effects of the 1832 cholera epidemic. The implication of this work was that one social aggregate—the poor—was being systematically excluded from the benefits of economic development and that the consequences of this exclusion included an irrefutable biological vulnerability. Such a conclusion worried figures such as Villermé, however, because of the possibility that membership in one or another social aggregate had more objective force and reality in determining life chances than individual behaviors. In other words, Villermé's statistical work seemed to indicate that collective destinies were more important than individual autonomy. Such a conclusion contradicted Villermé's own liberal assumptions about the place of individuals in a market economy, and his discomfort with this idea is evident in certain passages of his work. Other population researchers, such as the Belgian Adolphe Quetelet, remained unconcerned about this possibility and suggested radical new methods for capturing the diversity of individual lives in statistical constructions.

The population researchers who defended statistical aggregates found themselves challenged by both conservative and liberal skeptics. Conservatives disliked population statistics because quantitative arguments in the social sciences sounded too much like political arguments for mass democracy—in science as in politics they rejected the principle of majority rule. Liberals, like Villermé himself, were suspicious of any vision of social aggregates that threatened to subsume notions of individual autonomy and free will. At the back of everybody's mind in the turbulent 1830s and 1840s, of course, were the unacceptable proposals of socialists who were only too happy to see society in terms of social aggregates and to search for collective solutions to collectively defined problems. During these years, therefore, population researchers adopted interpretive strategies that paid special attention to the place of the individual in society, and they downplayed the aggregate nature of their conclusions.

The final three chapters of the book argue that population researchers soothed their anxieties about thinking in the aggregate by focusing ever more intently on the family and gendered division of roles within families. To avoid dealing with aggregates such as class, they concentrated on individuals who occupied particular places in the household: male wage earner, mother, and child. To avoid any hint of contradiction with a vision of a market-based economy of autonomous individuals, they embraced a series of gendered distinctions borrowed from liberal political economists. From Thomas Malthus, French population researchers adopted the population principle, which explained inequality as the natural result of scarcity and gave agency within the economy only to male heads of households. In much the same way, they adopted Jean-Baptiste Say's account of the place of the family in a market economy. Say overcame the potential for contradiction between a liberal vision of the economy based on individual liberty and a social order based on the family by making families representative of one particular interest: that of the male wage earner. Both Malthus and Say could thus blame the poverty of aggregates on the failures of individuals. The poverty of men was the result of improvidence and having more children than they could afford, while the poverty of women could result only from their inability to live in the dependent condition mandated by their sex.

Such accounts implied that single women were by definition an anomaly in the market economy. Unable to support themselves, they constituted a drain on public resources and a danger to the well-being of the social body as a whole. The attention to families thus led to intensified interest in two questions at mid-century: the role of women in the labor market and the importance of sexual differentiation for the social order. In early statistical work on the economy in the 1820s women's labor was not presented as a significant problem, but by the 1840s it had emerged as a central preoccupation of French political economy. Statistical work on women's labor helped to frame this discussion by presenting working women as aberrant figures who existed outside the lines of familial dependence that gave meaning to the lives of French wives, mothers, and daughters. Such studies also served to displace earlier anxieties about the results of aggregate analysis, since male workers retained their individuality and economic autonomy as *pères de famille*, and only women were relegated to a status that denied them such individuality.

This attention to the family and the social obligations borne by women survived the rejection of Malthusian ideas about population growth after the Franco-Prussian War. During the early years of the Third Republic, child welfare legislation and fears of depopulation dominated population research. Regulation of the wet-nursing industry in the 1870s reflected a concern with two groups of women in the economy: urban working women who preserved their wage-earning capacity by sending their infants to the countryside to nurse and rural women who used their own bodies to supplement their income by nursing other women's infants in exchange for money. Previous attempts at regulation had a limited effect because of official reluctance to challenge the authority of fathers in the family. Population researchers changed the terms of debate in the 1860s, however, by making the mother the most important component of the nursing child's environment. If infant death was solely a question of maternal responsibility, regulation of irresponsible mothers was not only feasible but necessary. The resulting regulatory legislation established an important precedent for government intervention in family life, in the name of the child's interest.

By the end of the nineteenth century, fears of slowing population growth had reached fever pitch, and women who sought economic and political autonomy bore much of the blame for the perceived decline in national fortunes. The very definition of marital fertility in the demographic literature of the 1880s and 1890s served to fix women irrevocably within a network of familial obligations, thus rendering their participation in the public world of the market or politics an aberration. Anybody who challenged these restrictions on women's behavior, such as the neo-Malthusians who campaigned for birth control rights at the turn of the century or liberal feminists who called for suffrage rights, were guilty of an unpatriotic egoism, a lack of concern for the good of the nation.

The critique of female individualism in the depopulation debate points to the central paradox of familial ideology in France in the second half of the nineteenth century. Interest in the family intensified in the 1840s and 1850s as population researchers and political economists looked for ways to preserve at least the potential for individual autonomy in a social world that seemed increasingly dominated by processes that functioned at the aggregate level—impersonal market forces, the accumulation of wealth, the incidence of poverty. Their solution to the question of individual autonomy was to defend a vision of the population that set expansive notions of male citizenship and social participation against a correspondingly restrictive definition of women's social roles within the family as procreators and mothers. By century's end, therefore, when French women increasingly demanded respect for their own claims of individual autonomy in the marketplace or the political sphere, they found themselves opposed by a populationist logic that could not see them as autonomous individuals. The familial ideology that soothed political economists in the 1850s by offering an unimpeded autonomy for males was used in the 1890s to deny the very same claims for autonomy when made by women.

This book, then, is not a history of the development of statistical institutions in France, nor is it a demographic study of population trends or an encyclopedic history of official family policies in the nineteenth century. A wide literature on all of these subjects already exists, and I have used and referred to this work in the chapters that follow. Instead, I have tried to trace the development of certain ideas about population across a broad chronology and in different areas: political arithmetic, medicine, political economy, and the administrative ethos of the modern French state. By close examination of the texts produced in these various fields, I suggest connections that have remained unexplored in the historical literature and probe the peculiar and often contradictory logic that one finds at the intersection of population thinking and liberal politics in nineteenth-century France.

THE UNIVERSAL AND THE PARTICULAR

POPULATION AND THE OLD REGIME

By the time Louis XVI came to the throne in 1774, the power of the centralized absolutist monarchy had largely superseded and weakened the political institutions associated with France's feudal past. The Estates General had not met since 1614, and although the provincial parliaments had not completely surrendered their authority, royal power was subject to many fewer checks than in the past. At the same time, however, the social institutions of feudalism still had a powerful hold over the organization of French society. The nobility retained many of their hereditary rights, and the strict hierarchies separating aristocrats from commoners still provided the basis for the complex system of privilege that determined the legal and financial structure of the realm.

When the monarchy stumbled and collapsed after the outbreak of popular unrest in 1789, the revolutionary leaders took on a twofold task. First, they reasserted the power of a strong and centralized national government, recognizing that any concessions to local intermediary bodies might allow for a resurgence of feudal political institutions. Second, they replaced the feudal society of orders and corporations with a more democratic and egalitarian society of individual citizens, whose relations with the state would be unimpeded by considerations of status, rank, or privilege. The first task was primarily political and depended on the ability of revolutionary leaders to preserve the consolidation of centralized authority that the monarchy had already accomplished across the eighteenth century. The second task was ultimately social and required a concerted attack on the society of orders that had been the basis of ancien régime France.[1]

The idea of "population" played a central role in this complex history.

1. Pierre Rosanvallon, *L'Etat en France de 1789 à nos jours* (Paris, 1990), pp. 97–99.

Before the Revolution, administrators in the service of the crown used studies of the population to increase the power of the absolutist state. Revenue assessments and economic research in different areas of the realm allowed the king's ministers to challenge the exemptions and privileges enjoyed by some regions and led them to hope that the complex system of tax collection could be placed on a more rational footing. When the provincial *parlements* protested that the abrogation of their privileges constituted an unacceptable extension of royal power, reforming ministers such as Turgot and Jacques Necker responded with reports composed in the scientific language of the Enlightenment, effectively cloaking the political consequences of their policies in a rhetoric of rational reform. Late eighteenth-century authors of population treatises shared with the king's reforming ministers both the optimism and the universalist outlook of Enlightenment science, and they used this broader view to challenge the particularism of those who sought to preserve the traditional interests of their rank or region. Believing that the organization of society was subject to general principles, the king's ministers defended the centralization of authority as the best means to establish a rational government within the dictates of natural laws. These laws, so the theory went, had their basis in a universal order that determined both the physical attributes and capacities of every citizen, as well as the cultural and political institutions that gave form to their collective life as a nation. This faith in universal laws suggested that all individuals shared an equal status as members of the larger agglomeration, thus providing the basis for an intellectual challenge to the hierarchical society of orders long before the Revolution actually put these ideas into practice.

In the seventeenth and eighteenth centuries various royal administrators perceived the value of population research, but none made such studies a regular and routine part of government. Jean-Baptiste Colbert, Louis XIV's innovative minister, envisioned regular reporting of population movements as a part of his ambitious mercantilist policies. Above all, Colbert sought to increase the king's tax revenues, and he was therefore interested in both the size of the population and its productive employment. Between 1663 and 1665 Colbert's subordinates produced studies of Rouen, Champagne, Bourgogne, Berry, and several other regions and *généralités*, but Colbert never succeeded in his attempts to give a detailed report on the kingdom's entire population. Beginning in 1670, however, his administration published regular reports of population movement in Paris based on parish records of births and deaths.[2]

2. On Colbert's population research, see Jay Smith, *The Culture of Merit: Nobility, Royal Service, and the Making of the Absolute Monarchy in France, 1600–1789* (Ann Arbor, 1996), pp. 133–34; and

Other attempts to establish a regular accounting of population in the seventeenth and eighteenth centuries were only partially successful. Between 1697 and 1700, the crown prince's preceptor, the duc de Beauvillier, commissioned the royal intendants to produce reports on their jurisdictions for the edification of the future Louis XV, but these reports remained in manuscript form and only a brief extract was later published.[3] In the latter years of Louis XIV's reign, Sebastien le Prestre, maréchal de Vauban, came up with a comprehensive plan for tax reform that entailed an annual accounting of the population, which he published as the *Dîme royal* in 1707. Unfortunately both for Vauban's reputation and for the fate of annual censuses, his enthusiasm for a more rational system of public finance led him to suggest that the crown do away with the tax-exempt status enjoyed by the nobility and the clergy. This early proposal for the use of *dénombrements* won Vauban only the condemnation of the king, and his plan was never implemented.[4] Most of his immediate successors saw no reason to push for similar accounts of the population. Only Charles Saugrain, an employee of the Royal Finances, attempted to continue in this vein, with the publication of his *Dénombrement de France par généralitéz, élections, paroisses et feux* (1709). Saugrain's work, based on reports by royal intendants, served as a model for much of the official work on population in the eighteenth century, but it made no attempt to estimate the number of people living in each election and generality. Instead, he contented himself with an alphabetic list of parishes, noting the number of *feux*, or hearths, in each one. In a footnote he admitted that the number of *feux* "must be regarded as more curious than certain, because nothing is more subject to change; but all the same it gives a near idea of [the parish's] size and composition."[5]

Beginning in 1772, Louis XV's last controller general of finance, the

Joseph Spengler, *French Predecessors of Malthus* (Durham, 1942), pp. 21–26. For a useful nineteenth-century view of pre-1789 population research, see Emile Levasseur, "France," in *25ème anniversaire de la Société statistique de Paris* (Paris, 1886), pp. 145–46.

3. Edmond Esmonin, "Les Mémoires des intendants pour l'instruction du duc de Bourgogne," in *Etudes sur la France des XVIIe et XVIIIe siècles* (Paris, 1964), pp. 113–30.

4. As early as 1686, Vauban had published *Méthode générale et facile pour faire le dénombrement des peuples*. See Jacques Dupâquier and René Le Mée, "La Connaissance des faits démographiques de 1789 à 1914," in *Histoire de la population française,* ed. Dupâquier 3:15, and Smith, *Culture of Merit,* pp. 134–35.

5. Charles Saugrain, *Dénombrement du royaume par généralitez, elections, paroisses et feux* (Paris, 1709), 1:iii. Another important although incomplete investigation into the French population in the mid-eighteenth century was that of Philibert Orry, controller general of finances under Louis XV. In 1745, Orry circulated a questionnaire on population and industry to every intendant in the realm and had the results compiled by a competent administrator. Nevertheless, the report was never published and the document lay unnoticed in the archives until the twentieth century. See Hervé Le Bras, "La Statistique Générale de la France," in *Les Lieux de mémoire,* vol. 2, *La Nation,* ed. Pierre Nora (Paris, 1986), pp. 320–21.

abbé Terray, succeeded in having the royal intendants of each generality provide the government with annual reports on population movement, culled from parish records of baptisms and deaths.[6] Not until Louis XVI's reforming controller general Jacques Necker published his famous *Compte-rendu de l'état du royaume et des affaires publiques* in 1781, however, did a royal official attempt a complete public accounting of the population. Necker's *Compte-rendu* came too late to help Louis XVI solve the looming financial crisis that ultimately led to his downfall in the Revolution of 1789. In any case, Necker's revelations about the size of the pensions that the king had granted to his courtiers, along with his less than honest reports about the size of the royal deficit, led to his dismissal soon after the publication of the *Compte-rendu*.

The financial crisis of the 1770s and 1780s brought a real urgency to the question of population because any reform of the monarchy's tax system required an accurate portrait of the kingdom's inhabitants. The failure of earlier administrators to establish the basis for a regular accounting of population made it difficult for the monarchy to gauge its future revenues. Moreover, because the king relied on the private accounts of independent financial agents and tax collectors to keep the royal treasury in the black, he had no reliable way of knowing how many people were paying how much and when, or how much the monarchy was owed at any given moment. Until 1779, when the former intendant of the Auvergne, Jean-François de La Michodière, became *inspecteur des dénombrements*, no royal official had primary responsibility for collecting information about the population, and finance ministers had no authority to demand that such information be gathered and kept in a central archive. In 1774, Turgot attempted to address this problem by radically restructuring the administration, but the powerful entrenched interests of the aristocracy, the financial elites, and the *parlements* successfully (but only temporarily) resisted the centralization of both authority and information.[7]

This conflict was essentially a political struggle between two groups of elites with very different notions of how the monarchy should be run. On the one hand stood a conservative group of aristocrats, financiers, and judicial officials, who were interested in preserving the complex layers of administrative and financial offices that the old regime had inherited from France's feudal past. Opposed to them stood the reformers recruited into state service by Turgot and later by Necker, who were interested in stripping away the intermediary bodies that stood as obstacles to the exercise

---

6. Eric Brian, *La Mesure de l'Etat: Administrateurs et géometres au XVIIIe siècle* (Paris, 1994), p. 19.
7. J. F. Bosher, *French Finances, 1775–1795: From Business to Bureaucracy* (Cambridge, 1970), pp. 42, 47–53.

of royal authority. When Necker published his *Compte-rendu* in 1781 he challenged the defenders of the old order by breaking the tradition of administrative secrecy which had hidden the royal government from public view. In so doing, he set a precedent for official accountability that was to have far-reaching consequences.[8] "Population" had not only become the target of state scrutiny, it was a topic fit for public consumption; from this point on, population was both object and audience of the new science.

Because the king's ministers failed to publish a regular census, the most innovative population research in the eighteenth century came from a wide variety of Enlightenment philosophes, members of the royal academies, lower-level royal officials, and assorted authors of political economy tracts. One historian has estimated that nineteen hundred works dealing with population questions and political economy were published in France between 1760 and 1789.[9] These writers published the results of their research on their own, and a few of them received wide attention in the decades leading up to the Revolution. Most of these philosophes carried the mercantilist emphasis on the size of population to its logical conclusion, claiming that the quantity, composition, and vitality of the population were signs of historical progress. In the preindustrial order of eighteenth-century France, they saw the size of the population as both an indicator and a guarantee of agricultural productivity. Furthermore, they reasoned, since the population contained the sum of human potential in a rationalized economic order, the quality of the government could be measured according to the relative prosperity of the people. "The population is the most certain sign indicating the health of the political body," wrote the abbé Jean-Joseph Expilly in 1768, "the moment where the population is the most flourishing is without doubt the moment of every state's greatest strength, in all governments."[10]

The work of these writers developed out of two important traditions: the "political arithmetic" pioneered by William Petty and John Graunt in England during the late seventeenth century and a roughly contemporary German academic tradition of *Statistik*, or state statistics. Petty's and Graunt's work was statistical in the modern sense, an attempt to quantify the resources that were important to the prosperity of the realm, including population, raw materials, manufacture, and trade. Important works

8. Keith Baker, *Inventing the French Revolution* (Cambridge, 1990), pp. 191–92. On Necker's interest in statistics, see Bourguet, *Déchiffrer la France*, p. 33. For a more general discussion of Necker's role, see Robert D. Harris, *Necker: Reform Statesman of the Ancien Régime* (Berkeley, 1979).
9. Brian, *La Mesure de l'Etat*, p. 12. See also Jean-Claude Perrot, "Les Economistes, les philosophes et la population," in *Histoire de la population française*, ed. Dupâquier, 2:499–551.
10. Jean-Joseph Expilly, *Dictionnaire géographique, historique et politique des Gaules et de la France*, 5 vols. (Paris, 1762–70), 5:787.

that were strongly influenced by the tradition of political arithmetic in France included Antoine Déparcieux, *Essai sur les probabilités de la durée de la vie humaine* (1746); Louis Messance, *Recherches sur la population des généralités d'Auvergne, de Lyon, de Rouen, et de quelques provinces et villes du Royaume* (1766); Jean-Joseph Expilly, *Dictionnaire géographique, historique et politique des Gaules et de la France* (1768); and Jean-Baptiste Moheau, *Recherches et considérations sur la population de la France* (1778). The German tradition of *Statistik*, in contrast, consisted of largely descriptive accounts of topography, climate, population, political institutions, and material wealth. Culminating in the eighteenth century with works by Gottfried Achenwall and Ludwig von Schlözer, both professors at Göttingen, *Statiskik* did not depend on quantitative information or calculation but strove instead to capture all the forms of knowledge important for government administration in an all-embracing system of classification. This tradition had a particularly strong influence on French population research during the early years of Napoleon's reign.[11] Not until the end of the first decade of the nineteenth century did the term *statistique* in France lose its more general meaning of "science of state" and come to mean a purely quantitative study of the state's population and resources.[12]

Much of the work on population produced in France during the eighteenth century was profoundly influenced by the Enlightenment tradition of universalism, which held that what was significant about humans was their common characteristics and behaviors, those aspects of their lives that allowed them to be grouped collectively. The eminent naturalist and director of the king's botanical gardens, the comte de Buffon, gave voice to this spirit when he claimed that "the history of an animal must not be the history of an individual, but that of the entire species of these animals."[13] Expressions of this universalism were bound to run into trouble, however. Simple observation of the human species seemed to give the lie to such assumptions. Men were different from women, peasants were different from town dwellers, the French were different from the British, and people in the Americas, in Africa, and in Asia seemed to exhibit remarkably different physical characteristics and behavior than Europeans. In other words, the perception of differences posed a problem

11. See Dupâquier and Le Mée, "La Connaissance des faits démographiques," p. 20.

12. On political arithmetic and the German tradition of *Statistik*, see Jacques Dupâquier and Michel Dupâquier, *Histoire de la démographie* (Paris, 1985), pp. 112–21 and 129–98. On the early definition of *statistique* see also Bourguet, *Déchiffrer la France*, pp. 21–52, and Brian, *La Mesure de l'Etat*, pp. 317–41.

13. Cited by P.-P. Gossiaux, "Anthropologie des Lumières (Culture 'naturelle' et racisme rituel)," in *L'Homme des lumières et la découverte de l'autre*, ed. D. Droixhe and P.-P. Gossiaux (Brussels, 1985), p. 52.

for Enlightenment universalism. Buffon found a historical explanation for this apparent paradox: the different cultures and peoples of the world were essentially the same, that is, subject to the same natural laws, but they occupied very different positions on a universal trajectory of historical development. Buffon could thus assert the essential unity of the human species while simultaneously reserving the right to rank different groups according to the degree of civilization that their culture had accomplished. Not surprisingly, he placed his own group, the Europeans, at the top of this list.[14]

The confident assumptions of Enlightenment universalism rested on a firm belief in a universe wholly determined by causal relations, a world of necessary linkages between successive events. Ignorance of this causal universe was the primary obstacle to good government. "So many circumstances . . . have contributed to the formation of societies," wrote the abbé Expilly in his 1768 article on population, "that those who find them already established believe them to be the work of chance. Most men exist without being aware of the causes, and they are the effects of them without knowing."[15] The most famous defender of this rigidly determinist position was the astronomer and mathematician Pierre Simon de Laplace, a leading member of the Académie royale des sciences, who was also deeply involved in research in political arithmetic. Laplace wrote, "We must envisage the present state of the universe as the effect of its anterior state, and as the cause of that which will follow."[16] For Laplace, causes could be minute, subtle, and even unknown, but they were always operative, and they always operated in exactly the same way. Most important, the utility of the knowledge that came out of early population studies depended on these determinist assumptions. Governments could not be expected to make predictions or act on the information gathered by their agents unless they were confident in their understanding of the causal nexus that resided at the heart of populations.

The universalism of Enlightenment thinkers was indispensable to the many accomplishments of eighteenth-century science, but in population

14. Tzvetan Todorov, *On Human Diversity: Racism, Nationalism, and Exoticism in French Thought* (Cambridge, Mass., 1993), p. 96. A similar logic had been used to account for sexual difference since the Renaissance. As Thomas Laqueur has demonstrated, early modern anatomists in Europe considered women's bodies to be essentially the same as men's though possessed of less heat. Their reproductive organs were thus folded inside their bodies and not external, but they were considered to be morphologically identical. In other words, as in Buffon's hierarchy of non-European peoples compared to Europeans, the early modern anatomists considered women to be the same as men, only less so (*Making Sex: Body and Gender from the Greeks to Freud* [Cambridge, Mass., 1990], pp. 63–113).
15. Expilly, *Dictionnaire géographique*, 5:787.
16. Cited in Joseph Lottin, *Quetelet, statisticien et sociologue* (Paris, 1912), p. 201.

research it did not always lead to reliable results. Many early theorists of population assumed that the ratios of births or deaths to the total number of inhabitants were constant expressions of universal law, and this idea persisted even after early measures of fertility and mortality revealed a high degree of variation from one region to the next. In Diderot's famous *Encyclopédie*, the author of the article "Population" used universalist assumptions to avoid the necessity of actually counting anybody when estimating the number of people who lived in France. Instead, he simply assumed a constant order at the most general and abstract level of planetary motion and inferred a symmetrical and reciprocal order for all lesser physical systems, including the agglomeration of individuals into social and political groups.[17] This procedure led him to assert that populations not subject to epidemic or human despoliation were unchanging, a claim that was severely tested as more regular statistics became available. In fact, the majority of eighteenth-century authors on population doubted the possibility of ever achieving an accurate count of the existing population. For this reason, the supporters of political arithmetic concentrated on attempts to determine the "normal" ratio of births and deaths to total population in the hopes of using such constants as multipliers for estimating the number of people in an area from parish records of baptisms and funerals.

The average print run of a political economy tract or a law treatise in the waning years of the old regime was probably less than fifteen hundred.[18] The champions of political arithmetic could not hope to reach a mass audience, but certain philosophes commanded a much wider public. Perhaps the most often repeated statement about population in prerevolutionary France was the baron Montesquieu's erroneous assertion in his bestselling work *De l'esprit des lois* (1748) that the population of Europe as a whole, and France in particular, had declined considerably since the age of Charlemagne. Many Enlightenment writers took Montesquieu's claim as a given, and when they called for political and economic reform in the last years of the old regime, they often blamed depopulation on royal mismanagement.[19] Montesquieu himself attributed this alleged population decline to an overly centralized government and an ill-

17. "All is linked in the universe, it is but a whole completely subsisting by the agreement and correspondence of all its parts. There exists nothing, down to the smallest atom, which is not necessary" (D'Amilaville, "Population," *Encyclopédie, ou Dictionnaire raisonné des sciences, des arts et des métiers*, vol. 13 [Neufchâtel, 1765], p. 91).
18. François Furet, ed., *Livre et société dans la France du XVIIIe siècle*, vol. 1 (Paris, 1965), p. 65.
19. Montesquieu's opinions on depopulation first appeared in *Lettres Persanes* (1721). In Letter 112, Montesquieu wrote "After making as exact a calculation as is possible with this sort of thing, I have come to the conclusion that there is scarcely a tenth of the number of men on earth that there was in former times" (*Persian Letters*, trans. J. C. Betts [New York, 1973], pp. 203–4). Montesquieu's

conceived distribution of wealth and resources, which gave the poor little incentive to labor for the sustenance necessary for population expansion. Such observations did not mean, however, that Montesquieu rejected all of the universalist assumptions that informed eighteenth-century thinking on population questions. On the contrary, he denied that the supposed decline had anything to do with a change in the fertility of humans as a species or women in particular, claiming instead that "the fertility of female animals is virtually consistent."[20] By extension, then, the presumed depopulation could have no relation to a defect in nature, for as he stated: "Wherever there is a place for two persons to live comfortably, a marriage is made. Nature very much inclines to this when she is not checked by the difficulty of subsistence."[21] The problem lay instead with a process of social and political development that had created incentives for people that conflicted with their physical capacities, most notably habits of luxury and accumulation on the part of elites.

The marquis de Mirabeau's *L'Ami des hommes* (1756) also brought the question of depopulation to a wide reading public in France. Mirabeau, later an active member of the group of physiocrats surrounding the economist François Quesnay, was not so much an original thinker on population as an effective popularizer. He seconded Montesquieu's opinions on population decline, and he too pointed to an inefficient division of labor that worked to the detriment of population growth. Mirabeau was also influenced by the economic writer Richard Cantillon, who had warned of the pernicious effects of luxury on the health of the economy. Following Cantillon's lead, Mirabeau wrote that "the measure of subsistence is that of the Population," and he called for concentrated efforts to increase agricultural production.[22] Mirabeau denied that the supposed depopulation of the realm had anything to do with religious celibacy, the exploration of foreign lands, or the depredations of war. Like Montesquieu before him, Mirabeau claimed that the problem of depopulation had no relation to

---

opinion was commonly cited, for example, by d'Amilaville in the article quoted above, and the depopulation hypothesis was accepted by an entire generation of political theorists and economists. See Jean-Claude Perrot, *Une Histoire intellectuelle de l'économie politique (XVIIe–XVIIIe siècle)* (Paris, 1992), p. 159, and Brian, *La Mesure de l'Etat*, p. 169. Other eighteenth-century writers who discussed the alleged depopulation of France included J. F. de Bielefeld, Plumart de Dangeul, Goyon de la Plombanie, Pierre Jaubert, the chevalier de Cerfvol, and Faiguet de Villeneuve. All of these authors are discussed in Spengler, *French Predecessors of Malthus*, pp. 77–109.

20. Montesquieu, *The Spirit of the Laws* (Cambridge, 1989), p. 427.

21. Ibid., p. 433.

22. Victor de Riqueti, marquis de Mirabeau, *L'Ami des hommes, ou Traité de la population* (1756; rpt. Darmstadt, 1970). Richard Cantillon's *Essai sur la nature du commerce en générale* was written during the 1730s but not published until 1755 as a result of Mirabeau's sponsorship. On Cantillon and Mirabeau, see Spengler, *French Predecessors of Malthus*, pp. 113–36.

changes in fertility.[23] And like Montesquieu and Cantillon, he criticized the development of large fortunes and the ostentatious luxury of the aristocracy, which he held to be evidence of an unhealthy "cupidity" on the part of the privileged. To counteract this tendency toward possessivness and self-interested accumulation, he called for the recognition of a collective good, embodied in the concept of population, now defined as "the first among society's possessions [le premier des biens de la société]."[24]

Montesquieu's and Mirabeau's overconfident assertions about depopulation earned them a riposte from Louis Messance, an official who was well-versed in the methods of political arithmetic in France. Messance was secretary to the intendant of the Auvergne, Jean-François de La Michodière, and he published his Recherches sur la population des généralités d'Auvergne, de Lyon, de Rouen, et de quelques provinces et villes du Royaume in 1766. Recognizing the impossibility of coming up with actual figures for the population of the realm, Messance sought to arrive at an estimate through a series of calculations from the figures for births that were available from baptismal records. He reasoned that if the "normal" number of births for a population of known size could be established, this proportion could be used to estimate the total number of people for much larger bodies from existing parish records of baptisms. After comparing the available figures for seven provinces and a large number of cities in France, Messance demonstrated that the population of these regions had increased by one-thirteenth in the previous sixty years. He admitted that this was not a great deal of growth, but it was enough to counter the arguments of those who believed that the population had declined.[25]

Messance's rebuttal of Montesquieu and Mirabeau became the first salvo in a concerted effort by the defenders of political arithmetic to place the government's population research on a more rational footing. In the

23. Mirabeau wrote: "If the multiplication of the species depended on its fecundity, there would certainly be a hundred more wolves in the world than sheep. Wolves give birth to large litters as often as sheep bear only one. Man condemns armies of sheep to celibacy, and I haven't heard that he commits the same type of injustice to wolves. He kills many more sheep than wolves, and meanwhile the earth is covered with the race of the former while that of the latter is very rare. Why? Because the grass [l'herbe, i.e., food] is very limited for wolves, and very widespread for sheep" (L'Ami des hommes, p. 12). Mirabeau's link between food supply and population would be more fully developed in the work of the English political economist Thomas Malthus.
24. Ibid., p. 171. To twentieth-century readers, Mirabeau's claim carries an almost tautological quality — to claim that "population" be regarded as a kind of social property is confusing, for we have assimilated "population" into our conception of what constitutes "society" in the modern world. In fact, Mirabeau's phrase exposes a discontinuity between the meaning of "population" today and its use in the eighteenth century. His "population" had not yet been fully invested with a social significance, and indeed, his statement is an early example of the attempt to do just that.
25. Louis Messance, Recherches sur la population des généralités d'Auvergne, de Lyon, de Rouen, et de quelques provinces et villes du Royaume (Paris, 1766), pp. 170–71. See also Messance's later work, Nouvelles recherches sur la population de la France (Lyon, 1788).

absence of a census, Messance's method for calculating the total population from the number of births became a standard technique of subsequent writers. First, they would determine the average number of births over a given period in a region of known population—an average they referred to as the *année commune des naissances*. Dividing the total population by the *année commune des naissances* gave them a relatively constant factor, a number that usually fell between 24 and 27. The goal of this procedure was to determine this factor as precisely as possible so that it could be used as a multiplier for the number of births in regions where the total population was unknown. This effort to find a more precise multiplier had an unintended effect, however. What began as an attempt to find a universal proportion between the number of births and the total number of inhabitants eventually led to a greater appreciation of the highly varied and complex relations between the population's composition and the number of births and deaths recorded. In the decade after the first appearance of Louis Messance's rebuttal to Montesquieu, these ideas were reinforced by an influential work of considerably wider scope, Jean-Baptiste Moheau's *Recherches et considérations sur la population de la France*, first published in 1778.

MOHEAU'S CHALLENGE TO THE SOCIETY OF ORDERS

Both nineteenth- and twentieth-century historians of demography have cited Jean-Baptiste Moheau as an important precedent for the vision of population that would become predominant after 1789. In 1805, an official in Napoleon's Interior Ministry, the indefatigable archivist Jacques Peuchet, wrote that "of all the authors who have written on the population of France, none did it better than Moheau." [26] Emile Levasseur, a prominent geographer and professor at the Collège de France, wrote in 1886 that Moheau's *Recherches et considérations sur la population de la France* was "remarkable," noting that "one is struck in reading it to find conclusions of great wisdom, in spite of the small amount of numerical data then possessed by science." [27] Writing in 1994, the historian Eric Brian wrote that Moheau's introductory chapters on the calculation of population estimates were "a scrupulous synthesis of the epoch." [28] In fact, Moheau's work received relatively little attention from a wider pub-

26. Jacques Peuchet, *Statistique élémentaire de la France* (Paris, 1805), p. 40.
27. Levasseur, "France," p. 146.
28. Brian, *La Mesure de l'Etat*, p. 393. Brian's opinion echoed that of Jean-Claude Perrot, who wrote that Moheau's *Recherches* "present a subtle synthesis of [population] science at the end of the 1770s." See Perrot, "Les économistes, les philosophes et la population," p. 531.

lic upon its publication in 1778, but his significance for later researchers makes him a worthwhile candidate for a more extended discussion of the state of population thinking in the years before 1789.

Moheau gained his familiarity with the royal administration from first-hand experience. He served as private secretary to the well-connected Auget de Montyon during the latter's term as royal intendant in La Rochelle and was thus familiar with the internal workings of the royal government. Montyon was better known to their contemporaries than Moheau. The intendant Montyon frequently attended learned salons during the last decades of the Bourbon regime, and he met the most famous philosophes of the day, including Montesquieu, d'Alembert, and Helvétius. Many subsequent authors assumed that Montyon himself was the primary author of the *Recherches*, and not his secretary. A recent study definitively established Moheau's responsibility for the most innovative sections of the work, however, including the highly sophisticated chapters on sex, age distribution, marital status, health, prosperity, mortality, and fertility.[29] Montyon may have been responsible for the work's initial dissemination among the learned elite of the ancien régime, but Moheau wrote the most important sections himself.

The most striking aspect of Moheau's *Recherches* is its thoroughly secular and instrumentalist focus and his determination to view the population solely in terms of the monarchy's material and administrative needs. "One cannot have a well-structured political machine," he wrote, "in a country where the state of the population is unknown."[30] In no place is Moheau's instrumentalist focus clearer than in his use of number. Moheau's *Recherches* appeared as the proponents of political arithmetic were beginning to redefine the meaning of *statistique*, and henceforth the term was increasingly associated with numerical figures. As in the work of his contemporaries, Moheau's numbers served an explicitly utilitarian calculation: they provided quantifiable standards for measuring the benefits that the king's administration could expect to draw from the lives and activities of individuals.

Moheau used numbers first to identify the size of smaller subgroups within the population—so many single men over age sixty, so many women who had not given birth before thirty, and so on. In each case, Moheau presented the fraction as a way of defining the precise contours

---

29. See René Le Mée, "Introduction," in Jean-Baptiste Moheau, *Recherches et considérations sur la population de la France*, ed. Eric Vilquin (Paris, 1994). On Montyon, see Bosher, *French Finances*, pp. 130–35.

30. Jean-Baptiste Moheau, *Recherches et considérations sur la population de la France* (Paris, 1778), p. 20. All future page references will be to this edition.

of a homogeneous group, each of which possessed certain capacities and abilities that were of potential benefit to the royal government. His second use of numbers compared the proportion of certain events to the total number of people present, so many births, so many marriages, so many deaths. This latter method, which followed up on the previous work of Déparcieux and Messance, prefigured the development of standardized techniques to measure the changes in mortality and fertility rates over time. It also allowed Moheau to gauge the extent to which members of different subgroups were fulfilling the obligations they owed to the realm.

Moheau left no doubt as to which distinctions were most important in determining both the essence and the obligations of each member of the population. "The principal distinction for humanity," wrote Moheau, "is that of sex: this immutable principle gives every individual, in the course of an entire life, a constitution, a manner of being, a degree of strength, a propensity to illnesses, a shape, qualities, a character, a mind, a heart, tastes, customs, rights, prerogatives, and duties, thus distinguishing [each individual] in an essential fashion."[31] In general, Moheau argued, men were a greater resource to the kingdom than women, and he listed the services that men provided to the state in the military, in government administration, in commerce, or simply through manual labor. But for reproduction of the species, Moheau was careful to add, "the state has the greatest obligations to the female sex, because it is she who produces."[32] Noting that he did not wish to address the controversial question of sex ratios at birth, he contented himself by observing that the French population possessed a slight but beneficial majority of women, at a ratio of approximately seventeen to sixteen.

Moheau's prescriptions on the sexual division of labor conformed to a conventional view that men were valuable for what they *did* and women for what they *were*. At the same time, however, his emphasis on the monarchy's obligations to women who fulfilled their social duties by becoming mothers set an important precedent for future legislation aimed at the family: women owed their children to the state, but in return, the state owed protection to mothers. In fact, Moheau's functionalist views went much further than a simple reflection of "traditional" gender roles. In a passage that demonstrated the extent to which he was willing to push his argument in the face of social convention, Moheau pointed out that one man could usefully fertilize several women, while "one woman's relations with several men have no more utility than the services of one."[33]

31. Ibid., p. 70.
32. Ibid., p. 129.
33. Ibid., p. 129.

Moheau's aside on sexual relations implicitly drew a distinction between traditional assumptions about the sanctity of marriage and the material needs of the monarchy. Although he made no recommendations that contravened the teachings of the church, his line of reasoning opened up the possibility of a secular revision of individual moral conduct in light of collective needs.

Moheau's functionalist concerns also framed his treatment of age and marital status. Certain ages, he wrote, "have no utility at the moment, but offer the hope of future utility." Others "offer no advantage to anybody, either in the present or the future."[34] For both men and women the productive age began at puberty, and he suggested fourteen for women and eighteen for men, noting, however, that men are not finished growing until they reach the age of twenty one. Moheau suggested that one-third of the population was under the age of sixteen and that half the population was twenty and under. Moheau justified the need to distinguish between the unmarried, the married, and the widowed, declaring: "The first duty of a citizen is to submit to the yoke of marriage and one of the greatest services that he can render to society is to increase the number of individuals that are its members."[35] In each case, then, Moheau's quantitative investigations into sex, age, and marital status aimed at measuring the extent to which individuals fulfilled the obligations they owed to their king by virtue of their membership in an identifiable subgroup of the population.

Once the important subgroups had been defined, Moheau proceeded to use numerical proportions to relate the frequency of certain events to the total number of people in each subgroup—so many births per inhabitant in a given year, so many marriages, so many deaths. In his treatment of these proportions, however, Moheau held two contradictory positions at once. Sometimes, like other eighteenth-century writers on population, Moheau proceeded as if the universal laws that governed humanity made the annual proportions of births, deaths, and marriages a constant figure, as if a population of a given size would always produce the same number of births, deaths, and marriages over a given period of time. This assumption is evident in his use of the *année commune des naissances* to calculate the total population of the realm. Having ascertained the average number of births a given population could be expected to show in a year, Moheau used this ratio to estimate the total population of the nation simply by multiplying the annual number of births by the

34. Ibid., p. 72.
35. Ibid., p. 81.
36. Assuming that actual counts were too difficult and prone to error, Moheau considered many different ratios as methods of estimating total population, including births, deaths, marriages, and even consumption (ibid., pp. 24–53).

derived constant.[36] At the same time, Moheau recognized that the *année commune des naissances* was not really a constant value but was highly variable depending on the fertility of different regions and the prosperity and health of the given populations.[37] Nevertheless, he proceeded as if the *année commune* really did express a universal constant, and he devoted a great deal of his discussion to ascertaining the likely quantity of births that could be expected for the total population.[38]

Moheau's use of number thus demonstrates a tension in eighteenth-century population work between the search for universal laws and the desire to describe what was unique and particular to specific individuals or groups in the population. His contemporaries exhibited the same ambiguity. An undated prerevolutionary report on the population in the National Archives (probably from the late 1780s) multiplied the annual number of births by 30 to estimate the population of Paris, while using a multiplier of 27 to estimate the population of cities with an episcopal seat, a multiplier of 26 to estimate the population of smaller cities, and finally, a multiplier of 25 to estimate the population of the realm as a whole. The author, presumably the *inspecteur de dénombrements* de La Michodière (who had formerly been Messance's employer as intendant of the Auvergne), justified these variations by pointing out that cities had larger populations of single men and women than did rural areas because cities contained more students, servants, and members of religious orders.[39] Because these groups had fewer children than their rural contemporaries, a larger multiplier was required to estimate the total population. Déparcieux had made the same observation about the age structure of urban populations as early as 1746, and Messance gave largely the same figures for these multipliers in his follow-up to his earlier study of Lyon, Auvergne, and Rouen, published in 1788.[40] These discussions were summarized and given the Académie royale des sciences's official stamp of approval in a series of papers submitted by Laplace, Condorcet, and du Séjour between 1783 and 1788.[41]

---

37. Ibid., p. 34.
38 Moheau concluded that the proportion of births to inhabitants for the entire realm was 25.5, noting that the proportion varied from province to province between 24 and 28 and that in a stable, healthy population with no outward emigration one could assume a figure of 26 (ibid., p. 42).
39. "Population du Roïaume," AN: H1 1444. Mémoires sur la population de la France et sur les rapports de la population avec l'impôt, XVIIIe siècle.
40. See Antoine Déparcieux, *Essai sur les probabilités de la durée de la vie humaine* (Paris, 1746), pp. 39–40; and Messance, *Nouvelles recherches*, p. 11.
41. See Pierre Simon de Laplace, "Sur les naissances, les mariages et les morts à Paris, depuis 1771 jusqu'en 1784; et dans toute l'étendue de la France, pendant les années 1781 et 1782," in *Histoire de l'Académie royale des sciences avec les mémoires de mathématique et de physique tirés des registres de cette Académie* (Paris, 1786), pp. 693–702; Marie-Jean-Antoine-Nicolas Condorcet, Pierre Simon de Laplace, and Achille-Pierre Dionis du Séjour, "Essai pour connoître la population du royaume et le

By the early decades of the nineteenth century, most population researchers gave up on their search for more precise multipliers of this nature, and they no longer sought to estimate the total population using the method of *année commune des naissances*. Instead, they began to express the frequency of births, deaths, and marriages in variable rates, usually given as a ratio of yearly births, deaths, or marriages to total population or occasionally as the proportion of such yearly events per single inhabitant. Eventually, they insisted on data from actual censuses to measure the denominator of these ratios. Nevertheless, the notion that specific groups in the population were possessed of certain social duties and obligations that could be measured numerically survived. In the nineteenth century, population researchers no longer devoted much energy to determining the "natural" levels of fertility that could be expected from a given population, but they continued to argue that reproduction was a social obligation that weighed particularly on women.

Regardless of the specific conclusions drawn on the question of universal law and variation, the works of Moheau, Messance, Expilly, and their peers are classic examples of what the historian Keith Baker has identified as the logic of "administrative rationality."[42] Baker described how the proponents of administrative centralization sought to legitimize their reforms by proposing scientific solutions to political problems. In doing so, they effectively moved the discussion of reform onto cognitive rather than political grounds and hid the exercise of power that this entailed behind a veil of technocratic efficiency. Moheau's *Recherches* illustrated this process in several ways. His use of numerical ratios such as the *année commune de mortalité* or the *année commune des naissances* provided a technical standard for measuring both the effects of government policies and the obligations of subgroups in the population. Furthermore, the all-encompassing scope of Moheau's *Recherches* also undermined the social distinctions that legally defined the members of the different estates un-

---

nombre des habitants de la campagne, en adaptant sur chacune des cartes de M. Cassini, l'année commune des naissances, tant des villes des bourgs et des villages dont il est fait mention sur chaque carte, presenté à l'Académie," in *Histoire de l'Académie royale des sciences avec les mémoires de mathématique et de physique tirés des registres de cette Académie* (Paris, 1786–91), pp. 703–18 (1786); pp. 577–92 (1787); pp. 601–89 (1788); pp. 703–17 (1789); pp. 601–10 (1790). See Eric Brian's discussion of these papers in *La Mesure de l'Etat*, pp. 256–71. In the first article, Laplace saw the discussion of the relation between births and total population as an opportunity to demonstrate newly developed techniques in the use of probability. He devoted his discussion to calculating how large a sample should be for arriving at the *année commune des naissances* to estimate a population as large as that of France with a reasonable margin of error. The series of articles by Condorcet, Laplace, and du Séjour were an attempt to arrive at a workable figure for the *année commune des naissances* by comparing the proportions of births to total population in as many locations as such data could be found.

42. Baker, *Inventing the French Revolution*, pp. 156–59.

der the old regime. Moheau's work recast the differences that separated man from woman, lord from peasant, lay from clergy, placing all in a singular relation with the power of the state.

Moheau's predecessors had been working up to this point for some time. In 1768, Expilly had divided the population into three categories by virtue of their dual relationship to the state and to production. First, he listed those who produced goods either directly or indirectly, including landowners, farmers, laborers, artisans, merchants, and manufacturers. Second, Expilly cited those who did not produce and whose subsistence came from the state, including the clergy, the army, the navy, and royal officials. Finally, he listed those who did not produce at all and whose subsistence was independent of the state: *rentiers*, beggars, and the unemployed. Messance, writing in 1788, was much more explicit, dividing the population into nine categories:

1) Cultivators, shepherds, and fishermen
2) Workers and artisans
3) Manufacturers and merchants
4) Businessmen and bankers
5) Financiers
6) Magistrates
7) Military officials and men of the court
8) The clergy
9) The sovereign and his family[43]

Expilly included the *rentier* class with beggars and the unemployed, while Messance placed the king, his family, the clergy, and men of the court in his list of productive occupations. Although it would be anachronistic to claim that these lists were purposefully incongruous, they point to the extent to which efforts to categorize the population in a functionalist manner were beginning to chafe against the social and legal distinctions that lay behind the old regime.

Moheau carried the logic of such categories much further than most of his contemporaries, explicitly acknowledging a principle of equality in membership that came with his idea of population. Nobody, no matter how powerful, was exempt from the all-encompassing gaze of the administrator. "Seeing man naked and stripped of all the prerogatives and distinctions introduced by social convention gives rise to a feeling of natural equality," wrote Moheau at the beginning of the *Recherches*.[44] At the same time, however, Moheau sought to show that very real differences existed

43. Messance, *Nouvelles recherches*, p. 56.
44. Moheau, *Recherches*, p. 2.

among people, and it was the duty of the administrator to take stock of these differences and determine their significance for the nation as a whole. In an extraordinary passage that is worth quoting at length, Moheau anticipated the coming strife of the Revolution, the utopian promise of a new technocracy, and the broad scope of social research that would be undertaken in the next several generations:

> All men are brothers. This is the first truth engraved in our hearts by nature, & confirmed by the infirmities that are common to all of us. Instead of regarding each other in light of what brings them together & unites them, these brothers only see what differentiates them, & these differences lead them to despise one another and persecute each other. Those whose skin is white and whose hair is long subjugate those whose color is black and whose hair is kinky. Those who carry a sword vex and at times mistreat those who carry only a spade. Those who wear a hat and fancy shoes believe themselves made of better stuff than those who wear only a cap and clogs, and those of the same sex, the same estate, the same profession have particular interests and pretensions. Within the nation, therefore, a multitude of divided and opposed nations live in secret and perpetual war. The Government is the ruling force, the institution that by serving some and hindering others, balances their interests and contains their reciprocal efforts. For this task it must know their respective strengths, for it is these strengths, and the number of individuals who compose these classes, which determine their rights and destinies.[45]

Even in Moheau's vision of universal fraternity there were no innocent differences; every physical variation, every mark of distinction signaled a new essence, a new identity, and a new potential for conflict. Fundamental to Moheau's project here was identification of polarities, which separated men from women, lord from peasant, wealthy from poor, dark-skinned from light. This multitude of nations within nations opened up the possibility of an infinite regress, whereby each subgroup would in turn dissolve before the observer into a constantly shifting morass of heterogeneity. From these premises, it is not difficult to see how the principle of equality in membership could be transformed into a utilitarian or instrumentalist doctrine founded on inequalities of function and value.

Not surprisingly, Moheau's suggestions for categorizing the influences that divide people into different groups do not correspond to our own. He did not, for example, distinguish between a given population's eco-

45. Ibid., pp. 78–79.

nomic, biological, social, or cultural characteristics—such categories had yet to be defined in the modern sense. Instead, Moheau contented himself with a simple division between "physical" factors, on the one hand, and the "political, civil, or moral" influences that acted on population, on the other. Under the former, Moheau considered the effects of climate, accidents in the workplace, wealth, indigence, and food; under the latter, he examined the influence of luxury, war, and capital punishment. If it is unclear to a twentieth-century reader why war is any less physical in its effects than accidents in the workplace, or why wealth should be treated in one section while luxury is discussed in another, it can only be because our own conception of what constitutes the "social" world is both different and more highly differentiated than Moheau's. For Moheau, the type of difference was less important than the fact of difference itself. His followers in the administration would soon begin the search for a more ordered and precise set of classifications, and in the nineteenth century, this search would lie at the heart of the emergent sciences of population.

Eighteenth-century population researchers thus established social complexity as both an epistemological and a political problem, and they insisted that statistics could play an important role in both understanding and governing large populations. Writers such as Montesquieu and Mirabeau had firmly established "population" as an object of public concern, and administrators such as Necker and Moheau took the first important steps toward making information about the population a regular part of government work. Much of the early impetus for this research came out of a faith in the influence of universal laws and the hope that such laws could be used in the service of administration. As more information about population became available, however, this faith in universal law began to cede ground to a different conception of social complexity. As in Moheau's work, this conception of population was based not on determinist assumptions of constancy but on a growing appreciation of the significance of variation and a desire to assign value to the new hierarchies that emerged from these differences.

During the Revolution this process continued as the authorities used population studies to undermine the social foundations of the hereditary monarchy. The establishment of the *état civil* in 1792 created the nation of citizens that was the political analogue of a population defined by equality in membership and marked the final dissolution of civic distinctions based on birth. From now on, each citizen was equal in the eyes of the law, and the significant events in his or her life were the subject of a unique record in the offices of the local town hall. But if the *état civil* gave the appearance of a commitment to an egalitarian individualism, the procedures for registering information about individuals in these records created the possibility of a new kind of aggregate thinking, based on distinctions of sex, age, profession, wealth, and regional identity. In other words, the principle of equality in membership, once established in the *état civil*, opened the way for population researchers to search for a new evaluation of every individual's function and value to society. They based this evaluation on a new set of categories and priorities that both reflected and gave shape to the emerging liberal social order. In this way, population research after 1789 helped to dismantle the older social hierarchies that had governed ancien régime society, offering in their place a newly rationalized vision of social differentiation. In this brave new world, the significance of individual lives was measured by the productive value offered to the nation as a whole by the particular aggregate groups that every individual belonged to by virtue of age, sex, profession, and civil status.

It was not a large step from instrumentalist arguments such as Moheau's to actual interventions in the lives of individuals, in the hopes of encouraging specific outcomes at the level of population. For Moheau, who after all still served a king, the standards for determining the utility of individual behavior ultimately referred back to the needs of the royal administration. After the Revolution, such bald statements of royal prerogative could no longer justify an active policy of state intervention, and the defenders of this new demographic instrumentalism were forced to look elsewhere for a means to legitimate official population policies. Eventually, this standard became the interest of the population itself, conceived on the one hand as a normally self-regulating social organism and on the other as the embodiment of a new political entity—the nation.

THE DESCENT INTO DETAILS

When government officials began counting in earnest, the sheer quantity of information they generated made social complexity as much a practical problem as a theoretical one. Dealing with this information required new bureaucratic offices, and during the revolutionary decade of the 1790s, statistical studies of the population took on a new prominence. Both the moderate National Assembly of 1789–92 and the radical National Convention of 1792–95 attempted to organize population counts, without succeeding in establishing the grounds for a general census. Under the Directory (1795–99) François de Neufchâteau established a statistical office in the Ministry of the Interior, which pushed for more accurate accounts from local officials about population, revenues, and productivity, but his definition of *statistique* was not limited to quantitative information.[46] Not until Lucien Bonaparte became minister of the interior under the Consulate (1799–1804), however, did a French government establish the nation's first real census in 1801. Alexis de Tocqueville was thus only partially correct in his assertion that the "government machinery" that emerged from the decade of revolution and war between 1789 and 1799 was "the same in all essentials" as the highly centralized institutions that characterized the French monarchy in the late eighteenth century.[47] The Revolution simultaneously created both new opportunities for the scientific study of population questions and new political uses for the knowledge that such study generated.

Initially, the events of 1789 disrupted the existing procedures for gathering information about population movements. Since 1772, the royal intendants of each administrative generality had been in the habit of sending regular "Etats de Population" to the ministers in Paris. These reports, which varied enormously in quality and scope, formed the basis of studies published by Necker, Moheau, and others in the years immediately before the Revolution. The system of intendants was one of the first victims of the events of 1789.[48] Almost immediately after its creation, the National Assembly sought to create an ambitious new system of departmental divisions in France, with the goal of establishing administrative units that would be homogenous with regard to population, resources, and territory. The eighty-three new departmental divisions became effective in February 1790, replacing the hodgepodge of ecclesiastical dioceses, military districts, judicial bailiwicks, and administrative generalities that had characterized the ancien régime. Population research on a national scale was now possible for the first time because each department was governed by an administrator who reported directly to the minister of the interior in Paris. The rapid pace of political change nevertheless prevented the implementation of full reforms. Despite a great deal of professed interest in official population research the first years of the Revolution saw few significant published results.[49]

46. Dupâquier and Le Mée, "La Connaissance des faits démographiques," p. 19.
47. Alexis de Tocqueville, *The Old Regime and the French Revolution*, trans. Stuart Gilbert (New York, 1955), p. 57.
48. Jacques Dupâquier and René Le Mée noted that the revolutionary government continued to receive the annual population tables until August 1792, when the monarchy was suspended and the Republic declared ("La Connaissance des faits démographiques," p. 16).
49. Ibid., p. 17. See also Bourguet, *Déchiffrer la France*, p. 54, and Rosanvallon, *L'Etat en France*, pp. 101–3. For an exchange of letters between Champion, the minister of the interior, and M. de La Michodière on the interruption of official investigations into population questions between 1789 and 1792, dated 4 August 1792 and 8 August 1792, see also AN: F20 103, n. 143.

The creation of new departmental divisions established a geometrically homogeneous political map of the nation; the revolutionary authorities in Paris now set about recasting the populations that inhabited these departments according to the new standards of citizenship. This task was accomplished by the Revolution's most significant contribution to the study of population, the *état civil*. The Legislative Assembly passed the "Loi sur la mode de constater l'état civil des citoyens" on 20 September 1792, the very day it disbanded.[50] This was a moment of intense crisis for the Revolution. Only two weeks earlier, organized crowds had massacred thousands of "counterrevolutionaries" in the prisons of Paris, and on the very day the law was passed, the revolutionary army was poised to win its crucial victory at Valmy, saving France from invasion. One day later, the newly constituted National Convention abolished the monarchy. Amid these dramatic events, the law of 20 September brought about a quieter revolution but one that served no less to transform the relationship between individuals and the French state: the law secularized the acts of birth, marriage, and death, defining them in purely civil terms. Aimed primarily at the continued power held by the clergy, the law of 20 September usurped the church's traditional role as the authority that supervised and recorded these pivotal moments in an individual's life. The mayors of each town were ordered to seize all parish records of baptisms, marriages, and burials and file them at the departmental archives. Henceforth, municipal authorities would keep the registers, and no individual could be born, marry, or die in France without official recognition of this act from the state. It would be difficult to underestimate the significance of this moment.[51]

Between 1789 and 1795, the revolutionary government undertook 446 separate investigations into population matters.[52] The frequency of these inquiries peaked during Year II of the Revolution (22 September 1793 – 21 September 1794) at an average rate of almost fifteen per month, or one every two days. Despite the uncertainty of these years, both the increasing centralization of authority under the Jacobins after the summer of 1792 and the simultaneous pressure of foreign invasion and internal op-

50. For the text of the law, see M. D. Dalloz, *Répertoire méthodique et alphabétique de législation de doctrine et de jurispridence en matière de droit civil, commercial, criminel, administratif, de droit des gens et de droit public*, 2 vols. (Paris, 1845), 2:489–91. For a nineteenth-century view of the law and its significance, see Maxime du Camp, "L'Etat civil à Paris," *Revue des deux mondes*, 18 March 1874, pp. 341–71.

51. Recognizing marriage as a form of civil contract between two people, the law also made provisions for divorce.

52. Isabelle Guégan, *Inventaire des enquêtes administratives et statistiques, 1789–1795* (Paris, 1991), pp. 9–18. I thank Sheryl Kroen for bringing this work to my attention.

position in the spring of 1793 worked to encourage the expansion of information channels between Paris and the provinces. Fully three-quarters of these investigations were of an economic or financial nature, concerning the resources available to the state during a time of revolution and war. Under these circumstances, the Revolution certainly impeded the development of long-term statistical investigations on the health and welfare of the population because this would have required an investment of official resources that the new government could ill afford. Nevertheless, the pressures of war and internal opposition galvanized the central authorities and encouraged an insatiable appetite for information that could be applied immediately to the urgent questions of the moment.

As might be expected, the tone of the revolutionary administration's proposals reflected both the anger and political discontent that drove events during these years. On the twenty-fifth day of Prairial, Year II (13 June 1794), during the most frenzied period of the Jacobin dictatorship, the Committee of Public Safety called for a general effort to determine the size of the population, as well as the number of births, deaths, and marriages in each district between 1789 and 1793. Accordingly, the Committee of Public Works sent out instructions, being careful to distinguish the effort from previous investigations undertaken during the old regime: "Under the Monarchy, pride and cupidity were the only motives for censuses, and this Operation, useful in itself, was not the least of the insults pronounced by Kings on the veritable sovereign . . . truth rarely crowned this insidious research." The committee's instructions concluded by reveling in the notion of a "census of Free men" performed by "Patriot Administrators." [53]

Despite these attempts to differentiate the intentions of the revolutionary government from the "insidious" research of the monarchy, however, the information requested was completely in line with the direction population research had been taking since the 1770s. District administrators were requested to record the number of births and marriages for the years 1789–93, for both sexes, alongside a column for recording the total number of inhabitants in each commune, as well as the number of houses and the number of households or hearths [feux]. The goal was clearly to provide information that would allow the officials in Paris to determine more precisely the kinds of universal multipliers used by Moheau and Necker to estimate the population of larger areas. In a special table devoted to mortality, however, space was provided for recording the

53. AN: F20 132, n. 53, letter from the Commission des Travaux Publics, Agence des Cartes et Plans, 3e Division, to district administrators, to accompany instructions for constructing "Etats de population" at the district level.

age distribution of those who died between 1789 and 1793, demonstrating a growing awareness that mortality rates varied according to the specific particularities of each individual region and community. In other words, the goals of the Committee of Public Safety with regard to population showed no clear sign of rupture with prerevolutionary population research. On the contrary, its investigations reflected the same mix of universalist assumptions with a growing empirical sense of the importance of difference and variation.[54]

Under the Directory, François de Neufchâteau's tenure at the Ministry of the Interior (July 1797–June 1799) marked a new departure point for official population research in France. To manage the accumulation of information that had overwhelmed administrators during the early years of the revolutionary decade, Neufchâteau created a special Bureau de statistique, often cited by historians as the first French office of population research in the modern era.[55] In his reports to his superiors, Neufchâteau noted the failure of royal administrators in the study of population. He gave strict instructions for the design of the tables that were to be distributed to every district administrator throughout the Republic, and he instituted a procedure by which each cantonal report would be forwarded to a central commission that would compile the information on a monthly basis.[56] His plans for the Bureau de statistique gave institutional expression to the distinction between Enlightenment universalism and the empirical interest in the particular. "To see the big picture is the duty of the legislator," he wrote, "to descend into the details is the task of the Administrator."[57]

Neufchâteau appreciated the value of numbers especially for their ability to reveal the slow and nearly imperceptible debilitating causes that could affect the population. "In its ordinary state," he wrote in a ministerial report, "nature acts by undetectable degrees, and its operations es-

---

54. AN: F20 132, n. 58, 59, and 60.
55. See Dupâquier and Le Mée, "La Connaissance des faits démographiques," p. 19.
56. Neufchâteau wrote, "Nothing is more certain than the number of births, marriages and deaths in a civilized State, when the Registers designated to make them known are in the hands of intelligent men. Nevertheless, under the old regime it was impossible to determine certain ratios which it would be so interesting to know, for example, that between births and population, or between population and death. . . . We have never determined the average life span of man" (AN: F20 105, "Rapport présenté au Ministère de l'Intérieure sur le travail relatif à la connaissance de l'Etat de la population de la République et de l'Etat civil des Citoyens, suivi d'un part de décision qui paroit nécessaire, pour utiliser cette partie du travail du 4eme Bureau," dated Thermidor, Year VI [July–August, 1798], p. 3).
57. AN: F20 105, "Rapport présenté au Ministère de l'Intérieure sur le travail relatif à la connaissance de l'Etat de la population de la République et de l'Etat civil des Citoyens, suivi d'un part de décision qui paroit nécessaire, pour utiliser cette partie du travail du 4eme Bureau," p. 4. On Neufchâteau, see also Bourguet, Déchiffrer la France, pp. 62–64.

cape us. An extraordinary event that ravages a department is sufficient to arouse the Government. But a continuous and almost imperceptible action that slowly undermines and destroys the human species might be felt only long years after it began. Its effects would be totally lost to mankind, if the power that governed them could not refer to comparative tables that register the traces of a fugitive action."[58]

This was the power of large numbers: taken over time, a large enough sample of observations could reveal the pernicious effects of hidden causes at work in the heart of the population. Neufchâteau's vision of the statistical bureau stood on the cusp between eighteenth-century political arithmetic, with its emphasis on a mechanical causality, and the view that would become more prevalent in the century to come, the understanding of causality based on aggregate observations and measurements of frequency.

Neufchâteau's successors were slow to pick up on the most innovative part of his plans for the statistical office however, and in the Napoleonic period, the bulk of population research was essentially descriptive, conforming to the older meaning of the term *statistique*. The golden age of descriptive statistics in Napeoleon's reign came under two ministers of the interior, Lucien Bonaparte (1800–1801), and his successor Jean-Antoine Chaptal (1801–4).[59] Lucien Bonaparte, the younger brother of the future emperor, enlisted the help of a state counselor with a deep interest in population, Adrien Duquesnoy. Together, Bonaparte and Duquesnoy pursued Neufchâteau's goal of an ongoing and constant correspondence between the ministry and departmental prefects. Their aim was to understand the fundamental situation in each department at the beginning of the new century, being careful to distinguish the purely short-term effects of war and the economic dislocations caused by military requisitioning.

Lucien Bonaparte had been an active Jacobin during the most radical phase of the Revolution, and under his tenure at the Ministry of Interior in 1800–1801, the Bureau de statistique discouraged the prefects of France from blaming the Revolution for any problems they perceived in their departments. A letter from the bureau to the prefect of l'Allier, dated 14 Frimaire, Year IX (5 December 1800) suggested that "the Revolution brought changes to all parts of the public body [*l'organisation publique*]

58. AN: F20 105, "Rapport présenté au Ministère de l'Intérieure sur le travail relatif à la connoissance de l'Etat de la population de la République et de l'Etat civil des Citoyens, suivi d'un part de décision qui paroit nécessaire, pour utiliser cette partie du travail du 4eme Bureau," p. 2.

59. The indispensable study of statistics during the Napoleonic period is Bourguet, *Déchiffrer la France*. See also Jean-Claude Perrot and Stuart Woolf, *State and Statistics in France, 1789–1815* (New York, 1984).

and the happy results of these changes remain to be perceived, rather than immediately felt. These happy results have been obscured by temporary and passing circumstances which no doubt have had their ill effects, but which are not fatal to a country." The bureau's letter went on to list the benefits the Revolution had brought to the French population: the suppression of the ecclesiastical *dîme* tax and feudal rents, the end of hereditary distinctions, and the abolition of monastic celibacy. "It is a certain fact," the letter concluded, "that in general, France's land is better cultivated, and the countryside is more populous than in 1789. Active causes have countered the inevitable evils that accompanied the long revolutionary torment and the destructive civil war. These causes must be found in the changes made since 1789. It is necessary, Citizen Prefect, to seize and study this observation with care, and to develop it in every way possible." [60] One might argue that this letter merely expressed a cynical desire to manipulate population research for political purposes. Cynical or not, however, the bureau's instructions illustrated the real connection between the universalizing rhetoric of revolutionary reforms—the push for equality, the end of privilege, the centralization of political authority—and the population question.

Lucien Bonaparte's successor, Jean-Antoine Chaptal, brought to the Ministry of Interior his extensive scientific experience as an industrial chemist, a doctor of medicine, and an agriculturist. Upon becoming minister in 1801, Chaptal separated the bureau of statistics from its connection with the ministry's archives and gave it a special status among the many offices in his administration. Almost immediately, he organized a large-scale investigation, the "Enquête sur l'état de France en l'an IX." In pursuing this project, Chaptal emphasized to the prefects under his authority the government's ignorance concerning population. "The more we busy ourselves with research on the population," he wrote to the nation's prefects on 30 Fructidor, Year X (21 September 1802), "the more we are convinced that we still lack the most fundamental foundations for our knowledge. The just proportions between population, births, deaths and marriages are not well known, and we are easily misled by speculation in the most important areas of political economy." [61]

The prefects' reports did not strive for exactitude, however, and they often contented themselves with round figures. Such lack of precision ran counter to developments in late eighteenth-century political arithmetic, which had suggested that numbers could be tabulated, arranged, and cal-

60. AN: F20 1, letter from the Bureau de Statistique to the prefect of Allier, p. 23.
61. Circular to departmental prefects from the Minister of Interior, dated 30 Fructidor Year X. The circular asked prefects to prepare a partial census of several communes in their jurisdiction, taking care to assign the task only to the most trustworthy mayors (AN: F20 27).

culated in such a way as explore the causal links between different phenomena. In spite of the clear precedent for such an analysis, the published work that emerged from Chaptal's tenure remained remarkably restrained in its enthusiasm for political arithmetic and the analytic use of numbers. The director of the Bureau de statistique under Chaptal, Alexandre de Ferrière, was an enthusiastic supporter of the investigations, but his interests, like those of Adrien Duquesnoy before him, were as much literary as they were quantitative. Duquesnoy, who served both Lucien Bonaparte and Chaptal, wrote: "We must not fool ourselves, a rigorous precision and a mathematical exactitude are impossible."[62]

A similar restraint was evident in one of the most ambitious works arising from the Ministry of the Interior's research, published by P.-Etienne Herbin de Halle, a judicial official under the Consulate. Herbin's seven-volume *Statistique générale et particulière de la France et de ses colonies* (1803–4) included an elaborate classificatory schema that encompassed France's topography and climate, the nation's political institutions and armed forces, the customs and characters of the people, the progress of science, literature, the arts, and education, and comprehensive sections on the products of industry, agriculture, and foreign trade. Herbin included numerical figures in his research, but they were not the primary focus of the work. In this sense, Herbin's *Statistique* was much more in line with the German academic tradition of *Statistik* than with the eighteenth-century French tradition of political arithmetic exemplified by writers such as Moheau and Messance.

Jacques Peuchet, one of Herbin's primary collaborators in this immense project, severely criticized the overconfident claims of political arithmetic, which he distinguished from a truly descriptive *statistique* and "political economy." In his "Discours préliminaire" to Herbin's first volume, Peuchet warned that political arithmetic could be misleading because of its tendency to produce "exaggerated or excessively variable values" that could never be a "solid foundation for knowledge."[63] In his own *Statistique élémentaire de la France* (1805), a work destined for *lycée* libraries, Peuchet criticized those authors who "garnished their books with calculations and tables that cut the thread and the succession of ideas, obscuring the narration, and leaving only slight traces in one's memory."[64] Peuchet's skepticism regarding the analytic uses of numbers points to the persistence of an older empirical tradition that sought to ground social

62. AN: F20 103, n. 126.
63. Jacques Peuchet, "Discours préliminaire," in P. Herbin de Halle, *Statistique générale et particulière de la France et de ses colonies, avec une nouvelle déscription topographique, physique, agricole, politique, industrielle et commerciale de cet état*, 7 vols. (Paris, 1803–4), 1:x.
64. Peuchet, *Statistique élémentaire de la France*, p. 2.

and political understanding in elaborate and totalizing systems of classification, rather than calculation.

Chaptal resigned from the Consulate's Interior Ministry in 1804, just before Napoleon crowned himself emperor of the French. His immediate successor, J.-B. de Champagny, allowed the statistical office to continue its research without a major change in personnel, but the bureau soon came under severe criticism from one of its own employees, Emmanuel Duvillard.[65] Duvillard's career in government administration had given him a thorough familiarity with the techniques of mathematical investigation developed by political arithmeticians in the last decades of the eighteenth century. Before the Revolution, Duvillard had worked in the office of the controller general of finances, and in 1791, under the sponsorship of Condorcet, he became director of the Bureau d'arithmétique politique at the National Treasury. From 1793 to 1800 he directed the government office responsible for liquidating life annuities, and in 1805, the secretary general of the Interior Ministry appointed Duvillard to be assistant director of the Bureau de statistique, under Alexandre de Ferrière. Duvillard's enthusiasm for political arithmetic soon brought him into conflict with the more literary intellectual interests of de Ferrière, Duquesnoy, and Peuchet. Without hiding his ambition to replace his superior, Duvillard published a stinging critique of the Interior Ministry's statistical office in January 1806. In the end, Duvillard did not get his wish. Alexandre de Ferrière resigned as director, and a new Bureau d'administration générale de la statistique was created at the Ministry of the Interior, under the directorship of Charles Etienne Coquebert de Montbret.

The episode is important for what it reveals about the tension within the administration concerning statistical research at the precise moment that the science was becoming institutionalized and made a routine part of government. Duvillard criticized the Bureau de statistique and its directors for conceiving of themselves as archivists instead of scientists who were capable of producing new knowledge about their object of study. De Ferrière's and Peuchet's zeal for classification led them to study aspects of the population in isolation from one another, and they did not attempt

65. On Duvillard's career and the debate over statistics under Napoleon, see Jean-Pierre Bardet, "Aux origines du bureau de la statistique, Duvillard de Durand, 1755–1832," *Population et société* 4 (1980): 154–64. See also "Duvillard et la statistique en 1806," *Etudes et documents. Comité pour l'histoire économique et financière de la France* 1 (1989): 425–26; Marie Noëlle Bourguet, "Décrire, Compter, Calculer: The Debate over Statistics during the Napoleonic Period," in *The Probabilistic Revolution*, ed. Lorenz Krüger, Lorraine J. Daston, and Michael Heidelberger, vol. 1 (Cambridge, Mass., 1987), pp. 305–16, and *Déchiffrer la France*, pp. 104–6; and Alain Desrosières, *La Politique des grands nombres, histoire de la raison statistique* (Paris, 1993), pp. 48–54. Duvillard's private papers are preserved in Bibliotheque Nationale, Manuscrits, nouvelles acquisitions françaises, 20576–91.

to establish the complex relationships between births and age cohorts or between populations with different proportions of adult men and women. Most disturbing to Duvillard was the bureau's apparent indifference to the need for greater precision in determining the exact proportions of births, deaths, and marriages to the total population, just the sort of ratios that were used to determine the *année commune des naissances*. Duvillard argued that if these proportions were well established and understood, the Bureau de statistique could use them to verify the data sent by each prefect.[66] In other words, Duvillard's confidence in political arithmetic led him to assert what Peuchet, Herbin, and Duquesnoy had been reluctant to concede, that calculation could reveal facts that were impossible to verify completely by observation. He listed the facts which he believed could be calculated from a well-kept statistical office: "the duration of marriage, of widowhood, the inventory of movable property [*la richesse mobiliaire*], the products of industry, raw materials and finished works, their dissemination, etc."[67]

Duvillard's failure to gain the directorship of the Bureau de statistique in 1806 left Napoleon's government without an active defender of political arithmetic in a position of authority, and in 1812 the bureau was suppressed altogether, its responsibilities dispersed to other offices. After the Restoration of the Bourbon monarchy in 1814, many of Napoleon's bureaucratic innovations remained in bad odor, and the statistical office was not reestablished under Louis XVIII (1814–24) or his successor, Charles X (1824–30). Not until another change of regime had made administrative reform politically acceptable again, in the late 1830s, did the French once more have a national office for centralizing and collecting statistical information about the population.

FROM *ÉTAT CIVIL* TO NEW SOCIAL AGGREGATES

The lack of a national statistical office between 1812 and 1835 meant that the most innovative developments in population research came from local studies based on information from the *état civil*. This office was now responsible for keeping records on every French citizen, and data gener-

66. "By combining the law of mortality with that of births, marriages, and deaths, one could ascertain what number of male, female, married, unmarried, and widowed individuals exist at every age, and in consequence, verify the population reports sent by the Prefects" (Emmanuel Duvillard, "Mémoire sur le travail du bureau de la statistique," *Etudes et documents. Comité pour l'histoire économique et financière de la France* 1 [1989]: 428).
67. Ibid., p. 429.

ated from these procedures provided the means for the "descent into details." At first, the primary purpose of the *état civil* was not statistical so much as juridical—it aimed to define "those facts which determine the rights of individuals with regard to family and society."[68] Under the ancien régime, individuals had no civil status as such, and whatever legal existence they possessed was derived from their position within a strictly defined hierarchy of estate, order, corps, and privilege. Under the new civic rules, however, all individuals possessed certain legal rights and obligations by virtue of their status as child, unmarried adult, father, wife, and eventually widow or widower. But if the ostensible function of the *état civil* was to provide the administration with information about individuals, statisticians soon found that they could rearrange this information to produce a body of knowledge about agglomerations within the population, organized by gender, marital status, and age. Eventually, researchers would use this information to assess frequencies and tendencies among different subgroups within the population and to make comparisons between different regions.

The most important area of research came out of the *état civil*'s complex procedures for registering death. The registration of births and marriages was relatively easy—the parents or the newly married couple simply presented themselves at the town hall and the event was recorded in the municipal register. The registration of death, however, required an official to leave his office, visit the corpse, verify its existence, and take the depositions of witnesses as to its identity. The presence of a government official in the house of the deceased created opportunities for exploring spaces that had previously remained outside the administration's purview. The interiors of bourgeois homes, the back streets and alleyways of poor neighborhoods, the drawing rooms and salons of the rich—all became components of a complex but increasingly visible social landscape that bound the population together as one organic unity, while simultaneously allowing officials to appreciate its heterogeneity. That these measures carried a coercive message for the population only served to underline the expansion of administrative power that accompanied the creation of the *état civil*: those who failed to report a death within three days, or before burial, faced two months in prison, six for a multiple offender.

Because collecting the information for the *état civil* was primarily the responsibility of local officials, many of the bureaucratic innovations required for this "descent into details" came from the departmental or municipal level. In this regard, the department of the Seine played an important role by expanding on the role played by the agents of the *état civil* in

68. Dalloz, *Répertoire*, 2:487.

collecting information on the population of Paris. On 13 October 1800, the prefect of the Seine decided that the local officials of the *état civil* could not be expected to have the time or the expertise to examine every dead body in their jurisdictions. To accomplish this task, the prefect created a special class of medical inspectors, recruited from the ranks of *officiers de santé*, for the express purpose of verifying the circumstances and causes of each death. Even at this point, however, the stated purpose of having a doctor present had little to do with the specialized information that an individual with medical training could hope to offer. Rather, the prefect desired to have a doctor present so as to avoid burying people who were not yet dead. Fearing unpleasant mistakes, the prefect warned that "any individual whose death is apparent but not yet verified must be considered to be still living." [69] Article 1 of the prefect's decree prohibited relatives from wrapping the body or face of those who were presumed to be dead and warned against exposing them to cold air before the medical examiner declared that the unfortunate person was dead.

In 1806, the Parisian authorities raised the standards of the *état civil* further by decreeing that the examining doctors could be selected only from those professionals who were already employed by the municipal *bureaux de bienfaisance* in dispensing care to the indigent. These medical officials, whose level of education and training had already been set by a previous decree, would now provide two of their members in each district for the office of *médecin vérificateur*. [70] Not until 1821, however, did the prefect of the Seine attempt to specify the information that would be recorded by the examining doctor in the case of death. [71] Prefect Chabrol de Volvic's decree of 31 December 1821 called upon the doctor of the *état civil* to record no less than thirteen particulars for each death: name, sex, marital status, age, profession, date (month, day, hour), quarter (street, number), floor and description of building, type of illness (if relevant to death, including reasons why an autopsy might be required), cause of illness and any complications, duration of illness, names of persons who furnished the deceased with medication, and names of persons who cared for the individual. The doctors were to record this information on pre-printed bulletins, filled out in duplicate, and filed with both the munic-

69. AdP: VD4 0001, n. 248, Inspection de la vérification des décès. Prefectural decree of 13 October 1800 (21 vendémiaire Year IX), signed by Frochot. Article 1.
70. AdP: VD4 0001, n. 248, Inspection de la vérification des décès. Prefectural decree of 2 June 1806, signed by Frochot.
71. Chabrol's successor, the comte de Rambuteau, summarized the significance of this moment later: "The administration . . . understood that the doctor called upon to verify each death was in a position by the nature of his functions to collect a great deal of information, not only useful for the medical police, but also of greatest interest to science and public hygiene" (AdP: VD4 0001, n. 247, p. 5).

ipal and the departmental authorities. Recognizing the greater burden that these duties placed on the *médecins vérificateurs*, Chabrol raised the sum they were paid for each visit from 1 franc 50 centimes to 2 francs.[72]

These bureaucratic procedures had two significant effects. First, the list of particulars that accompanied the registration of each death allowed for the municipal statistician to experiment with the construction of different social aggregates, based on the information contained on the death certificate. The information gleaned from observing these social aggregates eventually led statisticians to abandon the search for universal laws of population because death rates were found to vary according to age, sex, locality, profession, social status, climate, and season. Second, the *état civil* gradually opened up a gap between the "fact" of death and the moment of its legal recognition. A relatively trivial matter, perhaps, especially since in most cases this would simply have been a matter of time—time for the *officier de santé* or the *médecin vérificateur* to receive the report, make his way through the streets, enter the home, and make his investigation of the corpse. But this disjuncture between the death of the individual and the moment it became "official" effectively separated death into two distinct events—the first, biological, and the second, civic. The elements of biological death—the texture of the skin, the temperature of the body, the stiffness of the joints, the color of the tongue, the contents of the stomach—were in the medical domain and became the responsibility of the doctor. Civic death, on the other hand, was a matter of paperwork, bulletins to be filled out in duplicate, signed by witnesses, and filed with the appropriate authorities. This was the domain of the municipal statistician.[73]

The separation between the "fact" of a particular event and its moment of official recognition by a trained representative of the state thus became incorporated into the procedures that brought the complex world of the population into the workings of government during this period. Of course, many of the events that found their way into the statistical archives during this period required little interpretation or mediation by

72. AdP: VD4 0001, n. 248, Inspection de la vérification des décès. Prefectural decree of 31 December, 1821, signed by Chabrol. The culmination of Chabrol's work on the population of Paris came in a series of volumes published by the Prefecture of the Seine in the 1820s, collectively titled *Recherches statistiques de la ville de Paris*. These volumes are discussed in Chapter 2.
73. One might argue that a similar separation between biological death and "civic death" also existed for the old regime's parish records of baptisms and funerals. Nevertheless, the linkage of this separation to the emerging scientific disciplines of statistics and medicine was undoubtedly a new and significant departure from previous practices. In Chapter 3 I examine in detail the conflicts that emerged between these two scientific fields as they discussed the empirical procedures for ascertaining the causes of illness and death.

any other expert than the municipal statistician himself. Weekly variations in the depth of the Seine and fluctuations in the price and quantity of theater tickets could be transformed into civic events through simple acts of registration in a municipal table. Nevertheless, statisticians could not interpret many of the complex events that made up the life of the population without the help of other scientific disciplines. The causes of death could not be registered without the cooperation of medical doctors. Patterns of production and consumption could not be interpreted without the help of political economists. The relationship between public health and environmental conditions could not be clearly understood without the assistance of trained hygienists. In such cases, the separation between the actual event under observation and its eventual inscription in the statistical table opened up the possibility of conflict between the representatives of science and the agents of the administration, for they did not always agree about the significance of their respective observations.

Between the 1770s and the 1820s, the modern notion of "population" came into much sharper focus in France as a result of two related developments: increased sophistication in the use of statistics for social research and the rapid growth of a centralized government. The steady growth of a rationalized system of bureaucratic offices that extended from the village commune all the way up to the highest levels of government brought peripheral areas of the nation into regular contact with the authorities in Paris. This process had already begun well before the Revolution. Turgot and Necker were especially energetic in encouraging population research during Louis XVI's reign in the 1770s and early 1780s. Works such as Moheau's *Recherches et considérations sur la population de la France* firmly established the principle of equality in membership, effectively challenging the social hierarchies that structured French society during this period. Simultaneously, Moheau's work laid the foundations for a new secular utilitarianism based on numerical assessments of the obligations that every individual owed to the sovereign.

This enthusiasm was matched by the new administrators who came to power during the tumultuous decade of the 1790s. Substituting the interest of the nation for the interest of the monarchy, the successive regimes of the revolutionary period refined and augmented the instrumentalist procedures they inherited from their predecessors, most notably with the establishment of the *état civil* in 1792. In so doing, they replaced the ancien régime's preoccupation with estate and corporate identity with a new set of social hierarchies—sex, age, marital status, residence, and profession. Studying these new aggregates statistically over the long term promised to reveal the subtle causes at work affecting the condition of the social body, offering administrators a view of the population that was both totalizing and differentiated, attuned to the constant fluctuations of a complex society. Above all, this new work on population held out to administrators the comforting objectivity of procedures that could be reproduced ad infinitum. It was not only a theory of population, it was a practice of government.

The very audacity of these claims aroused considerable controversy, however. Every innovation carried with it the possibility of a more active population policy, whereby the state might act on the information now at its command, intervening in the lives of individuals to ensure the continuing health and prosperity of the nation. Improvements in statistical measurements ensured their continued use while simultaneously opening up complex questions about the reliability of the new knowledge and the representational status of numbers. Most significantly, the *état civil*'s procedural separation between the *médecin vérificateur* and the municipal official paved the way for a debate between doctors and statisticians beginning in the 1830s. Breaking out soon after what should have been the statistician's most triumphant moment—the establishment of the Statistique Générale de la France in 1835—this controversy revealed a surprising uncertainty within the French scientific community about the ability of population statistics to reveal anything about causality in the social world.

CHAPTER 2

THE CHAOS OF PARTICULAR FACTS

Numbers and Social Complexity

In 1837, a prominent French doctor named Casimir Broussais looked at the new field of knowledge opened up by statistics and could not contain his delight. "How they unravel the chaos of particular facts!" he exclaimed.[1] From our twentieth-century vantage point, it is difficult to recapture this sense of wonder. A new order had emerged from the assembled figures and tables, giving structure and form to the infinite variety of human experience. When grouped together in series, the most random events of social life were found to exhibit recognizable and consistent patterns, hinting at an unsuspected universe of exquisite precision. The result was an unbridled enthusiasm among those who found themselves seduced by the science of numbers. Announcing the new era, the political economist and statistician L.-F. Benoiston de Chateauneuf wrote in 1821: "Let us multiply our research, collect facts everywhere, and occupy ourselves with their assembly. Thus united they will speak loudly of their own accord, and from their unity will emerge transparent truths [*des vérités assez claires*]."[2]

Despite the advances made since the late eighteenth century, however, the organization of a centralized and permanent agency for the collection of official statistics developed remarkably slowly in France. The statistical office established by Neufchâteau during the Revolution and developed by Lucien Bonaparte and Jean-Antoine Chaptal disappeared in a reorganization of Napoleon's administration in 1812, when its activities were absorbed into other offices.[3] Not until 1833, when Adolphe Thiers pro-

---

1. Casimir Broussais, *Hygiène morale, ou application de la physiologie à la morale et à l'éducation* (Paris, 1837), p. 28.
2. L.-F. Benoiston de Chateauneuf, *Recherches sur les consommations de tout genre de la ville de Paris* (Paris, 1821), p. 23.
3. See Gille, *Les Sources statistiques*, p. 140, and Perrot and Woolf, *State and Statistics*, p. 120.

posed the creation of what eventually became the Statistique Générale de la France, did anyone suggest that it be replaced. Throughout the period of the conservative Restoration Monarchy (1814–30) and into the early years of the July Monarchy (1830–48) statistical work on population remained the domain of local or regional officials complemented by a looser community of private savants and academic researchers.[4] Under the leadership of Chabrol de Volvic, the Prefecture of the Seine published four large volumes on the capital in 1821, 1823, 1826, and 1829. These volumes, the *Recherches statistiques sur la ville de Paris*, possessed a wealth of demographic, economic, and meteorological information and provided the next generation of statistical researchers with an enormous compendium of raw data on the population of Paris.

Chabrol de Volvic had a brilliant career as an administrator, one that spanned both the Empire and the Restoration Monarchy. He had been a senior official under Napoleon and remained in office as prefect of the Seine from 1812 until 1830, an unusual feat given the antipathy of Restoration officials to the accomplishments of Napoleon's government. To supervise the *Recherches statistiques*, Chabrol recruited one of the most able mathematicians of the period, Jean-Baptiste Fourier, who had been Chabrol's professor at the Ecole polytechnique in the 1790s. Both Chabrol and Fourier had accompanied Napoleon on his expedition to Egypt, and both had extensive contacts in the scientific world of early nineteenth-century France. In 1817, Chabrol ordered the director of the prefecture's statistical bureau, the archivist Frédéric Villot, to undertake a census of the capital. Villot's remarkable accomplishments in this difficult task served as the basis for the volumes published in the 1820s.[5] Together, Chabrol, Fourier, and Villot made the *Recherches statistiques sur la ville de Paris* the most significant source of raw data on population in France dur-

4. Eric Brian argued that the establishment of the Montyon Prize for statistical research in 1817 by the Académie des sciences marked the moment at which the academic establishment took control of population research from the state administration ("Le Prix Montyon de Statistique à l'Académie royale des sciences pendant la Restauration," *Revue de synthèse* ser. 4, no. 2 [1991]: 207–36). See also Libby Schweber, "The Assertion of Disciplinary Claims in Demography and Vital Statistics: France and England, 1830–1885" (Ph.D. dissertation, Princeton University, 1996), p. 298.

5. Chabrol, Fourier, and Villot collaborated on four volumes, the *Recherches statistiques sur la ville de Paris*, published in 1821, 1823, 1826, and 1829. Two supplementary volumes were published in 1844 and 1860 by Chabrol's successors as prefect of the Seine, the comte de Rambuteau and the Baron Haussman. Chabrol gave the impetus for the first four works with his supervision of the pathbreaking Parisian census of 1817, which formed the basis for all the work done in the 1820s. Fourier offered technical assistance and wrote the introductory articles to each of the first four volumes. The bulk of the calculation and tabulation was probably done by Villot. See Coleman, *Death Is a Social Disease*, pp. 141–48; and Ann F. La Berge, *Mission and Method: The Early Nineteenth-Century French Public Health Movement* (Cambridge, 1992), pp. 76–81. On Fourier, see Ivor Grattan-Guinness, *Joseph Fourier, 1768–1830* (Cambridge, Mass., 1972). On Villot's role, see footnote in *RSVP*, 1821, p. iii.

ing the first third of the nineteenth century. Most important, the *Recherches statistique* provided the basis for Louis-René Villermé's path-breaking examination of differential mortality between rich and poor, published first in the 1820s and then continued in a series of articles he wrote for the *Annales d'hygiène publique et de médecine légale* in the 1830s.

In his introduction to the first volume of the *Recherches statistiques* in 1821, Fourier made clear that the term *statistique* in the title did not refer to simple descriptive categories in the older sense associated with the German tradition of *Statistik*. For Chabrol, Fourier, and Villot, *connaissances statistiques* referred to quantitative knowledge "of territory and climate, of public institutions, and the exact enumeration of all products of consumption, and all elements of industry, agriculture and commerce."[6] Of all of these elements, claimed Fourier, the "most important of all" was population. The editors of the *Recherches statistiques* did not bother to justify their preference for number over prose with a theoretical discussion of the power of calculation, as Duvillard had done in 1806. Instead, they offered their statistical tables as the most pragmatic solution to the problem of finding meaningful comparisons between different times and places and as a means of "excluding useless discussions." The *Recherches*, they promised, would provide administrators with a "methodical enumeration of facts."[7] Fourier was careful, however, to emphasize that the aim of the *Recherches* was not absolute truth in the scientific sense but only "the degree of precision required by questions of government and administration."[8] Conscious of those who had criticized quantification for achieving only the appearance of rigor at the expense of truly subtle and accurate verbal descriptions, Fourier justified the use of quantification on practical grounds.

Their ultimate goal, wrote Fourier, was to determine "the current law of population [*la loi actuelle de la population*] in this country."[9] The key to determining the "law of population" lay in accurate mortality tables, which would indicate the survival rate from year to year of different age cohorts in the population. Such tables, in turn, could be deemed reliable only if they were constructed from actual nominative lists of the population: a census that noted every individual, along with name, age, and date and place of birth. By comparing the number of individuals aged zero to one year with the number of individuals aged thirty to thirty one or sixty to sixty one, the administrator could measure with precision the rate of survival and the effects of mortality on the body politic over time. To

6. *RSVP*, 1821, p. ii.
7. Ibid., p. iv–v.
8. Ibid., p. vi.
9. Ibid., p. x.

monitor this law of population effectively, Fourier noted, the administration had to accomplish two primary tasks: regular and periodic censuses and careful annual registration of the number of births and the
number and age of deceased individuals. Throughout this discussion,
Fourier's vocabulary retained the connotation of universalism inherent in
eighteenth-century political arithmetic, especially with his reference to
"laws" of population and the underlying assumption that the survival
rates of each cohort were the product of constant causes. Nevertheless,
his use of the modifier "current" [actuelle] revealed his awareness that this
so-called law was in fact highly variable according to time and place. The
"law" of population was, according to Fourier, the ultimate and primary
cause which acted on the collective body of a population, once all of the
"accidental causes" had canceled each other out, but it did not necessarily act on all populations in the same way.[10]

Given the clear and programmatic agenda for population research announced as early as 1821 by Chabrol, Fourier, and Villot in the *Recherches
statistiques de la ville de Paris*, what can account for the delays in establishing a truly comprehensive official statistical bureaucracy in France? In
part, the answer to this question can be found in political obstacles. The
absence of a centralized national office for population research between
1814 and 1830 resulted from the association of such investigations in the
minds of Restoration officials with the administrative structure set up
during the Revolution and under Napoleon.[11] Equally important as these
political obstacles, however, was a persistent uncertainty among some scientists concerning the power of statistics to represent real phenomena
faithfully. The first director of the Statistique Générale, Alexandre Moreau de Jonnès, wrote that statistics "are like the hieroglyphics of ancient
Egypt, where the lessons of history, the precepts of wisdom, and the
secrets of the future were concealed in mysterious characters."[12] Such
statements were not easily juxtaposed to Benoiston's celebration of facts,
"which spoke loudly of their own accord."[13] Together, these conflicting
images point to the paradox faced by social investigators who were forced
to reconcile two contradictory ideas at the heart of their project. On the
one hand they found it necessary to claim, as did Fourier in his introduction to the *Recherches*, that statistics would speak for themselves and that
their status as truth necessitated a rejection of the dangerous vagaries of

10. Ibid., pp. xxxvi–xxxvii.
11. René Le Mée, "La statistique démographique officielle de 1815 à 1870 en France," *Annales de démographie historique* (1975): 251.
12. Quoted in Theodore Porter, *The Rise of Statistical Thinking, 1820–1900* (Princeton, 1986),
p. 29, translation Porter's.
13. See note 2 above.

interpretation. On the other hand, the ability of statistics to reveal the hidden processes that lay behind social phenomena required the creation of an aura of mystery, a promise of truths to come that were inaccessible to other methods of analysis. Moreau de Jonnès's reference to Egyptian hieroglyphs was not fortuitous because it simultaneously opened up and closed down the possibility of signification in social science by positing a new symbolic order and reserving the key to its reading to a select few.

Until recently, most histories of the statistical explosion in the first half of the nineteenth century in Europe concentrated primarily on methodological breakthroughs.[14] Recognition of important technical developments is of course necessary, but it is also important to avoid simplifying the history of the new science into a progression of "cognitive steps" that unfolded as if their destination had been foreordained.[15] Such a view risks overlooking the peculiar and contradictory history of population studies during a key period in its development. Was the development of population statistics in France simply a history of technical questions overcome by patient experimentation? Even the most astute of historians have fallen into this reductive perspective, as evidenced by Louis Chevalier's comment that the "population expert" became more important early in the nineteenth century simply because "the facts of population themselves were making an ever-increasing impact."[16] Chevalier's summary explanation, although clearly not wrong, is insufficient, for it makes no attempt to understand how the language of the population sciences achieved its legitimacy. The new statistical knowledge of population changed the relationship between government and the governed, challenged established conceptions of the state's responsibility to protect the public welfare, and brought newly emergent corporate groups, such as public functionaries and doctors, to levels of power and prominence that they had never before possessed. Obviously there was more to this transformation than a greater impact of "population" itself on the life of the nation.

Having rejected a purely functionalist account of the development of statistical thinking, one may well ask what it was about statistics that

14. Excellent works that are an exception to this trend include Lorraine Daston, *Classical Probability in the Enlightenment* (Princeton, 1988); Desrosières, *La Politique des grands nombres*; Gigerenzer et al., *Empire of Chance*; Ian Hacking, *The Emergence of Probability* (Cambridge, 1975) and *Taming of Chance*; Porter, *Rise of Statistical Thinking*; Steven Stigler, *The History of Statistics: The Measurement of Uncertainty before 1900* (Cambridge, Mass., 1986); and the many essays in Lorenz Krüger, Lorraine Daston, and Michael Heidelberger, eds., *The Probabilistic Revolution* (Cambridge, Mass., 1987). Works dealing specifically with social statistics in France include Bourguet, *Déchiffrer la France*; Le Bras, "Statistique Générale"; *Pour une histoire de la statistique* (Paris, 1977); Perrot and Woolf, *State and Statistics*; Gille, *Les Sources statistiques de l'histoire de France*.
15. The phrase is Marie-Noëlle Bourguet's in "Décrire, Compter, Calculer," p. 305.
16. Louis Chevalier, *Laboring Classes and Dangerous Classes in Paris during the First Half of the Nineteenth Century* (Princeton, 1973), p. 47.

made them resonate so well with the community of experts who first championed their use. An important ingredient in this transformation was not immediately related to a greater success in explaining the complexity of the social world but in representing this complexity in a particularly attractive way. A close look at the representational status of numbers during this period should help in understanding a particular paradox about the history of statistics: that widespread enthusiasm for the science of number predated the development of effective and reliable statistical techniques. In other words, many people became excited about statistics long before they actually began to produce reliable results. They did so, at least in part, because of the powerful significance attributed to numbers as signs of precision and rigor in the face of seemingly impenetrable complexity.

Focusing on the question of representation can also help to explain much of the resistance faced by statisticians as they attempted to apply their science of number in medicine, political economy, public hygiene, and other human sciences. Many of the debates on the advantages of statistical methods focused on fundamental theoretical questions concerning the nature of empirical observation and the ability of numbers to capture the fluidity of social and biological events as they unfolded in the world. Rarely did these debates actually broach specific methodological questions relating to the use of averages or the calculation of rates, the isolation of different variables, or other aspects of quantification. Numbers were clearly fascinating (or repugnant) to these scientists as signs of complexity, and their representational status was just as much at stake in the debates as was their simple functional utility. This was not a simple disagreement, therefore, between the defenders of scientific progress and the reactionary protectors of an outdated status quo. Much of the dissent came from scientists who were firmly committed to empirical research but who disagreed about how to draw conclusions from particular observations and how to represent those conclusions convincingly. Part of the problem for dissenting scientists was the extravagant confidence of the Enlightenment tradition itself, which refused to settle for anything so timid as statistical frequencies when it could call for a rigid and determinist law to explain a given phenomenon.

To a great degree, the ubiquitous use of quantitative information in all branches of the human sciences has inured us to the representative status of numbers and obscured the history of their acceptance in scientific research. As they are used today, statistics are a form of realist description; applied to population, they purport to represent social and biological processes as they unfold in time through series of numerical signs, tables, and graphs. This form of realist representation is not at all mimetic; it is a complex abstraction that creates the possibility of new meaning by constructing a new context for judging the significance of particular observations. This new context is established through the juxtaposition of similar phenomena, which one can count, tabulate, average, and measure in changes over time.

Behind the calculations, however, statistics are haunted by the absence of individual narratives, the untold stories of each particular case. For perfectly understandable reasons, these narratives are deemed irrelevant to the goals of quantitative analysis. Nevertheless, the statistician must necessarily suppress the possibility that these individual narratives might diverge significantly from the history being written at the level of the collective—and the necessity of this suppression lends an unavoidable allegorical quality to the numbers themselves, which stand as the signs of such absent narratives.[17] An important achievement of statistical knowledge in the nineteenth century lay in the containment of this inescapable allegorical tendency by the conventions and standards of mathematical analysis. Clearly one should be aware of the history of technical developments that established such standards, but an overemphasis on a teleological progression runs the risk of misinterpreting the resistance statistical knowledge faced and ignores the often elaborate schemes that the proponents of statistics constructed around their "breakthroughs."[18] In fact, an important part of the resistance to statistical methods was precisely a defense of these absent narratives and a rejection of the attempt by statisticians to dismiss their significance through what was initially perceived as a kind of representational sleight of hand.

POPULATION AND CAUSALITY

Central to the debate about statistics in the first half of the nineteenth century was a growing awareness among mathematicians, doctors, economists, and statisticians that Enlightenment accounts of causality were insufficient to explain the complexity of the social world. In 1857, a Malthusian political economist, Joseph Garnier, noted with some exasperation that "the majority of causes become effects, and that these effects in

17. I am indebted to Thomas Pepper for drawing my attention to the allegorical quality of statistical work.
18. A list of such breakthroughs would include Laplace's notion of inverse probability, which made statistical inference possible; Gauss and Legendre's perfection of the method of least squares for calculating degrees of error; Poisson's recognition of the dual nature of probability; Quetelet's use of the binomial law to examine distribution around mean values; and later, Galton's development of laws of regression for treating problems with multiple variables. All of these developments are treated at length in Stigler, *History of Statistics*.

turn act as causes, such that it appears difficult in this regard to arrive at an absolutely logical classification." [19] Garnier's statement stands as eloquent testimony to the difficulty that nineteenth-century social observers had with causality. No one doubted that the question of cause and effect was central to their research into population. In 1845 Michel Levy, a doctor and specialist in public and private hygiene, wrote "The specific population comprises not only all the current elements of a country, but also all the influences which have acted upon it in preceding centuries." [20] By mid-century, then, "population" had come to mean more than the mere collectivity of bodies found in a given geographical area. "Population" also meant the signs of the history of these bodies, signs that could be read in their environment, in their behavior, and even in signs on the bodies themselves. Unraveling the chaos of particular facts depended on being able to see "population" as the sum of the effects of its past and the cause of its future.

Part of the difficulty lay in the inductive character of statistical analysis, which led the quantifiers to speak in terms of frequencies and tendencies among large populations, rather than pinpointing specific causes that acted the same way in each individual case. The indeterminacy of statistical reasoning was disturbing to many scientists during the first half of the nineteenth century because of the implication that ignorance about the outcome of any particular event was irrelevant to an understanding of a large number of events. As we have already seen, eighteenth-century predecessors of social statisticians in France believed firmly in a mechanistic determinism, which assumed that every occurrence was necessarily located within a minute and intricate web of interlocking causes. When determinists like Pierre Simon de Laplace used the term "probability" they were referring to the limits of human understanding in the face of such complexity. Statements of probability in such a context were never descriptions of real events, but rather measurements of uncertainty in the mind of the human observer. "The curve described by a simple molecule of air or vapor," wrote Laplace, "is regulated in a manner just as certain as the planetary orbits; the only difference between them is that which comes from our own ignorance." [21]

Laplace pointed out, however, that in observing repeated events of a

19. Joseph Garnier, "Tableau des causes de la misère et des remèdes qu'on peut y apporter," *Journal des économistes* ser. 2, 14 (1857): 340.

20. Michel Levy, *Traité d'hygiène publique et privée*, 2 vols. (Paris, 1844), 2:492.

21. Pierre Simon de Laplace, *A Philosophical Essay on Probabilities*, trans. Frederick Wilson Truscott and Frederick Lincoln Emery (New York, 1951), p. 6. In Ian Hacking's terminology, Laplace's probability was primarily "epistemic." Hacking contrasted "epistemic" probabilities with "aleatory"

similar nature, such as flipping a coin, our ignorance often diminished over the long term. Although we might never know the precise combination of initial velocity, air currents, and momentum that determined any particular toss, we might be able to hazard a reasonably accurate guess as to the proportion of heads and tails in a sufficiently large number of throws. From his observation of such long-term regularities Laplace drew a very big conclusion, that "the ratios of the acts of nature are very nearly constant when these acts are considered in great number."[22] In his subsequent discussion, Laplace made clear that under "acts of nature" he included observed regularities that depended on human volition or "moral causes," such as the proportion of births to the total population, the ratio of marriages to births, or the number of undeliverable letters deposited at the post office in a normal year. Every statistical regularity, Laplace reasoned, must result from the effects of "constant causes" that prevailed in the long term over any variable or accidental causes that might intervene at any particular moment. Ultimately, Laplace drew a political lesson from this observation, claiming (without much evidence) that "the eternal principles of reason, of justice, and of humanity" functioned as constant causes on the well-being of populations and their institutions.[23] It was incumbent upon legislators, therefore, to recognize the effects of such constant causes and avoid contravening them in any way.

Laplace's system of mechanistic determinism jostled uncomfortably in the 1820s and 1830s with another use of "probability," one that threatened the neatness of Laplace's pronouncements on causality and made the moral lesson less certain. This new use of probability made no claims to be about knowledge but was rather an attempt to describe the observed frequencies of events occurring in the world, such as the "probability" of rolling snake-eyes with dice or of drawing a full house in poker.[24] Defining probability as observed frequencies, or as ratios that actually existed

---

or "stochastic" probabilities, those that are objective frequencies that actually occur in the world. According to Hacking's account, these two versions of probability coexisted uneasily in philosophy from the late seventeenth century until Siméon-Denis Poisson made the distinction explicit in 1837 (*Emergence of Probability*, pp. 12–13; *Taming of Chance*, pp. 96–97). Gigerenzer et al. have preferred the term "subjective" probability over "epistemic" probability because the former emphasizes that such statements can only be the product of particular observations with limited information. Likewise, for "aleatory" probability they substitute the expression "objective frequency" (*Empire of Chance*, pp. 7–18).

22. Laplace, *Philosophical Essay*, p. 60.
23. Ibid., p. 63.
24. The most famous early example of this use of probability occurred in Jakob Bernoulli's *Ars conjectandi* (1713). Bernoulli placed a fixed proportion of colored balls in an urn and attempted to find a measurement of this proportion by making a series of drawings, replacing the balls each time. He determined that as the number of drawings increases to infinity, the probability that the observed

independently of human awareness, was potentially disruptive to a rigidly mechanistic determinism because it separated the occurrence of an individual event from its cause, making its outcome a matter of tendency rather than inevitability. Such stochastic probabilities (i.e., probabilities that were purely the result of chance) had no place in the universe of eighteenth-century philosophes because their notion of an absolute determinism would not allow for any uncertainty to exist except in the fallible mind of the human observer.[25] One can imagine their dismay, as well, at the difficulty of drawing the same moral conclusions that Laplace drew from his analysis of "constant causes." If regularity was only a matter of tendency observable among large populations, how was one to draw a moral lesson from the particularities of any individual case?

The transition in thinking from Laplace's subjective conception of probability to that of objective frequencies occurred not through any philosophical breakthrough but in a gradual shift of emphasis that accompanied the great expansion of statistical work in the first decades of the nineteenth century.[26] In the meantime, the rigid determinism of the eighteenth-century theorists of probability lingered on, giving much impetus to social science and inspiring many with the hope that the investigation of society would soon achieve the exactitude and precision of the physical sciences. Conflict arose, however, when population researchers sought to use their observations of particular facts to make generalizations about the "constant causes" that acted on larger groups or society as a whole.

In concrete matters such as public health, these theoretical questions

---

proportion of colors equals the actual proportion in the urn approaches certainty. Gigerenzer et al. claim that Bernoulli's theorem is both "revolutionary" and "banal," the latter because common sense shows it to be true, and the former because "it linked the probabilities of degrees of certainty to the probabilities of frequencies, and because it created a model of causation that was essentially devoid of causes. Heretofore causes had been understood as essences, or as microscopic mechanisms. In either case, they produced their effects necessarily, if obscurely. Causes were more loosely connected to effects in Bernoulli's model of a posteriori reasoning, just as the results of individual drawings were only loosely connected to the actual proportion of balls. Necessity obtained only in the long run" (*Empire of Chance*, pp. 29–30). On Bernoulli's influence on Laplace, see Victor L. Hilts, "Statistics and Social Science," in *Foundations of Scientific Method: The Nineteenth Century*, ed. Ronald N. Giere and Richard S. Westfall (Bloomington, 1973), pp. 209–11.

25. In addition to Hacking and Gigerenzer et al., other historians have discussed the transformation in the meaning of probability from the "classical" definition to the "frequentist" model. See especially Charles Gillispie, "Probability and Politics: Laplace, Condorcet, and Turgot," *Proceedings of the American Philosophical Society* 116 (1972): 1–20; Porter, *Rise of Statistical Thinking*, pp. 71–88; and Daston, *Classical Probability*, pp. 210–25.

26. Early attempts to set up "life tables" for the purposes of selling insurance and annuities are a notable case of gathering statistics long before sufficient techniques existed to ensure that such transactions would prove profitable. See Gigerenzer et al., *Empire of Chance*, pp. 25–26; and Hacking, *Taming of Chance*, pp. 111–21.

could have perplexing repercussions. For example, when French hygienists attempted to introduce smallpox vaccination programs soon after Edward Jenner's vaccine was introduced in 1798, they often encountered opposition among local populations.[27] The doctors tried to explain that vaccinations would help prevent the spread of disease, even if some people who received vaccinations subsequently became ill during epidemics. In fact, they could point to real successes with these vaccination programs between 1800 and 1820, especially in the Bas-Rhin region. Despite this progress in preventing the spread of disease, however, the hygienists' efforts continued to be resisted by communities that refused to allow their children to be vaccinated. Some people held to the traditional belief that smallpox was a necessary purgative that strengthened the constitution of those who survived the disease; others blamed any subsequent illness on the vaccine. Confronting such beliefs with a statistical argument about the decline in mortality rates experienced by vaccinated populations could have little meaning to people in rural communities who were more accustomed to thinking of disease as individual misfortune or, at most, a local calamity. The historian Ann La Berge concluded that the hygienists ultimately failed to achieve wider success because of the government's unwillingness to make vaccination obligatory, arguing that "compulsory vaccination raised the basic public health question, then as now: the right of individual liberty versus the good of society."[28] It is important to remember, however, that the very terms of this opposition were being transformed by the new techniques of population research. Both the realm of individual autonomy and the concept of public health were recast by the language of number, the former by a set of linkages that privileged certain aspects of an individual's life at the expense of the rich and varied texture of his or her own experience, and the latter by a process of mathematical generalization that sought to establish socialized standards of well-being in the place of individual measurements of self-satisfaction.

For the proponents of statistics the answer seemed clear enough. In matters of public health, hygiene, and the well-being of the nation, statistics allowed them to measure the internal and external dynamics of specific populations, be they rich or poor, male or female, young or old, urban or rural. Armed with this information, administrators would be able to evaluate in quantitative terms the effect of individual behavior on society. The public, however, remained suspicious of any bureaucratic procedures associated with the census, taxation, or novel medical practices. Even in the scientific community, many doctors insisted that quantifi-

27. La Berge, *Mission and Method*, pp. 101–8.
28. Ibid., p. 108.

cation could explain nothing of significance at the level of individual behavior because statements of probability could not account for the mechanical sequence of cause and effect that they assumed to be the determinant force in human society. And even the liberal supporters of population research were disturbed by the fact that statistical generalizations lent weight to analyses of social problems cast in terms of larger aggregates such as class. In the uncertain political climate of the first half of the nineteenth century, any population study that treated the emergence of social classes as objectively real entities was bound to be disturbing. If economic and biological processes were capable of producing homogeneous aggregates such as class as effects, what was to prevent these aggregates from acting as causes in turn? The lessons of revolution in 1789, 1830, and 1848 only served to compound this anxiety, making the identification of social aggregates both an empirical and a political problem, and as we shall see, the specter of revolution was never far from these debates.

HEALTH AND WEALTH IN PARIS

In the 1820s, the prominent hygienist Louis-René Villermé lent new legitimacy to the quantitative treatment of social aggregates when he published the first results of his research on the differential mortality of rich and poor populations in Paris. Villermé was well placed to undertake this study. The son of a lawyer, he was one of the first students of the newly founded Ecole de médecine in 1801, and he entered Napoleon's army as a military surgeon in 1803. For eleven years, Villermé followed the emperor's armies across Europe, coming to know firsthand the suffering and deprivation of societies at war. The emperor's defeat in 1814 allowed Villermé to complete his formal medical studies, and he launched a career as a doctor in Paris in the first years of the Restoration Monarchy. He was an associate of the innovative Société médicale d'émulation, a gathering of clinicians founded in 1796 by the inventor of pathological anatomy, Xavier Bichat. In 1823 Villermé was elected adjunct member of the recently refounded Académie royale de médecine, and throughout the rest of the 1820s he devoted himself to medical research. He helped to found an influential journal, the *Annales d'hygiène publique et de médecine légale*, in 1829, and he resumed medical practice in 1832 during the deadly cholera epidemic that swept through the country. In 1835, in recognition of his research on mortality and his participation on the official commission that wrote the report on the cholera epidemic in the capital, Villermé became a full member of the Académie de médecine. During the 1830s, he was also active in the prestigious Académie des sciences morales et politiques, a section of the French Institute known for its association with liberal ideas of social reform, and in 1849 he became the president of this body. At the end of his career, Villermé was named honorary president of the Société de statistique de Paris upon its founding in 1860. In short, Villermé was at the center of an increasingly professionalized world of social and scientific expertise, one in which doctors, hygienists, lawyers, political economists and government administrators conferred with one another about social and political matters and debated proposals for reform.[29]

In the 1820s, Villermé studied with great interest the rapidly growing population of Paris. The capital's dangerous and unhealthy neighborhoods were standard themes of medical and literary description from the end of the eighteenth century through the July Monarchy, but Villermé's work on Paris was the first to test these assumptions rigorously with the help of statistics.[30] Villermé, along with his hygienist colleague François Benoiston de Chateauneuf, used data from Frédéric Villot's *Recherches statistiques sur la ville de Paris* to demonstrate that wealth and poverty had a far stronger impact on mortality rates than the meterological or environmental factors that were commonly thought to influence health in early nineteenth-century France. Published in the most important medical and scientific journals of the period, these pathbreaking articles were the first to take advantage of the vastly increased body of information on mortality made available through the services of the *état civil*.[31]

The construction of aggregates was central to Villermé's project.[32] At

29. On Villermé's career, see Coleman, *Death Is a Social Disease*, pp. 4–14.

30. Chevalier, *Laboring Classes*, pp. 27–144. Villermé's influence on later investigators can be gauged by the words of a Parisian municipal counselor who stated on the occasion of the founding of a new statistical office in Paris in 1877 that "[Villermé's] observations have become what one could call banal truths" ("Rapport présenté par M. Lamouroux sur la réorganisation de la Statistique municipale de la ville de Paris," *Conseil Municipale de Paris, Rapports et Documents*, 1877, no. 12, p. 3).

31. Louis-François Benoiston de Chateauneuf, "De la durée de la vie chez le riche et le pauvre," *Annales d'hygiène publique et de médecine légale* 3 (1830): 5–15; and Louis-René Villermé, "De la mortalité dans les divers quartiers de la ville de Paris, et des causes qui la rendent très différente dans plusieurs d'entre eux, ainsi que dans les divers quartiers de beaucoup de grandes villes," *Annales d'hygiène publique et de médecine légale* 3 (1830): 294–341. Villermé published earlier versions of this work as "Rapport fait par M. Villermé et lu à l'Académie royale de médecine, au nom de la Commission de statistique, sur une série de tableaux relatifs au mouvement de la population dans les douze arrondissements municipaux de la ville de Paris pendant les cinq années 1817, 1818, 1819, 1820, et 1821," *Archives générales de médecine* 10 (1826): 216–47; and "Mémoire sur la mortalité en France dans la classe aisée et dans la classe indigente," *Mémoires de l'Académie royale de la médecine* 1 (1828): 51–98. For a detailed account of Villermé's publications on this question and his use of Villot's data, see William Coleman's indispensable account, *Death Is a Social Disease*, p. xxi. See also Bernard-Pierre Lécuyer, "Démographie, statistique et hygiène publique sous la monarchie censitaire," *Annales de démographie historique* (1977): 215–45.

32. This was a central theme of political economy in the 1820s, as theorists turned from the study of governments to the study of economic behavior and the social question. Charles Dunoyer, a

the most fundamental level, Villermé assumed that each neighborhood of the capital possessed a homogeneous population. "I considered each district of Paris as if it formed a distinct city," he wrote, so as to dismiss the complicating factor of internal migration from his calculations.[33] One might argue that Villermé's assumption here was simply a product of the limitations of his data: Frédéric Villot's tables in the *Recherches statistiques* did not allow him to make more precise determinations of the composition of each neighborhood or of movements in or out of each district. But even as he acknowledged this problem, Villermé revealed his essential preconceptions about the composition of these various district populations. He admitted that "the inhabitants of one district pass easily to others" but claimed that "these are almost always individuals of the same classes, individuals of analogous occupations and whose status reflects the same degree of wealth, possessions or poverty." [34] In other words, Villermé believed as a matter of course that the different *quartiers* of Paris possessed their own character, attracting people of similar trades, status and wealth. The populations of Parisian districts were not simply random composites produced by the principle of equality in membership and the accident of being neighbors. On the contrary, they were real collective bodies, whose common characteristics allowed one to make assumptions about the lives of individual members. The overt goal of the research—proving a connection between wealth and longevity—was thus complemented by a second, tacit, goal: defining the objective reality of social classes in terms of a few shared characteristics such as health, wealth, or geographical proximity.

Villermé's procedure can be summed up simply as follows. Using the data provided by Frédéric Villot's studies of the Parisian population between 1817 and 1826, Villermé noted that the ratio of inhabitants per death in the north and west of the capital was considerably more favorable than in the southern and eastern districts. In calculating these ratios Villermé limited himself to deaths that occurred in the home (*à domicile*) and set aside the large number of deaths that occurred in hospitals for the

---

noted liberal political economist, announced the significance of this turn in 1825: "First, I will not speak of governments, or at least what I do say about them will be indistinguishable from what I say about populations. I will not cast my gaze on anything but the masses; their industry and their morality will be the subject of all my observations, the material of all my experiments" (*L'Industrie et la morale considerées dans leurs rapports avec la liberté* [Paris, 1825], pp. 7–8).

33. Villermé, "De la mortalité dans les divers quartiers de la ville de Paris," p. 295.

34. Ibid. From the perspective of today's standards in population research this assumption was undoubtedly an error. William Coleman, for example, called Villermé's neglect of migration a mistake (*Death Is a Social Disease*, p. 154).

poor and indigent because these were unevenly distributed throughout the city. After ranking the twelve districts according to the ratio of deaths per inhabitant for each of the years 1818–26 and finding that the same ranking occurred almost every year, Villermé concluded that these differences in mortality were not the effects of random fluctuations but of "constant causes."[35] His analysis thus far was completely in keeping with the agenda for population research outlined by Chabrol, Fourier, and Villot in the early volumes of the *Recherches statistiques sur la ville de Paris*.

Villermé then sought to compare these rankings by examining other factors in turn: proximity to the Seine, elevation and drainage, nature of the soil, narrowness and sinuousity of the streets, height of the buildings, direction of prevailing winds and major thoroughfares (thought to influence air currents), quality and source of water, and density of population. Each of these factors was commonly linked to health, both in the medical literature and in popular opinion. Villermé reasoned that if he could demonstrate that one of these factors consistently coincided with the ranking for mortality, he could then claim to have identified a "constant cause" that produced the observed statistical regularity. One by one, however, he eliminated all of these possibilities by demonstrating that there was no discernible pattern of coincidence.

Villermé then remarked that it would be convenient to have accurate information on "cleanliness or uncleanliness, clothing, food, drink, etc." for each district because these factors could be assumed "to sustain life or to abridge it."[36] Lacking such detailed information, he settled for a table from Villot's *Recherches statistiques* that gave the percentage of houses in each district that were not subjected to a tax on rent. Rents under 150 francs were untaxed, and Villermé assumed that a neighborhood with a high percentage of untaxed rents was one with a high proportion of poorer inhabitants. Villermé summed up his logic with the painstaking care that was typical of his prose: "Untaxed rents represent the poor, and the others [represent] people who are more or less well-off or leisured [*les gens plus ou moins aisés*]. The ratio of the first to the second has as its corollary the relative wealth of the inhabitants of the twelve districts taken each one in mass; and because food, clothing, and cleanliness are linked to wealth, the latter represents them faithfully enough." Villermé must have been aware that his argument here depended as much on common

---

35. Villermé, "De la mortalité dans les divers quartiers de la ville de Paris," p. 298. Of course, no demographer today would speak of "deaths per inhabitant" when discussing mortality rates, now usually calculated as deaths per 1,000 total population. Because Villermé's specific methods are the issue here, however, I will use his terminology throughout this discussion.
36. Ibid., p. 309, also cited in Coleman, *Death Is a Social Disease*, p. 160.

Table 2.1.   Average annual mortality *à domicile* in Paris, by arrondissement, 1817–26

Arrondis- sement	Quarters	Untaxed rents (%), 1820	Average rent (francs), 1820	Average inhabitants per 1 death, 1817–21	Average inhabitants per 1 death 1822–26
2	Chaussée-d'Antin, Palais Royal, Feydeau, faub. Montmartre	7	604.99	62	71
3	Montmartre, faub. Poissonière, Saint-Eustache et Mail	11	425.81	60	67
1	Roule, Champs-Élysées, place Vendôme et Tuileries	11	497.80	58	66
4	Saint-Honoré, Louvre, Marchés et Banque	15	328.25	58	62
6	Porte St.-Denis, St. Martin des Champs, Lombards et Temple	21	242.13	54	58
5	Faubourg St.-Denis, Porte St. Martin, Bonne-Nouvelle et Montorgueil	22	225.70	53	64

sense as it did on a rigorous standard of proof. Nevertheless, his language revealed the purpose of this scrupulous attention to detail. Even more than the connection between rent and standard of living (which was never really in doubt) Villermé sought to establish the legitimacy of seeing "the inhabitants of the twelve districts taken each one in mass."[37]

None of this information would have been available even ten years earlier, and none of Villermé's data had been collected with his purposes specifically in mind. His figures for mortality came originally from the *état civil*, an office set up ostensibly to assemble information about individual citizens living in a secular nation. In Villot's *Recherches statistiques*, where Villermé first encountered these figures, they were divided up into groups according to district. There was no reason to suppose that district boundaries reflected clear social distinctions. In fact, many neighbor-

37. Villermé, "De la mortalité dans les divers quartiers de la ville de Paris," p. 310.

Table 2.1. (*continued*)

Arrondissement	Quarters	Untaxed rents (%), 1820	Average rent (francs), 1820	Average inhabitants per 1 death, 1817–21	Average inhabitants per 1 death 1822–26
7	Sainte-Avoie, Mont-de Piété, Marché St.-Jean, Arcis	22	217.46	52	59
11	Luxembourg, École de Médecine, Sorbonne et Palais de Justice	19	257.62	51	61
10	Monnaie, St.-Thomas-d'Aquin, Invalides et faub. St.-Germain	23	285.41	50	49
9	Ile St.-Louis, Hôtel-de-Ville, Cité et Arsenal	31	172.41	44	50
8	St.-Antoine, Quinze-Vingts, Marais et Popincourt	32	172.86	43	46
12	Jardin du Roi, St.-Marcel, St.-Jacques et Observatoire	38	147.62	43	44
	All Paris	NA	289.06	51	56

Source: Villermé, "De la mortalité dans les divers quartiers de la ville de Paris," pp. 296–97, 310; and *RSVP*, 1823, table 102. See also Coleman, *Death Is a Social Disease*, p. 161.

hoods contained highly mixed proportions of propertied and indigent people, though, of course, Villermé was relying on broader patterns that connected the wealthy to certain neighborhoods and the poor to others. The figures for percentages of untaxed rent came from tax records assembled by the prefect of the Seine as part of a system of accounting that registered the sums paid by the capital to the national government. From these disparate sources, Villermé assembled a portrait of each district, as if they reflected a larger social reality.

Confident that the proportion of untaxed rents was a strong indicator of relative wealth, Villermé compared the rankings of the twelve districts according to this factor for 1820 with the rankings for mortality (averaged over the periods 1817–21 and 1822–26) and found an almost perfect correlation (see Table 2.1). He concluded: "In the current state of things, wealth, possessions, and poverty are the principal causes (we do not say unique causes) to which one must attribute the great differences in mortality that one observes for the inhabitants of the various districts of Paris."[38] Villermé did not claim to have demonstrated that wealth or poverty actually caused or prevented individual deaths in any mechanistic sense; he relied on the common sense of the reader to accept these possibilities as within the realm of reason. Instead, he considered wealth and poverty to be principal causes of "the differences in mortality" observed in each of the twelve districts. Villermé's "principal causes" did not depend on any necessary linkages between particular events in any one individual's life because the summary of his research contained no particular events or life stories. Wealth and poverty did not preserve or kill individuals, they produced different ratios of inhabitant per death among social aggregates. With these procedures, Villermé had moved from Laplace's world of mechanical causality and subjective probability into the more uncertain world of observed frequencies. In seeking to understand the collective in terms of "constant causes," Villermé succeeded in placing the individual citizen in a newly conceptualized social realm, where fate had been replaced by risk and one death could be understood only in its relation to all deaths. There were no autonomous individuals here, only populations taken "en masse," social classes produced by "constant causes."

Perhaps uncomfortable with the implications of his own argument, Villermé attempted to reinsert a portion of individual agency into his study of collective populations by asking whether the relative proportion of "productive" or "unproductive" wealth had any influence over the mortality of the twelve Parisian districts. The same table from Villot's *Recherches statistiques* that gave the breakdown for untaxed rents also recorded the number of renters taxed *à la contribution personelle seulement* ("people who live solely from their revenues or from a vocation not subject to the *patente*") and those *imposés à la patente* ("merchants, businessmen, manufacturers, entrepreneurs, commercial agents, etc."). In examining these figures, Villermé hardly hid his hope, which was to prove that there were two kinds of wealthy social aggregates. The first, marked by a certain passivity, lived like the aristocracy of the old regime, off the profits of other people's labor. The second, characterized by a measurable dynamism and vitality, was in control of their own destinies, filled with the entrepreneurial spirit of the newly ascendant commercial and professional classes.

As can be seen from Tables 2.2 and 2.3, Villermé's rankings by "pro-

38. Ibid., p. 312.

Table 2.2. Average annual mortality *à domicile* for each district in Paris ranked by percentage of population living from their own revenues (Villermé's definition of "unproductive wealth"), 1817–26

Arrondissement	Percent living from own revenue	Average inhabitants per 1 death, 1817–21	Average top and bottom, 1817–21	Average inhabitants per 1 death, 1822–26	Average top and bottom half, 1822–26
1	49	58		66	
10	46	50	Top half:	49	Top half:
2	40	62	55.50	71	62.17
11	39	51		61	
3	38	60		67	
7	29	52		59	
5	28	55		64	
9	26	54	Bottom half:	50	Bottom half:
8	25	43	51.17	46	54.00
4	23	58		62	
6	20	54		58	
12	19	43		44	

Source: Villermé, "De la mortalité dans les divers quartiers de la ville de Paris," p. 313.

ductive" and "unproductive" wealth were not as conclusive as his initial data on untaxed rents. Nevertheless, he was content to compare the average for the top six districts in both categories to the average for the bottom six and conclude from the resulting differences that both "productive" and "unproductive" wealth contributed to lower mortality rates. As he had hoped, however, the differences between the top six and the bottom six were particularly marked when districts were compared according to the proportion of their inhabitants who paid the *patente*. Unsure of his data, Villermé concluded somewhat tentatively that "induction would lead one to conclude that in Paris, large industry and high finance [*haut commerce*] serve the public health better than unproductive wealth . . . but I dare not make definite claims in this regard."[39]

Despite this caution, Villermé found a conclusion that suited his liberal views on politics and economics. He may have been appalled to discover a statistical connection between poverty and death, but he could comfort himself with the thought that the same data connected wealth and health. In fact, Villermé had definite ideological reasons for prefer-

39. Ibid., p. 315. On the greater differences of mortality produced by "productive wealth" Villermé commented: "This is no doubt because the payers of large patents employ a great number of persons who procure, according to their occupations, a greater degree of well-being [*aisance*]" (ibid.).

Table 2.3. Average annual mortality *à domicile* for each district in Paris ranked by percentage of population who pay the *patente* above 30 francs (Villermé's definition of "productive wealth"), 1817–26

Arrondissement	Percent inhabitants paying the *patente* (over 30 fr.)	Average inhabitants per 1 death, 1817–21	Average top and bottom half, 1817–21	Average inhabitants per 1 death, 1822–26	Average top and bottom half, 1822–26
4	49	58		62	
2	47	62	Top half:	71	Top half:
6	45	54	57.50	58	64.67
3	44	60		67	
5	36	53		64	
1	35	58		66	
7	35	52		59	
11	32	51	Bottom half:	61	Bottom half:
8	31	43	47.17	46	51.50
9	30	44		50	
12	29	43		44	
10	24	50		49	

Source: Villermé, "De la mortalité dans les divers quartiers de la ville de Paris," p. 314.

ring a demonstration of the latter rather than an unpleasant reminder of the former. To his credit, Villermé spent a great deal of time attempting to demonstrate the validity of both propositions, and one might have expected them to go hand in hand. In his concluding sentences, however, Villermé chose to emphasize only the optimistic side of the equation: since a lower mortality was linked to the possession of wealth, he concluded, then the disparities he perceived would diminish with "the development of civilization" as "the gross ignorance of the people" was replaced "with a spirit of industry" and "a greater number of people" procured "those objects necessary for life."[40] Such a conclusion was consonant with Villermé's liberal political and economic beliefs, but it ran counter to the principal implications of his mortality research, which pointed to the existence of social aggregates that were distinguishable both by their lack of wealth and their greater susceptibility to disease, malnutrition, and death. The contradiction between Villermé's liberal faith in individualism and his scientific concern with the nature and significance of social aggregates was compounded by his use of statistics, which effectively effaced the individual as a social actor.

This tension between a scientific interest in aggregates and a liberal

40. Ibid., pp. 338–39.

defense of individual autonomy can also be found in official reactions to
the most important public health crisis of the period, the terrifying and
deadly cholera epidemic of 1832. Between March and September of that
year, 18,402 Parisians died of the disease, most succumbing within a few
days to the extreme dehydration brought on by the cholera bacterium.
The fact that the years 1830–32 had witnessed the most severe outbreaks
of revolutionary unrest since the Revolution of 1789 only compounded
the anxiety felt by officials as they contemplated the overburdened burial services, the cemeteries filled to overflowing, and the breakdown of
public order in the face of a disease whose origins were poorly understood. Villermé himself played an important role on the royal commission that prepared the official report on the cholera epidemic in the capital, as did Frédéric Villot, who was by then the director of the office of
the *état civil* and statistics at the Prefecture of the Seine.[41]

The official report's conclusions on the cholera epidemic were cautious, considering the amount of medical controversy generated by the
disease, but in large part the commission's study confirmed Villermé's earlier conclusions concerning the connection between income, neighborhood, and mortality. The commission emphasized above all the heavy
price paid by inhabitants of the city's numerous *maisons garnies*. These
lodgings, mostly furnished rooms rented by the poorest of the poor, lined
the twisted and narrow streets in the oldest areas of Paris's central districts. The report estimated that the total population of this group was
between thirty-five thousand and forty thousand people and that their
mortality from cholera was thirty-two per thousand, compared with
twenty-three per thousand for the city as a whole.[42] "Placed at the lowest
social position," the report claimed, "this class is incessantly generated
by downturns in industry, lack of foresight, and disorderly behavior. Nowhere more numerous than in Paris, [this class] continues to grow from
the crowd of vagabonds [*gens sans aveu*] drawn by the lure of gain. After
wandering the entire day on the public thoroughfares, this class retires for
the night in the furnished rooms of the capital's various districts."[43] The
commission's report thus vacillated between a desire to portray this group
as a homogenous aggregate body, a dangerous element at the heart of
the city produced by inexorable economic forces ("the downturns in in-

---

41. The report was published as *Rapport sur la marche et les effets du choléra morbus dans Paris et les
communes rurales du département de la Seine* (Paris, 1834). Also on the commission were Alexandre
Parent-Duchâtelet and Benoiston de Chateauneuf. On the medical community's reaction to the
cholera epidemic, see especially Catherine Kudlick, *Cholera in Post-Revolutionary Paris: A Cultural
History* (Berkeley, 1996), pp. 67–81, and Coleman, *Death Is a Social Disease*, pp. 171–78.
42. *Rapport sur la marche et les effets du choléra morbus*, p. 192.
43. Ibid., pp. 191–92.

dustry"), and a wish to see this body as the sum of individual failures ("disorderly behavior" and "lack of foresight"). The cholera commission's emphasis on the vulnerability of the *maisons garnies* functioned in the same way as Villermé's earlier distinction between productive and unproductive wealth in the 1820s. In the face of a frighteningly convincing argument for the reality of biological and social distinctions whose effects were best measured in aggregate terms, both Villermé and his colleagues on the cholera commission sought to show that individual behaviors could have some effect in determining the outcomes of individual experiences.

In Villermé's later work, especially in his monumental study of textile workers published in 1840, he continued to examine the complex relationship that linked wealth and mortality among different social classes.[44] In this work, however, he revealed signs of a continued ambivalence toward the political lesson to be gleaned from work on social aggregates. When Villermé described his methods of research in 1840, he wasted little time in laying out the principles of statistical analysis. Instead, he described a different approach, one that allowed him to appreciate workers as individuals within the surroundings of their daily lives. His insistence on firsthand observation, he claimed, allowed him to "see everything, hear everything, know everything."[45] His own description of his role testified to the scope of this ambition:

> Such is the care that I desired to bring to this type of investigation that I followed the worker from his shop to his home. I entered his house and studied him in the heart of his family; I joined him in his meals. I did more: I saw him in his work and in his household, I wanted to see him partaking of his pleasures, and to see him in the places where he joined his fellows. There, listening to his conversations, partaking of them at times, I became without his knowledge the confidant of his joys and complaints, his regrets and hopes, the witness to his vices and his virtues.[46]

In the ten years between Villermé's work on differential mortality and that on textile workers, his overall research goals did not change much, but the manner in which he presented his own position in relation to his material changed a great deal. In the later work his examination of workers' lives required his presence; his earlier work contained no authorial intrusions whatsoever. Count how many times he used the first person pro-

44. Villermé, *Tableau*.
45. Ibid., 1:vi.
46. Ibid.

noun in the above citation. To understand the worker, Villermé felt obligated to enter into a relation with him, to become his "confidant." His role was both sympathetic and judgmental, and as both an observer and a participant in the scene, Villermé embodied a heroic model of the public health researcher who abandoned the solitude of his study and literally got his feet wet in Parisian gutters. Villermé's self-consciousness in his study of textile workers lent an explicitly subjective tone to his observations of working-class life. His refusal to distinguish between strict observation and moral participation was a departure from the coldly objective procedures he had pioneered in his earlier work and countered his earlier aim of constructing a vision of homogeneous social aggregates.[47] Interestingly, in an elegy of Villermé published after his death, Antony Roulliet of the Société de statistique de Paris emphasized above all Villermé's empathy with the individuals who were the object of his study, evoking "the love [Villermé] bore for the unfortunate, the sympathy he felt with regard to workers."[48] Such a statement might not be unusual in an elegy of a celebrated doctor, but it indicates the extent to which both Villermé and his colleagues in statistical research felt obliged to emphasize that their interest in social aggregates did not obscure their commitment to the lives of individuals.

By the time Villermé published his 1840 study of textile workers, two important events had changed the atmosphere surrounding population statistics in France. First, in 1835, a Belgian statistician named Adolphe Quetelet published a large and controversial work, *Sur l'homme et le développement de ses facultés*. Second, in 1837, the Académie royale de médecine debated the use of statistics in medical research. Whereas Villermé had been content to present his work on social aggregates as a modest illustration of the utility of statistics, Quetelet presented his version of quantification as a brave new world, with broad implications for the nature of human understanding. Quetelet's enthusiastic tone irritated more than a few powerful men of science in Paris, especially in the medical profession, and the 1837 debate in the Académie de médecine focused almost

47. Villermé's conscious invocation of the split between public and private was also the moment in which he pointed to his own difference, bourgeois social observer that he was, and his active role in constructing the scenes that he describes. Marie-Noëlle Bourguet pointed to the class bias of researchers such as Villermé, who saw the elites as beyond the pale of their research because of their privileged status but were happy to penetrate to the heart of working-class or rural families in an effort to expand the horizons of their knowledge. Bourguet interpreted their hesitation in the matter of elites as an early recognition of a private sphere that should remain impervious to official intervention ("Décrire, Compter, Calculer," p. 311).
48. Antony Roulliet, "Les présidents de la Société de statistique de Paris," *25ème anniversaire de la Société de statistique de Paris, 1860–1885* (Paris, 1886), p. 27.

entirely on Quetelet's vision of statistical aggregates. Villermé's insistence in 1840 that his observations of textile workers had taken him into their neighborhoods, across their thresholds, and to a seat at their tables may well have been a way of insisting that his quantitative work had not lost sight of the uniqueness of particular facts. Before taking a look at this debate in closer detail in the next chapter, however, we must first examine Quetelet's contribution to the unraveling of the social world and its apparent chaos.

QUETELET'S ALLEGORY OF DIFFERENCE

Adolphe Quetelet was a Belgian mathematician, astronomer, and statistical enthusiast who helped to found the Royal Observatory in Brussels in 1832. Having studied in Paris, Quetelet corresponded with many French researchers, including Laplace, Fourier, Villermé, and the inventor of judicial statistics, A. M. Guerry. Quetelet's major work, *Sur l'homme et le développement de ses facultés* (1835), became an important reference for the generation of researchers who founded the demographic sciences in France at mid-century, including Achille Guillard (who coined the term *démographie*) and Guillard's son-in-law, Louis-Adolphe Bertillon. Through his tireless efforts to organize a series of international statistical congresses in the 1850s, Quetelet also had an important influence on the creation of an international network of population researchers and statisticians.[49]

Like Laplace and others before him, Quetelet observed that despite the presence of a potentially disruptive element at work in society—human agency—definite patterns could be observed in statistical studies of social phenomena. He was struck by the regularity of crime statistics gathered by the municipal authorities of Brussels and Paris—the fact that the

---

49. For a useful and detailed study of Quetelet's life and work, see Lottin, *Quetelet*. An early appraisal in English is Frank H. Hankins, *Adolphe Quetelet as Statistician* (New York, 1908). See also Maurice Halbwachs, *La Théorie de l'homme moyen: Essai sur Quetelet et la statistique morale* (Paris, 1912). Important recent discussions can be found in Georges Canguilhem, *The Normal and the Pathological* (New York, 1989), pp. 156–64; Ewald, *L'Etat providence*; Hacking, *Taming of Chance*, pp. 105–14; Porter, *Rise of Statistical Thinking*, pp. 41–57; Paul Rabinow, *French Modern: Norms and Forms of the Social Environment* (Cambridge, Mass., 1989), pp. 60–67; Stigler, *History of Statistics*, pp. 161–220; and Hilts, "Statistics and Social Science," pp. 208–19. My own reading of Quetelet has been heavily influenced by these writers, and especially by Ian Hacking. On Achille Guillard and Louis-Adolphe Bertillon and their contributions to the formation of demography as a distinct discipline, see Michel Dupâquier, "La famille Bertillon et la naissance d'une nouvelle science sociale, la démographie," *Annales de démographie historique* (1983): 293–311, and Schweber, "Assertion of Disciplinary Claims," esp. chaps. 1–4.

number of robberies, murders, and arrests remained relatively constant from year to year. He speculated that such regularity could only be evidence of laws, hidden structures that contained the possible futures resulting from the sum of individual actions.[50] The observed regularity, he reasoned, could only mean that the multiplicity of individual actors and motivations had little effect on the social organization as a whole. Following this line of reasoning, Quetelet asserted that, a posteriori, society was ruled by laws that acted not on individuals but on the collective and whose results were observable only in the long term.[51]

As in Villermé's work on differential mortality in Paris, Quetelet's focus on the aggregate statistics loosened—but did not break—the bonds that held cause to effect in the determinist universe. Quetelet's vision of society thus functioned according to principles that departed significantly from Laplace's mechanical model of cause and effect; his laws were not "causes" in the earlier sense, though they were no less inescapable. They were accessible only through enumeration, through the agglomeration of individuals into collective bodies whose underlying tendencies would thus be allowed expression despite their seeming heterogeneity. Elements of such an argument were already implicit in Villermé's work of the 1820s, but unlike Villermé, Quetelet explicitly announced his rejection of the older models of causality that depended on knowledge of particular cases. "We must above all lose sight of man taken in isolation, and see him only as a fraction of the species," he wrote, in perhaps his most cited passage. "In stripping him of his individuality," he continued, "we will eliminate all that is only accidental; and the individual particularities which have little or no effect on the mass will efface themselves, and permit one to grasp the general results."[52] Quetelet's system of calculation, which he

50. Quetelet wrote, "Society contains within itself the germs of all the crimes which are going to be committed, and at the same time the factors necessary for their development. It is [society] that in some way prepares the crimes, and the guilty are only the instruments that execute them. Every social system [*Tout état social*] supposes therefore a certain number and a certain order of crimes resulting as the necessary consequence of its organization" (*Sur l'homme et le développment de ses facultés ou Essai de physique sociale*, 2 vols. [Paris, 1835], 1:10). Theodore Porter found Quetelet's astonishment at the regularity of social statistics somewhat surprising. Quetelet was certainly familiar with the work of probabilists such as Bernoulli, who were satisfied that stable ratios would arise if probabilistic events were repeated often enough. Porter takes Quetelet's reaction to indicate that no one had anticipated that social phenomena would reveal the same patterns observed in sciences such as astronomy and physics. See Porter, *Rise of Statistical Thinking*, pp. 49–50.

51. Michelle Perrot wrote: "That the 'science of man' began as a 'science of crime' testifies simultaneously to the urban mutations and social psychologies which valorized property, order, and sexual continence. It is born of the fascination with crime, a disorder in a rational society of production" ("Premières mesures des faits sociaux: Les debuts de la statistique criminelle en France, 1780–1830," in *Pour une histoire de la statistique*, vol. 1 [Paris, 1977], p. 134.)

52. Quetelet, *Sur l'homme*, 1:4–5.

termed "*physique sociale*," [53] would create the blindness necessary for true insight by literally averaging out "accidental" differences, a category that included emotion, temperament, motive, and all the attributes of the individual personality. "The greater the number of observed individuals, the more the individual particularities, be they physical or moral, are effaced [and the more] the general facts by virtue of which society exists and conserves itself are allowed to predominate." [54]

The culmination of Quetelet's work was the theory of *l'homme moyen*—the average man—a composite abstraction that emerged from his system of calculation as the idealization of the collective in the form of a singular object. The basis of this concept lay in Quetelet's ingenious importation of a method for calculating the probability of error in astronomical measurements to the statistical study of human attributes. An early example of this method—called the "method of least squares"—had been clearly stated by the mathematician A. M. Legendre in 1805 but had most likely been introduced to Quetelet by the work of J. B. Fourier in 1826. [55] Roughly stated, Fourier had written that if repeated measurements of an object's size are taken, the *average* of these measurements approaches the true value as the number of measurements increases toward infinity. Assuming that there is no reason to believe that one type of error occurs more often than another, the values of each individual measurement generate the familiar bell curve when placed on a graph. [56] Quetelet's innovation lay in applying this method to measurements not of one single object but a multitude of similar objects: people. Finding that a bell curve could be charted for the height of military recruits, he postulated the existence of an objective average height that somehow dictated the distribution of varying measurements. [57] With this observation, the

53. Quetelet borrowed this term from Auguste Comte's early writings. Comte, who disapproved of Quetelet's statistical claims to positivism, was thus led to come up with "sociologie" in response. See Lottin, *Quetelet*, pp. 357–67.

54. Quetelet, *Sur l'homme*, 1:12.

55. See Stigler, *History of Statistics*, pp. 55–61, 162. Quetelet cited Fourier's "Mémoire sur les résultats déduits d'un grand nombre d'observations" (1826) in *Recherches statistiques* (Brussels, 1844), p. 5. His wording is very similar to that used by Fourier in an article originally published in 1826. Fourier wrote: "In an immense number of observations, the multiplicity of chances eliminates all that is fortuitous and accidental, and only the constant causes remain; there is no chance for natural facts considered in large numbers" ("Mémoire sur les résultats moyens déduits d'un grand nombre d'observations," in *Oeuvres de Fourier*, vol. 2, ed. Gaston Darboux [Paris, 1890], p. 527).

56. This "normal distribution" or "probability curve" already formed the basis of astronomical measurement in Quetelet's time, having been articulated most explicitly by Carl Friedrich Gauss in 1809 and in subsequent work by Laplace. See Stigler, *History of Statistics*, pp. 139–58.

57. Alain Desrosières has suggested that Quetelet's assertion of the objective existence of averages was an important antecedent to Durkheim's pronouncement that one must treat social facts as if they are things ("Comment faire des choses qui tiennent: Histoire sociale et statistique," *Histoire & mesure* 4 [1989]: 225–26, 229–30).

average man became "the analog of the center of gravity in the body . . . the average around which oscillate the social elements." [58]

Just as averages could be ascertained for a population's physical attributes—height, weight, strength—so too did Quetelet believe that a population's intellectual and moral capacity could be calculated. Furthermore, he intended to use averages as normative standards for measuring progress; by doing so, he made the average man a unit of comparison for populations of different time periods as well as for different geographical areas. The average man was not only an identifiable "type," he was also the telos of history. [59] At first simply a methodological expedient for eliminating the confusion of accidental influence, the average man thus became incorporated into a political ideal, whereby the perpetual oscillations and variations around the mean would eventually narrow and approach the happy medium. Quetelet's speculations on the unequal distribution of positive and negative character traits differed from the eugenic programs of the later nineteenth century because, unlike later eugenicists, Quetelet believed that the evolution toward perfection was automatic. Nevertheless, his utopian vision provided an important precedent for eugenics: human variation, definable in quantitative terms and interpreted as deviations from a norm, had become the legitimate concern of the state. [60]

Quetelet broke new ground by jettisoning the reliance on an absolute determinism that had characterized social science up to that point, while simultaneously asserting that the values arrived at through calculation and comparison had objective force and reality. [61] He insisted that "man" could be understood only as a collective body and not in the uniqueness of particular examples. In so doing, Quetelet transformed the abstract individual of liberal political theory into a "social" being, a creature whose significance lay not in the primacy of some sphere of individual moral autonomy but in the network of relations that connected him to the social

58. Quetelet, *Sur l'homme*, 1:21. According to Hacking, Quetelet's concept of the average man "transformed the mean into a real quantity" (*Taming of Chance*, p. 107).

59. Quetelet wrote, "One of the principal characteristics of civilization is to progressively narrow the limits in which the various elements relative to man oscillate. The greater the spread of enlightenment, the more the deviations from the average diminish; and in consequence, the closer we approach that which is beautiful and good. . . . Defects and monstrosities increasingly disappear in the physical realm. Medical science combats the frequency and gravity of illness with increasing success; the moral qualities of man are subject to no less evident improvement, and as we advance, the less reason we will have to fear the consequences and effects of great political upheavals and wars" (*Sur l'homme*, 2:326–27).

60. On Quetelet's contribution to the development of a distinctly eugenic line of thought, see Hacking, *Taming of Chance*, pp. 107–8.

61. François Ewald has written that this insight of Quetelet's marked a "fundamental epistemological displacement" (*L'Etat providence*, p. 149).

and physical environment. Simultaneously, by reducing the individual to a simple product of accidental influence with no general significance for a science of society, Quetelet's epistemological insight had a profound message for politics. Quetelet's *physique sociale* was incompatible with a politics of moral reform and philanthropy, which aimed at improving the individual through paternalist assistance and education. Instead, he called on government to focus its attention on the influences that acted on the collective, to act on the milieu as opposed to the individual. Quetelet tied the fortunes of his science to his vision of government; both were concerned with the elaboration of a science of social aggregates, the former in the pursuit of enlightenment, the latter in the interest of social improvement.

Historians of science and probability have not hesitated to accuse Quetelet of misapplying the probability curve to biological and physical events and erroneously concluding that the average man was an objectively real entity. In his appraisal of Quetelet's theory, published in 1912, Maurice Halbwachs held that the regularity of statistical variation was not the result of a Gaussian distribution of "error" around a bell curve but rather the complex result of "the constant causes, organic constitution, physical milieu, and the relations of adaptation between the one and the other." [62] The authors of a more recent study have concluded that Quetelet's theory was "the purest form of positivism, requiring no knowledge of actual causes but only the identification of regularities and, if possible, their antecedents." [63] Stephen Stigler concurred, concluding that although Quetelet was successful in stimulating a wide interest in the description of "types" through normal distribution, his method ultimately failed to provide an analytically coherent method for distinguishing between mere regularity and significant evidence of causal influence.[64] The philosopher of science Ian Hacking went a step further in his criticism, stating that in Quetelet's theory of the average man "the mathematics of probability and the metaphysics of underlying cause were cobbled together by loose argument to bring an 'understanding' of the statistical stability of all phenomena." [65] Such criticisms may well explain why there is no place for Quetelet's theory of the average man in contemporary demography. Nevertheless, by treating Quetelet's innovations as merely an episodic aberration in the development of a unified statistical theory, these authors cannot take into account the power of such an "error" in the

62. Halbwachs, *Théorie de l'homme moyen*, p. 68.
63. Gigerenzer et al., *Empire of Chance*, p. 42.
64. Stigler, *History of Statistics*, pp. 203–20.
65. Hacking, *Taming of Chance*, p. 112.

context of the nineteenth-century social sciences, or indeed, Quetelet's own text.

Far from being a simple stage in the development of an efficient social calculus, however, Quetelet's "average man" should be read as an essentially allegorical figure, even as an attempt to assert the power of statistical allegory as a privileged mode of social description. In no place is Quetelet's insistence on an allegorical reading of the average man more clear than in his attempt to assert its utility for medicine. He argued that no doctor could diagnose a patient's illness without referring to "a fictive being that one regards as being the normal state and who is nothing but the [average man]." [66] Judging the quickness of the pulse, the rate of breath, the temperature of the patient—all of these decisions could only be made with reference to a composite image assembed from the doctor's previous experiences. Quetelet's claim in this regard was beguiling in its simplicity. On the one hand, he appeared to be making a argument for the progress of medical knowledge based on the standardization of conventional analogies. On the other hand, he made no effort to hide his belief that these conventions were artificial and that artifice—the creation of a "fictive being" in the form of the average man—was a necessary step on the path toward understanding the truth of the individual case. Of course, this artifice existed within limits dictated by a normal distribution curve (which allowed him to escape the apparent contradiction between his assertion that the average has objective reality and his reference to a "fictive being"), but it was artifice nonetheless.

Quetelet's observations on the utility of the concept of the average man for medical research would seem to support Michel Foucault's contention that early nineteenth-century medicine was more concerned about "normality" than about health.[67] But his frank admission of the ambiguity inherent in these norms—their "fictive" quality—raises new questions about the epistemological status of Quetelet's claims for statistical

---

66. Quetelet continued: "A doctor is called to the side of an invalid, and, after having examined him, finds that his pulse is too quick, that his breathing is excessively agitated, etc. . . . Each doctor, in making such observations, refers to the knowledge established by the present state of science, or even to his own experience; this is fundamentally the same estimation which we would like to make on a wider scale and with more precision" (Sur l'homme, 2:267).

67. Foucault wrote: "Up to the end of the eighteenth century medicine related much more to health than to normality; it did not begin by analyzing a 'regular' functioning of the organism and go on to seek where it had deviated, what it was disturbed by, and how it could be brought back into normal working order; it referred, rather to qualities of vigour, suppleness, and fluidity, which were lost in illness and which it was the task of medicine to restore. . . . Nineteenth-century medicine, on the other hand, was regulated more in accordance with normality than with health; it formed its concepts and prescribed its interventions in relation to a standard of functioning and organic structure" (The Birth of the Clinic [New York, 1973], p. 35).

knowledge. Quetelet's statements point to a quest for a transcendent metaphor, a form of description that would bridge the gap between the empirical observation of individual cases and a more general understanding of the patterns that emerge from the heterogeneous mass of collective phenomena. The "average man" was Quetelet's allegory of difference, an avowedly fictional representation for multiplicity and variety in a single object. Quetelet's *physique sociale* was thus not merely an epistemological turning point in the social sciences; it also marked a rhetorical transition in the treatment of numbers as signs of social phenomena. No longer merely descriptive or enumerating, Quetelet's averages eliminated the one-to-one correspondence between objects in the world and digits in the statistical table, and in so doing, they released social statisticians from the constraints of a rigid determinism.

Between the fall of the Napoleonic Empire in 1814 and the creation of the Statistique Générale de la France in 1835, France did not have a national office for statistical research on population questions. Owing to the initiative of local officials and individual researchers, however, the period was fruitful in the consolidation of research strategies and the collection of important bodies of raw data, such as those undertaken by the Prefecture of the Seine in the 1820s and following the cholera epidemic in 1832. The most important population research to emerge in France during this time was Louis-René Villermé's studies of differential mortality in Paris, which established a statistical basis for understanding the connection between wealth and health and provided later investigators with an important model for further studies.

Villermé's work on mortality exhibited an innovative and enthusiastic awareness of the potentials of statistical analysis, especially in his careful and methodical comparison of mortality rates in different districts of the capital. He chose to portray these districts as if their social composition made them "distinct cities" unto themselves, partly because of the limitations of his data but also because such assumptions about social and economic status were necessary to his hypothesis. His conclusions were irrefutable by the standards of the day: he ranked each district according to its mortality rate and relative wealth (determined by the payment of taxes) and found that the rankings reproduced themselves exactly. He concluded that the poor died in greater number than the wealthy, and his argument lent great weight to the idea of a population divided irrevocably into aggregate groups whose lives and destinies could be accurately charted with careful statistics. At the same time, however, Villermé remained ideologically committed to a liberal vision of the social body and placed great emphasis on the ability of individuals to determine their own destinies. He therefore sought to demonstrate, both in his earlier examination of the different effects of "productive" and "unproductive" wealth and in his later studies of textile workers, that the social aggregates made visible by statistical analysis in no way prevented him from seeing clearly the individual stories of particular people. The esteem with which Villermé was held by his colleagues and the extensive role he played after the 1830s in the Académie royale de médecine, the Académie des sciences morales et politiques, and the Société de statistique de Paris are evidence enough of the influence of his ideas. Most important to our discussion here, however, is the extent to which the tension in his work between an interest in aggregate analysis and the desire to conserve a vision of individual behaviors found echoes in other discussions of population research. The next chapter will discuss the 1837 debate on statistics in the Académie de médecine, and as we shall see, much of the debate turned on the defense of individual narratives in the face of the collective embrace of statistical analysis.

The clinicians in the Académie de médecine who remained skeptical of statistical analysis reacted strongly to the enthusiastic endorsement of aggregate thinking put forth by Adolphe Quetelet. In his 1835 work, *Sur l'homme et le développement de ses facultés*, Quetelet proposed his *physique sociale* and his concept of the "average man" as the key to understanding both humanity's past and its potential for development in the future. He brazenly rejected any critics who might worry about the tendency of his collective vision to overwhelm the particular stories of individual lives. Instead, he announced, "We only wish to study the social body, and not the particularities that distinguish the individuals who are a part of it. Our study is of interest above all to the philosopher and the legislator. The literary person and the artist, on the other hand, will prefer to dedicate themselves to the pursuit of those particulars . . . that give society its physiognomy and its picturesque aspects."[68] Many doctors with a keen interest in "those particulars" took offense at Quetelet's condescending tone and were outraged that he might relegate their tradition of clinical observation to a mere interest in the "picturesque." The 1837 debate in the Académie de médecine demonstrated that the representational status of Quetelet's numbers was still up for grabs. The "chaos of particular facts" remained an uncertain field.

68. Quetelet, *Sur l'homme*, 1:15.

THE INDIVIDUAL BODY
AND THE BODY SOCIAL

THE MEDICAL DEFENSE OF MINORITY FACTS

The publication and reception of Quetelet's work on the "average man" and Villermé's pathbreaking work on social aggregates coincided with two important events: the reestablishment of a national office for population research in 1835 and a heated debate in the Académie royale de médecine in 1837 on the scientific validity of statistical methods. The foundation of the Statistique Générale de la France in 1835 began a tradition of regular and published statistical research into population and the economy that continued uninterrupted until the office was reorganized in 1941. The 1837 debate in the Académie de médecine, however, revealed a significant kernel of opposition to statistical research among leading members of the French scientific community at the precise moment when statistics were becoming both ubiquitous and indispensable in the administration.

All of these events unfolded against the background of political turmoil unsurpassed since the Revolution of 1789. The popular uprising of July 1830 put a more moderate Louis-Philippe on the throne in the place of the conservative Charles X, but the new king's government proved a great disappointment to the crowds of artisans and journeymen who had fought for his cause. Under the new regime only the propertied elite could vote or hold office and Louis-Philippe subsequently distanced himself from the revolutionary enthusiasm that had made his accession possible. Unhappy workers in Paris and Lyon rebelled in 1831, 1832, and 1834, calling for an extension of the suffrage, the right of association, and an end to oligarchic rule. In each case the monarchy used troops to quell the disturbances, but this did not prevent an assassination attempt on Louis Philippe's life on 28 July 1835 — the fifth anniversary of the revolution that had put him in power. In response, the government passed a series of repressive laws that aimed to silence the republican opposition and strengthen the hand of the courts in cases of rebellion and inciting violence.

In the middle of this crisis, the effort to reestablish a central office for population research began in 1833. In that year, Adolphe Thiers, then minister of the interior, noted the benefits that the British reaped from the Board of Trade's official statistical portrait of the nation and called for the creation of a similar office in France. Thiers's proposition, supported by his successor C.-M.-T. Duchâtel, resulted in the creation of the Statistique Générale de la France in 1835, under the authority of the Ministry of Commerce. Alexandre Moreau de Jonnès, a veteran of the administration with an interest in public health, served as the SGF's first director. Moreau de Jonnès was loyal to the memory of the Bonapartist regime, and he modeled the SGF's research and publications on the example of the empire's Bureau de statistique. Like many of the earlier imperial administrators, Moreau de Jonnès was conservative in the use of statistics. Throughout his career, he remained suspicious of any attempt to manipulate data by the calculation of rates and averages. Instead, he insisted on using only absolute quantities, claiming that statistics were valuable only if one could be sure of a one-to-one relationship between objects in the world and numbers in a statistical table.[1]

Even taking Moreau de Jonnès's methodological conservatism into account, one might have thought that France in 1835 was poised for a new and fruitful period of population research. Since 1812, when Napoleon's statistical office was disbanded, population research had depended on the initiative and individual efforts of local officials and private savants. Responsibility for judging the quality of this work had largely been left up to the scientific academies and professional journals. Now, under the SGF population studies would be supported by the highest levels of the nation's administration. Nevertheless, there was no immediate breakthrough. In his initial and ambitious program for the SGF, Moreau de Jonnès announced that its work would be divided into fourteen categories: territory, population, agriculture, mines, industry, commerce, navigation, colonies, interior administration, finances, military forces, navy, justice, and public instruction. Only six of these categories became the object of separate publications in the coming years, and Moreau de Jon-

---

1. On Moreau de Jonnès and the foundation of the SGF, see Le Mée, "La Statistique démographique officielle," pp. 253–55; Dupâquier and Le Mée, "La Connaissance des faits démographiques," pp. 34–36; Le Bras, "La Statistique Générale," pp. 340–44; and Schweber, "Assertion of Disciplinary Claims," pp. 299–313.

nès had difficulty obtaining the complete cooperation of the nation's prefects. Throughout the July Monarchy (1830–48) the SGF remained essentially a centralized depository for information and never succeeded in establishing more innovative and coordinated national investigations into the population or the economy. Furthermore, Moreau de Jonnès's administration came under attack by his rival, Alfred Legoyt, who directed a separate statistical office at the Ministry of Interior. In 1852 the office was reorganized under the new regime of Napoléon III (1852–70), and Legoyt became the new director of the SGF.[2]

Meanwhile, the defenders of statistics faced resistance from unexpected quarters. Doctors who expressed their discomfort with quantification in the 1837 Académie de médecine debate may have been disturbed to find their area of expertise encroached on by new state institutions, such as the SGF, that remained largely outside of their control. As the procedures for gathering information on the population since the 1790s had become more elaborate, doctors had increasingly been called on to cooperate with municipal and national administrations. Doctors filled out the death certificates that were so important for the *état civil*, and the success of official research into public health depended on both their accuracy and their willingness to cooperate with the statisticians and archivists who put together the eventual reports. Villermé's work on mortality in Paris districts, for example, would have been impossible without the cooperation of the medical community. Meanwhile, the organization and practice of medicine in France had undergone great changes since the Revolution of 1789, and the opposition of some doctors to statistical methods may have reflected strains and insecurities felt by members of this newly professionalized field.

The generation of doctors who debated statistical methods in 1837 had witnessed unprecedented change in the profession during their lifetimes. The corporate bodies that had governed the training and practice of physicians and surgeons under the old regime had been swept away by the Le Chapelier law of 1791, which prohibited individual members of trades and occupations from organizing in defense of their professional interests. Two categories of medical practitioner emerged from the period of revolutionary reforms. The *officiers de santé* received their licenses after

2. Under Moreau de Jonnès, the SGF published a limited series of tables on the years 1800–1835 in 1837 and thirteen more volumes between 1835 and 1852. Legoyt replaced Moreau de Jonnès as director of the SGF in 1852, when the two offices at the Ministry of Commerce and the Ministry of Interior were combined. On the controversy between Moreau de Jonnès and Legoyt, see the latter's own commentary in Alfred Legoyt, *La France statistique* (Paris, 1848), pp. 4–7. On Moreau de Jonnès and the SGF, see Le Mée, "La statistique démographique officielle," pp. 253–54; and Le Bras, "La Statistique Générale," p. 343.

passing an exam and completing either a six-year apprenticeship with a doctor or three years of study in a medical school. Possessing more prestige, and considerably less numerous, were the *médecins*, who studied for at least four years and passed a rigorous national exam. By the end of the revolutionary decade, France possessed just three medical faculties, in Paris, Montpellier, and Strasbourg.[3]

The Le Chapelier law and subsequent legislation did not prohibit professional associations with a primarily scientific orientation, and from the 1790s onward, several important medical associations were created, bringing together some of the most prominent and innovative medical practitioners of the period. These included the Société de santé (1796), which acted as an advisory body to the city of Paris; the Société médicale d'émulation (1796) founded by the pathological anatomist Xavier Bichat; and the Société de l'Ecole de médecine (1800), which brought together the faculty of the prestigious medical school in Paris. Not until 1820, however, under the Restoration monarchy, did a full-fledged medical academy emerge, the Académie royale de médecine, heir to the eighteenth-century Société royale de médecine. The Académie de médecine served as the supreme forum for examining new developments in the field, and members were elected only after making significant contributions to their area of specialization. Most important, since France did not have a national office for overseeing matters of public health until 1848, the Académie de médecine served an important advisory role to government officials in the 1820s and 1830s on matters pertaining to the health and well-being of the population.[4] When doctors in the academy debated the use of statistics in the spring of 1837, therefore, the presence of a significant group opposed to quantitative methods threatened to disrupt the relationship between the medical establishment and the newly founded institutions for population research.

The political questions that beset the regime of Louis Philippe affected the academy's debate in curious ways, most notably in its discussion of how statisticians drew conclusions from a preponderance of evidence. The main voice of antistatistical skepticism was Risueño d'Amador, a

3. On the professionalization of medicine in France, see Toby Gelfand, *Professionalizing Modern Medicine: Paris Surgeons, Medical Science, and Institutions in the 18th Century* (Westport, Conn., 1980); Matthew Ramsey, *Professional and Popular Medicine in France, 1770–1830: The Social World of Medical Practice* (Cambridge, 1988); and Jacques Léonard, *La Médecine entre les pouvoirs et les savoirs* (Paris, 1981).
4. In 1848, the government established a national commission on public health. This advisory body was linked to a network of locally organized health councils that brought together doctors, pharmacists, and local officials to discuss and implement public health policies. On this matter and on the formation of medical associations and the Académie de médecine, see Ramsey, *Professional and Popular Medicine*, pp. 105–6.

professor of pathology and general therapeutics at the medical faculty of Montpellier. Amador claimed that statisticians were fascinated by "majorities" and disdained "minorities." What becomes of the "minority fact" in medical statistics, he wondered. "Will you condemn to death those sick people placed in this unhappy category? I see only an attention paid to majority facts in statistical work, but the minority, gentlemen, is also a fact; and science as well as conscience obliges us [*nous font une loi*] to take it into consideration." [5] Amador was openly reaching here, stretching to make a point that must have seemed tenuous to his colleagues who were more familiar with quantification and its procedures. Convincing or not, however, his argument is striking simply for the fact that he made it at all: Amador's politically charged language demonstrated the urgency imparted to discussions of statistics and social aggregates during the 1830s. In his mind, at least, it was only a small step from the question of popular sovereignty—the power of the people taken en masse to determine the direction of political reform—to the question of quantitative reasoning or the power of large numbers to reveal the truth.

Risueño d'Amador's attempt to cast the defenders of statistics in the same light as the supporters of unrestricted democracy may have had more than a grain of truth to it. Certain members of the Académie de médecine who supported the use of statistics were indeed associated with liberal circles, and one of them, Jean Bouillaud, would become a member of the National Assembly and dean of the medical faculty after the revolution of February 1848. But this slippage between the vocabulary of the empirical scientist and the terms of contemporary political debate hints at a conflict that goes beyond a simple professional spat between contesting power blocs within the academy. Amador's choice of imagery suggests that it was difficult for doctors to debate fundamental questions about knowledge without talking simultaneously about power. Epistemology had become inseparable from politics, and the fear of the revolutionary crowd expressed itself in an anxiety about the ability of numerical aggregates to capture the complexity of human life and behavior. This anxiety shaped in important ways the participation of doctors in the elaboration of population studies in France between 1830 and the end of the Second Empire in 1870.

Like Amador, the opponents of statistics in the academy rejected the idea that aggregate generalizations could have any empirical value in

---

5. *BARM*, 1 (1836–37): 634. The minutes of the academy debate on statistics and all the relevant papers appeared in this volume.

medicine, and they did so in the name of minority facts. The academy's 1837 debates made little mention of specific experiments or research—no one mentioned Villermé's work on differential mortality between rich and poor, for example. Instead, most of the participants in the debate kept their comments at an abstract and general level, preferring to question the ability of mathematical averages to represent general trends in a heterogeneous population. Did observed regularities in the measurement of averages indicate underlying cause? The emphasis on averages testified to the impact of Quetelet's work (he was often paraphrased, although not mentioned by name), and in fact, much of the academy's debate seemed less about statistics in general than about Quetelet's particular vision of their applicability. This indicates more than a little confusion among French doctors about what statistical analysis actually was, and some of their arguments seem quaint today. But the peculiarity of their counter-arguments—and the epistemological unease they reveal—demonstrate that many doctors did not view statistical innovations as merely another element of technical progress. Rather, they recognized in the new methods a radical transformation both in the conventions for representing the complexity of human life and in the political conclusions that could be drawn from the new understanding of this complexity.

During the debates in the Académie de médecine, two clear opinions emerged as crucial. The first was clinical in its orientation, emphasizing both the uniqueness of each particular visual observation that the scientist made in the course of his research and the necessity of the doctor's presence in the face of the event in question. The purpose of such unique observations was to explain the strict mechanical causality that lay behind the unfolding of successive events. Because each event was unique, this mode of empirical research was skeptical of any attempts at quantification and relied instead on narrative descriptions and analogies for its larger conclusions. It was this clinical perspective that led Amador to defend "minority facts" in the face of the statistician's confident "majorities."

The second conception of empirical research was avowedly statistical. The researchers who defended this method sought to make quantitative generalizations about tendencies and frequencies among large and unwieldy bodies of data, and they claimed that these techniques were superior to the narrative descriptions offered by their opponents. Unlike Quetelet, however, they did not insist that the knowledge gained from statistical aggregates represented anything radically new in comparison to older methods of research. Rather, they attempted to demonstrate that numbers were a more accurate means of measuring the significance and extent of phenomena that were the traditional concerns of medicine, such as the duration of illness and treatment, the quantity of medication, the temperature of the patient's body, or the age at death.

The academy's debates thus offer a glimpse into the ways in which professional bodies of experts and agents of the administration cooperated in determining the form official population statistics would take. Ultimately, the statistical representation of populations allowed policy makers and government officials to reify collective interests such as the "nation" or "society" in numerical terms. Before the nineteenth century, of course, such collective interests remained comfortably abstract. French liberals, following the Enlightenment tradition, could defend *both* the nation (or society) *and* individual freedoms without fear of irreconcilable contradictions. Accordingly, liberals in France defended the autonomy of the (male) individual from outside interference and made this autonomy the basis for demands for extensions of the suffrage in the political sphere and for the principle of free markets in the economic realm. The subsequent widespread adoption of a statistical understanding of populations challenged the eighteenth-century view of individual autonomy. By offering a considerably more precise reckoning of the social consequences of individual actions and by recasting scientists' understanding of the combined forces of milieu and heredity, statistics both enlarged and deepened the perceived connections between individuals and the society in which they lived. Used as a tool of government, in other words, statistics forced social scientists and political figures to reinterpret the freedom and autonomy that individuals could exercise in pursuance of their goals and desires. At times, statistics forced them even to reconsider the very nature of the "individual" itself.

The Académie de médecine debates were an important forum for these issues in three specific ways. First, the academy's discussion of the doctor's position as observer probed the extent to which the individual—in this case the doctor himself—could be seen as a reliable knowing *subject*, whose accounts of his observations could be relied on for scientific validity. For the clinicians, of course, the reliability of the medical observer was never in doubt; their brand of empiricism was based on the presumed accuracy of the observer's sensory perceptions. For statisticians, on the other hand, the primary benefit of quantification lay in its ability to eliminate the idiosyncrasies of individual perspective through the homogenizing effects of statistical generalization. Both of these epistemological positions were compatible with a liberal politics, but their difference in emphasis was crucial. Both could be used to support an extension of the suffrage to a larger proportion of the population because both assumed that individual decisions could result in a general good or truth. In the clinician's view of subjectivity, however, the general truth—in science as in politics—was only as good as the reason and care taken by the individual observer; such a view lent itself to a more restricted and elitist view of political participation. The statistician, on the other hand, worried less about the accuracy of each individual belief and more about the cumulative effect of their combined opinions or judgments. For the statistician, justice in the political realm would function along the same lines as truth in the scientific realm: as in Quetelet's *physique sociale*, the effects of particular errors and individual bad faith would cancel each other out in favor of a general good.

The academy's discussion of the nature, origins, causes, and signs of illness also posed difficult questions about the status of the individual patient as an autonomous object. How much of the body's health and vitality was the result of internal processes, and how much could be attributed to the effects of the environment or of interaction with other individuals? For the clinician, it was impossible to generalize on a matter of such complexity, and each case needed to be explored solely in terms of its own particularities. For the statistician, on the other hand, it was precisely this complexity that required the use of quantitative generalizations, for only statistics could reveal the relative importance of internal constitution, of the environment, of family life, and of social interactions on the health of populations. The statistician's research into these matters eventually recast the classic opposition between "individual" and "society" that French social science had inherited from Enlightenment thought and allowed for a politics of social reform that linked individual behavior to the national interest in a new and incontrovertible fashion. Representing the national interest in quantitative terms leant a new power to calls for a more active and interventionist social policy in France, especially in areas where individual actions could be shown to have a significant effect on the health and vitality of the population.

The academy's debates thus provided a forum for adjudicating between the twin goals of scientific truth and political authority. Eighteenth-century authors, such as Moheau, had assumed that the goals of science and the state were one and the same, and their vision of a technocratic state was perfectly compatible with an authoritarian monarchy precisely because they could not imagine a situation in which a rational government and truth would conflict.[6] The nineteenth-century disagreements between clinicians and the statisticians in the Académie de médecine re-

6. See Chapter 1.

vealed, however, that unanimity between science and the state was not automatic but subject to continual negotiation.

THE CLINICAL VS. THE STATISTICAL

Although many of the earliest practitioners of social statistics had medical training, the science of medicine would not have appeared to be a fertile field for the application of quantitative analysis in the early years of the nineteenth century. Philippe Pinel, who dominated the Paris school of medicine from the 1790s to the end of the Napoleonic period, began his 1819 essay "Observation" in the *Dictionnaire des sciences médicales* by pronouncing that "the most solid foundation of medicine rests on the knowledge of particular facts, that is to say, the individual histories of illnesses."[7] On a purely theoretical level, as well as in practice, such an emphasis on the individual illness and on the necessity of careful observation made doctors suspicious of generalizations made solely on the basis of statistical averages or frequencies. The medical philosopher P. J. G. Cabanis, a prominent physiologist and ideologue of the revolutionary period, had formalized this mistrust of quantitative methods by invoking the sensationalist psychology of Condillac. Condillac's form of radical empiricism posited a material correspondence between events in the world and their apprehension in the mind; he believed in a physiological connection between physical sensation and rational thought.[8] Such a psychology encouraged physicians to learn about the body by dissecting them in great numbers, and Cabanis's work provided the basis for early research in clinical and pathological anatomy. Many clinicians perceived this approach

---

7. Philippe Pinel, "Observation," in *Dictionnaire des sciences médicales*, vol. 37 (Paris, 1819), p. 29. Pinel went on to state that "the method [*ordre*] that one follows in the editing of medical observations varies almost as much as there are observers. This uncertainty seems at first to produce ill consequences; but as all good minds are in agreement as to the foundation, the result is that often men of real talent arrive at the same end by different paths." Terence Murphy pointed out that Pinel was open to the calculus of probabilities, even though he never used such methods in his own work. ("Medical Knowledge and Statistical Methods in Early Nineteenth-Century France," *Medical History* 25 [1981]: 308). Today, Pinel is primarily remembered for his contributions to psychiatry, but he was primarily known at the time for his attempts to arrive at a systematic classification of all diseases. See E. A. Ackerknecht, *Medicine at the Paris Hospital, 1794–1848* (Baltimore, 1967), p. 47.
8. "Ideology" was the name given to the work of a group of philosophers during the French Revolution who attempted to unify a psychology of the passive mind, which they viewed as dependent on sensation for its thought processes, with a program for empirical research in the sciences. Cabanis, Condillac, and Destutt de Tracy were the primary defenders of "Ideology." See George Rosen, "The Philosophy of Ideology and the Emergence of Modern Medicine in France," *Bulletin of the History of Medicine* 20 (1946): 328–39; on Cabanis specifically, see especially Martin Staum, *Cabanis: Enlightenment and Medical Philosophy in the French Revolution* (Princeton, 1980).

to be incommensurate with the calculus of probabilities, however, because such calculus gave no priority to the doctor's specific observations and perceptions of individual patients.

At the same time, however, some doctors were anxious to extend the purview of medicine to include society as a whole. In a work titled *De la médecine politique en générale et son objet* (1814) a doctor from the famous medical school in Montpellier,[9] Clément-Gabriel Prunelle, made an early claim for an expanded political role for medicine. "A profound knowledge of the animal organism, and of the bodies which exercise salutary or noxious effects upon our own [bodies]," wrote Prunelle, "becomes even more necessary when . . . science no longer contents itself with being of use to the individual and applies itself to the social body, supporting Legislators and Magistrates in their greatest endeavors, and in their most sacred duties."[10] By establishing average life spans and life expectancy tables, scientists could measure the impact of government reforms on society as a whole. Doctors could use such information to gauge the effectiveness of hygienic measures, proper nutrition and eating habits, even the appropriateness of certain types of dress.[11] The culmination of this strand of public medicine, of course, was the work of Louis-René Villermé on differential mortality in Paris and the accompanying studies published in the ensuing decades in the *Annales d'hygiène publique et de médecine légale*.

Taken together, Pinel's description of the doctor's responsibility to the individual body and Prunelle's characterization of medicine's role with regard to the *corps social* mirrors what Michel Foucault called the "great bipolar technology" of early nineteenth-century medicine, "anatomic and biological, individualizing and specifying, directed toward the performances of the body, with attention to the processes of life."[12] This bipolar technology did not, however, emerge fully formed from the ad-

9. The medical school at Montpellier had been marked by an early enthusiasm for social medicine and the application of the calculus of probabilities to the science of therapeutics. In the year XII, its director, Charles-Louis Dumas, had remarked on the advances made in the physical sciences by the use of such calculus and asked if these methods could not be fruitfully applied to medicine (Murphy, "Medical Knowledge," p. 306).

10. C. G. Prunelle, *De la médecine politique en général et de son objet; de la médecine-légale en particulier, de son origine, de ses progrès, et des secours qu'elle fournit au magistrat dans l'exercice de ses fonctions* (Montpellier, 1814), p. 1.

11. In a subsequent work Prunelle wrote: "Medicine can indicate to manufacturers the means to preserve their materials from waste and rot. It can make known the form of clothing that is the most advantageous to health. It can proscribe all the finery required by luxury and disavowed by good taste that cause the destruction of the individual and the degeneration of the race" (*De l'action de la médecine sur la population des états* [Paris, 1818], p. 5).

12. Foucault, *History of Sexuality*, p. 139; see also Hacking, "Biopower," p. 279.

vances made in clinical and pathological anatomy in the late eighteenth century, although certain doctors supported Prunelle's claim that such an extension of medicine to the social world was a natural one. Rather, the two fields of research emerged as part of an ongoing epistemological debate about the acceptability of statistical reasoning in medicine.

Michel Levy, a prominent hygienist who later became the president of the Académie de médecine, claimed that the distinction between the two realms of medical practice was essentially methodological. "Public hygiene," he argued, differed from "individual hygiene" only in scope and in its reliance on medical statistics. "Private hygiene," he continued, "encloses itself around the organism, and interrogates each part . . . , social hygiene embraces a class of men, a population, a nation, all of humanity."[13] Despite Levy's confident assertion that the two branches of medical research differed only "by the scale of their applications," his characterization of their separate spheres revealed the extent to which the medical metaphor was being stretched beyond recognition as it attempted to encompass a new set of objects. The strains were evident in the invocation of a nonmedical vocabulary—public and private—to justify the division of labor between the two disciplines, and in fact, the two branches of science did not coexist comfortably. Their respective territories were ultimately defined by default, as a result of an inability of the medical community to accept the application of quantitative methods to the treatment of individuals.

When the issue of statistical reasoning came up in the Académie de médecine, these tensions rose to the surface.[14] The issue was broached when Pierre Louis, the president of the Société médicale d'observation, published a paper attacking the practice of bloodletting. Louis supported his arguments with a polemic based on the quantitative analysis of patients' rates of survival and asserting the superiority of his own methods, repeated purgings and the administration of emetics.[15] The debate was complicated by the fact that bleeding had been championed by a powerful Parisian doctor, François-Joseph-Victor Broussais, an influential and combative member of the faculty at the Ecole de médecine.

Broussais was the dominant clinician of the generation that came after Pinel, and his views on disease and therapeutics reigned supreme over the

13. Levy, *Traité*, 1:50.
14. Léonard, *La Médecine*, pp. 119, 135; Murphy, "Medical Knowledge," pp. 310–17; Desrosières, "Comment faire des choses qui tiennent," p. 229.
15. Pierre Louis, *Recherches sur les effets de la saignée dans quelques maladies inflammatoires et sur l'action émétique et des vésicatoires dans la pneumonie* (Paris, 1835).

Paris medical faculty for much of the 1820s and 1830s.[16] His 1816 work, *Examen de la doctrine médicale généralement adoptée*, attacked Pinel's *Nosographie philosophique* of 1798 and effectively replaced that work, which had been the unquestioned authority for the earlier generation of doctors. Broussais rejected Pinel's "ontological" classification of disease according to symptom and suggested instead that all diseases had their origins in specific anatomical lesions or inflammations—for this reason his theory came to be known as "physiological medicine." Broussais concluded that in almost all cases the cause of these inflammations was overstimulation of the affected tissues, and he recommended bleeding and restrictions in diet to treat almost all ailments.[17] By the 1830s, a new generation of pragmatically minded doctors—the so-called eclectics—began to challenge Broussais's authority, announcing their rejection of his all-embracing systems and theories, as well as those of Pinel. Many of these doctors, including Pierre Louis, François Chomel, and Jean Bouillaud, showed a decidedly liberal bias in their politics, and many of them spoke out in favor of statistics in the academy debate. The eclectic school's support for Louis stemmed in part from their opposition to Broussais, and the debate can also be seen as a tactical episode in a generational conflict between powerful doctors.[18]

In 1837, then, the Académie de médecine was already divided politically, generationally, and scientifically. The debate on statistics could not remain immune to these divisions. Many of the clinicians associated with Broussais's *physiologisme* loudly resisted the use of statistical techniques in medicine, and members of the eclectic group rallied to defend their use. The transition from eighteenth-century systems of disease classification to nineteenth-century procedures of anatomical investigation did not

16. Ackerknecht, *Medicine at the Paris Hospital*, pp. 61–80.

17. Ackerknecht strikingly demonstrated the impact of Broussais's theories on French medical practice by documenting the increase in the importation of leeches to France in the 1820s and 1830s. In 1823 320,000 leeches were imported. Ten years later, the figure had increased to 41,654,300 (ibid., p. 62).

18. Michel Foucault made much of the transition in medicine from a classificatory system of diseases and their species to a descriptive "anatamo-clinical" method which located disease in the body of the individual—a transformation that he saw occurring between Pinel's nosology of 1798 and Broussais's *physiologisme* of 1816. Foucault saw this transformation as part of a process whereby doctors began to locate pathology within bodies, departing from their previous habit of treating each disease as a distinct realm with its own particular natural history. As they extended their research into the bodies of patients, Foucault argued, doctors developed a new way of seeing, a new way of confronting the unwell body, and this "medical gaze" became the organizing principle of a new political consciousness, with its own institutions and practices: the hospital, the autopsy, the morgue, the death certificate. Foucault's instructive analysis implied a close fit between the new medical knowledge made possible by this epistemological transformation, and the new aggregate sciences of population (*Birth of the Clinic*, esp. pp. 3–21 and 175–94).

necessarily mean that doctors complacently accepted a medicalized vision of the social body, laid open before their eyes like a patient etherized on a table. They had to be convinced.

The debate began on 11 April 1837, when a skeptic in the academy, the pathological anatomist Jean Cruveilhier, suggested that a full session be devoted to a discussion of "the utility of statistics in its medical applications, and the limits of this utility."[19] Accordingly, the session opened on 2 May when Risueño d'Amador gave a long paper titled "Mémoire sur le calcul des probabilités appliqué à la médecine," in which he attacked Pierre Louis's advocacy of statistics and listed the reasons for refusing to admit such methods to the practice of medicine.[20] The discussion occupied the academy for the next six sessions.

Amador based his condemnation of statistical reasoning on what he perceived to be the inadequacy of probability in the face of "the great question of certainty in medicine."[21] He stuck to an understanding of probability compatible with that of eighteenth-century writers on the subject, claiming that "to invoke probability . . . is to invoke chance. It is the renunciation of all medical certainty, surrendering all the rational rules which are a part of induction, experiment, observation, and reason to the mechanical and inflexible operation of calculation."[22] He insisted that statistics was "a dead science," capable merely of counting and categorizing on the basis of surface similarities but unable to capture the "mobility of real pathological states even while outward organic appearances remain the same."[23] For Amador, the dynamism of living organisms, the inherent unreliability of the body's surface as a sign of illness, and the invisibility of interior pathologies precluded the categorization entailed by statistical reasoning.

Amador's characterization of the problem revealed the standards behind the task of vitalist medical description in this period, standards founded on the traditional Hippocratic interpretation of the signs of disease, what Amador's medical contemporaries called the science of *sémiotique*.[24] According to this orthodoxy, doctors needed to make an important distinction between mere "symptoms" and the "signs" that revealed the progress of the disease in the body, its future course, and the possibilities for treatment. On the one hand, then, the essence of disease lay

19. *BARM*, p. 597.
20. *BARM*, pp. 622–80.
21. *BARM*, p. 624.
22. Ibid.
23. *BARM*, p. 660.
24. For a good contemporary summation of this science, see J. B. T. Serrurier, "Sémiotique," *Dictionnaire des sciences médicales*, vol. 50 (Paris, 1820), pp. 556–69.

inside the body, hence Amador's rhetorical emphasis on depth. What one could see—the symptoms and "outward appearances"—did not necessarily correspond directly to this inner truth, and it was the responsibility of the doctor to navigate this thicket of signs to arrive at the correct diagnosis.[25] Only the doctor's careful observation could bridge this gap between the superficially visible and the reality of the disease in the patient's body. Statistics, on the other hand, only magnified and expanded upon the gap between physical sign and pathological essence. By organizing the groups under observation by their outward signs and by concerning themselves only with surfaces, statistics made the notion of an internal essence at the heart of each pathological case irrelevant. In studies of the etiology of disease, according to Amador, statistics were "preoccupied with occasional causes" and "accorded little attention to internal causes or predisposition." In diagnosis, the numerical method "placed an external and visible symptomology entirely in the place of *sémiotique*."[26]

Amador did not categorically oppose the use of inductive reasoning—he realized that "where one cannot demonstrate one must infer [*induire*]."[27] But he refused to recognize the inductive nature of statistics. A proper use of induction in science would function by careful analogy, he argued, because analogy was based on the congruence between two signs and their respective referents, whereas the statistician was forced to assume that like phenomena were identical.[28] Amador could not accept this procedure because it established such congruence only at the level of the signifier and left the referent to chance. His conclusion was firm: "Numbers, as such, signify nothing in therapeutics."[29]

The question of medical certainty was thus reduced in Amador's discussion to an anxiety about the ability of signs—whether on the body or

25. Michel Foucault emphasized the medical expert's perception of bodily depth as an important part of what he termed the clinical "regard" or gaze: "The structure, at once perceptual and epistemological, that commands clinical anatomy, and all medicine that derives from it is that of invisible visibility. Truth, which, by right of nature, is made for the eye, is taken from her, but at once surreptitiously revealed by that which tries to evade it. Knowledge develops in accordance with a whole interplay of envelopes; the hidden element takes on the form and rhythm of the hidden content, which means that, like a veil, it is transparent" (*Birth of the Clinic*, pp. 165–66).
26. *BARM*, p. 662.
27. *BARM*, p. 646.
28. Amador wrote: "Induction only brings facts together by virtue of their common qualities, the only ones which are comparable, and leaves aside the special traits which give them their individual character [*qui les individualisent*]. In contrast, addition supposes not a simple analogy but an identity. It is precisely because the experimental sciences only operate on the basis of analogy and never on the basis of identity, that the human mind uses induction and not numeration" (*BARM*, p. 646). These words are a paraphrase of Auguste-Charles Savary's comments in his article "Analogie," *Dictionnaire des sciences médicales*, 58 vols. (Paris, 1812–22), 2:18. Savary is cited as well by Murphy, "Medical Knowledge," p. 309.
29. *BARM*, p. 678.

in the statistical table—to represent their object. The only possible recourse in the face of such uncertainty was the intervention of the doctor's
knowledge of the particular case, which he compared to that of the artist
approaching a difficult subject. "Recently many mechanical procedures
have perfected the art of the portrait," he wrote, "but none of these procedures can replace a good painter's able hand, even if they take as their
principle the complete reproduction of the model's smallest details. It is
the same with the procedures of the numerists, who believe that the art
of observing requires nothing more than the manipulation of observations."[30] In a subsequent passage, Amador went even further, writing that
the choice of therapeutic methods is "the result of a spontaneous conviction and is in some manner instinctive." Claiming that medical diagnosis had more in common with the moral deliberation of a jury than with
the strict application of judicial science, he concluded that such decisions
were the result of "a conviction produced more by the real value of witnesses, than by their number."[31]

Amador's choice of examples—the painter approaching a canvas, the
moral deliberation of a jury—show his need to preserve a special realm
for subjective intuition that could not be reduced to rule-bound mathematical procedures. The doctor's diagnosis, he believed, required a sympathy or affinity with the body of the patient that a statistical approach
would not permit. This view could be interpreted as an attempt to preserve the privileged status of medicine as an art in the face of a rational-
izing and potentially reductive technique that might diminish a physician's social prestige. Nevertheless, Amador did not reject rationality. On
the contrary, he sought to defend it, so long as it remained the prerogative of a privileged elite. In the political context of the July Monarchy, of
course, such claims resonated with the conservative supporters of the regime. Louis-Philippe and his ministers sought to limit extension of the
suffrage to the propertied on the grounds that only an elite was capable
of participating in the political process. In so doing, he hoped to fore-
stall the kinds of social unrest that had been fatal to the Bourbon regime
in the 1790s and again in 1830. The same logic lay behind Amador's defense of the "minority fact" against the tyrannical majorities supported
by statisticians.

The intrusion into the debate of a very real political anxiety about mass
democracy explains why it was possible for the opponents of statistics to
refute Adolphe Quetelet's arguments simply by quoting them. François
Double, the author of an important three-volume clinical study of *sémi-*

30. *BARM*, p. 663.
31. *BARM*, p. 668.

otique, announced in an unashamed (and unattributed) plagiarism of Quetelet that "in statistical matters . . . the first care before all else is to ignore that man is an isolated individual and only to consider him as a fraction of the species. It is necessary to strip him of his individuality in order to eliminate any accidental qualities from the question. In applied medicine, on the other hand, the problem is always individual."[32] Frédéric Dubois d'Amiens, later permanent secretary to the academy and one of its most prominent orators, took a similar position. Certainly, Dubois d'Amiens admitted, one might perform dissections on a large number of individuals and deduce from these observations a series of averages for every anatomical variation, a composite "anatomical average man" such as that imagined by Quetelet. "Well!" he exclaimed, "that would be a fictive being, a creation of reason! Far from having an exact idea of what one had found in the dissections, one would have a master plan [*patron*] whose form one could never find in nature, because it would be a mere assemblage of *anatomical averages*."[33] Double's and Dubois d'Amien's arguments made no sense as refutations of Quetelet's work—they were simply quoting him—but in the highly charged political atmosphere of the academy's debate, Quetelet's emphasis on the *volume* of observations as opposed to their *quality* made his work suspect and vulnerable to attack. Even more telling, the opponents of statistical research were able to cloak their defense of their own professional status and autonomy with the spirited language of a defense of individual rights, thus beating the liberals at their own game.

Dubois d'Amiens, Double, and Amador all championed the cause of variety and flux in organic life, and they clearly feared a tendency of statistical work to treat individual patients as interchangeable units. Double claimed that, for pathologists, "individuality is an incontrovertible truth: a sickness is not a simple fixed or invariable being; it is a series of multiple actions, mobile, ever-changing; consequently, any exclusive theory makes no sense in pathology, and any absolute method is the opposite of therapeutics."[34] Perhaps the most curious rhetorical ploy in this argument was Double's assertion that the complexity of organic life was of the same order as the complexity of language. "Morbid states," he wrote, "are no less numerous than the letters that make up the composition of our alphabet. Look at the wealth of alphabetic language, what number, what variety, what multiplicity of words it produces. Imagine what a quantity of particular and distinct cases could arise from the direct combination of the

32. Quoted in Murphy, "Medical Knowledge," p. 312, translation Murphy's. See also discussion of Quetelet in Chapter 2.
33. *BARM*, p. 692, emphasis in original.
34. *BARM*, p. 714.

elements of our morbid states. To push the analogy even further, one finds that some of these elements are more common, more important than others; in our pathological alphabet there are also vowels and consonants."[35] Double's peculiar arguments point to the paradox faced by empirical scientists during this period. On the one hand, they were committed to a vision of the natural world that exhibited a nearly boundless complexity. On the other hand, they sought to define a representational system that would do justice to this complexity while simultaneously reducing its variety and multiplicity to understandable and reproducible procedures. Double solved this dilemma by making a virtue out of the instability of his chosen representational system. Words could be just as infinite as numbers, and their ability to move in a multitude of directions as they recombined, in short, their pliability, made them superior to statistics, which could only reproduce a monotonous cadence of similitude.

The defenders of statistics—many of them members of the anti-Broussais "eclectic" school—attempted to calm the offended sensibilities of their opposition. Jean Bouillaud, the liberal professor of clinical medicine who served as the model for the character of Bianchon in Balzac's novel *Père Goriot*, announced (with no detectable irony): "I fear we differ more on words than on things."[36] Bouillaud criticized Amador for his dated views on probability, claiming that counting was an integral part of medical practice: in the periodization of illness, in determining the morbidity of contagious disease, or in the proper dosage of medicines. François Chomel repeated Quetelet's observation that statistical reasoning was merely a more exact method for the sort of reasoning that physicians had always performed.[37] Pierre Louis, whose paper had initiated the controversy, criticized the imprecision of an adverbial medical vocabulary that continually resorted to expressions such as "more or less, rarely or frequently." "More or less," he exclaimed, "is it ten, twenty, or eighty percent? Who can say? The best dictionary in the language could not resolve such a problem."[38] This cautious defense on the part of the statisticians, who would not admit the more radical implications of their own method, indicates how difficult it was for the *probabilistes* themselves to let go of the older models of empirical observation.

Louis attempted to make clear that statistics should not be understood simply in terms of Quetelet's work, but to little avail.[39] The goal of sta-

35. *BARM*, pp. 708–9.
36. *BARM*, p. 698.
37. *BARM*, p. 721.
38. *BARM*, p. 732.
39. *BARM*, p. 741.

tistics was not "an average or imaginary man," he argued, but he could do little to overcome the association in his opponents' mind between quantification and the work of the Belgian statistician. Perhaps more fatal to the numerists, as they were called, was the unwise defense of quantification by J. A. Rochoux, a physician from the Bicêtre hospital who was well known for his work on apoplexy and typhus. Rochoux managed to muddle the issue of statistical regularity and mechanistic causality to such an extent that he ended by claiming that the minds of scientists themselves were subject to inexorable statistical laws. "The maniac who is prey to the most stormy delirium and Newton calmly calculating the most elevated problems of analysis are one and the other under the empire of laws so regular, so necessary, so fatal, that if the conditions in which they found themselves could suddenly change, their roles would be instantaneously reversed." [40] One is hard-pressed to imagine the esteemed members of the academy finding such arguments attractive.

This failure to mount an effective rebuttal to Amador's attack left the outcome of the 1837 debate inconclusive. Neither side could be convinced by the other, and at the end of the debate Amador reasserted his total and absolute rejection of the numerical method. Such opinions persisted long after the debate in the academy was closed. As late as 1865, the most noted physiologist of the century, Claude Bernard, wrote that the strict determinism required by experimental medicine precluded the use of statistics, famously commenting that "statistics have never taught nor will they ever teach us anything about the nature of phenomena." [41] Quetelet's hopes for a universally applied statistical science of "man" would seem to have been soundly rejected.

Despite continued opposition, however, the proponents of statistics continued to make their case. The positive reception given Jules Gavarret's *Principes généraux de statistique médicale* (1840) indicated a shift in medical opinion, and despite Bernard's skepticism, no one seriously contested after this point that the calculation of probabilities had a place in the medical arsenal. [42] The result was the establishment of two distinct

40. *BARM*, p. 751. Rochoux also stated that "statistics are stronger than the Faculty, stronger than the Academy and all the Academies in the world; in a word, medical statistics are true and have an answer for everything" (quoted in Léonard, *La Médecine entre les pouvoirs et les savoirs*, p. 135). On Rochoux, see also Ackerknecht, *Medicine at the Paris Hospital*, p. 104.
41. Quoted in Murphy, "Medical Knowledge," p. 318.
42. Gavarret chastised both the supporters and opponents of the numerical method in the Académie de médecine, demonstrating that neither side fully understood the mathematical principles behind the calculation of probabilities. See William Coleman's discusion of Gavarret in *Death Is a Social Disease*, pp. 134–37. Another contemporary work dealing with the academy debate is Casimir Broussais, *De la statistique appliquée à la pathologie et la thérapeutique* (Paris, 1840).

fields of medical inquiry and practice. The first, the diagnosis and thera-peutics of individual cases, would remain the domain of the clinical prac-titioner. The second would focus on the species body conceived as a so-cial organism.[43] Initially, statistical reasoning would be admitted as an acceptable tool only in the latter case. In other words, the medical com-munity was prepared to allow the looser connection between cause and effect which allowed for the establishment of "social laws" but still in-sisted on the classical notion of a mechanical causality when speaking of the individual body.

The ultimate irony of this history lay in the successful importation of a medical metaphor of the clinical researcher into the social realm. De-spite the clear rejection by powerful figures in the academy such as Du-bois d'Amiens, Double, and Amador, later proponents of the numerical method were able to legitimize their own activities by comparing them-selves to anatomists and physiologists. When the pioneering demogra-pher Louis-Adolphe Bertillon introduced his newly minted science to the world in 1855, he began by claiming that "statistics has taken on another role in our day." "This modest science," he continued, ". . . is the scalpel that one uses to isolate the smallest fibers of the social body. It is the mi-croscope that with its magnification renders the smallest influences vis-ible. It is the sensitive reactant that tells us of the presence and extent of a disturbing element whose effects may have long escaped the keenest observer."[44] Bertillon's announcement pulled the rug out from under the clinicians. Their own cherished empirical practice, which had so ada-mantly refused the statistical allegory put forth by Quetelet and the pro-ponents of quantification, had been reduced to a metaphor for the very procedures they abhorred.

In 1821 Benoiston de Chateauneuf had rejoiced in the quantitative treatment of facts, which "speak loudly of their own accord."[45] Why, then, was it necessary in 1855 for Bertillon to have recourse to the more subtly evocative image of the careful empiricist peering through a micro-scope at a social body laid open with the scalpel of statistics? The answer to this question can be found in the resistance offered by doctors in the Académie de médecine to aggregate analysis. In their frame of reference, the complexity of the world could be captured only in a continual parade of discrete observations—the chaos of particular facts. Bertillon's meta-phor addressed this residual desire to retain the individual narratives whose suppression lent the number in the statistical table all of its alle-

43. See Murphy's comments on this split, "Medical Knowledge," p. 311.
44. Louis-Adolphe Bertillon, *Congrès internationale de statistique* (Paris, 1855), p. 3.
45. See Chapter 2, note 2.

gorical power—and by doing so he effectively de-allegorized his numbers. Unlike Quetelet, who discredited his own project by admitting the "fictive" nature of his statistical constructions, Bertillon succeeded simply by appropriating the metaphor of the anatomists and claiming their rigor as his own.

STANDARDIZING THE CAUSES OF DEATH

Did the clinicians' mistrust of statistics have any wider impact on population research during this period? There is some evidence that a lingering reluctance to treat social aggregates as objectively real phenomena may have influenced the course of research on mortality during the 1830s, 1840s, and 1850s. Bertillon's metaphor of the anatomist may have soothed the lingering anxieties that some members of the academy felt about aggregate analysis, but it could not entirely dispel the political uneasiness that many population researchers felt about the reality of social aggregates themselves.

Villermé's 1829 work on differential mortality in Paris had pointed to the existence of distinct populations in the capital, distinguished by a disturbing inequality before death that correlated all too well with inequalities of wealth. The renewed outbreak of revolution in 1848—centered in the same poverty-stricken neighborhoods identified by Villermé in his 1829 work—only confirmed the enormous social cost of these inequalities. One might have expected, therefore, that population researchers between 1830 and 1860 would have concentrated on further explorations of this correlation, in studies of mortality by profession, for example. Historians of demography, however, have pointed out that studies of mortality by profession at mid-century, though plentiful enough in the medical journals of the period, are universally rudimentary, partial, and lacking in systematic conclusions. Studies that did exist were undertaken almost exclusively by private savants, and the state-sponsored statistical institutions expressed little interest in following up on Villermé's conclusions. Not until 1892 did somebody publish a table of mortality by profession in France.[46]

Part of the problem was certainly a lack of reliable data. Information on the occupation of the deceased was available on death certificates in

46. See Dupâquier and Dupâquier, *Histoire de la démographie*, pp. 347–48. Jacques Bertillon claimed that his 1892 study was the first publication of a table of mortality by profession in France. See Bertillon, "De la morbidité et de la mortalité par profession," *Journal de la Société de statistique de Paris* 33 (1892): 341–87.

Paris as early as the 1820s, but without reliable information on the number of people in each profession it was impossible to calculate and compare the different rates at which these groups died. Nevertheless, when the prefect of Paris, the comte de Rambuteau, published one of the few officially sponsored studies of death by profession as part of the 1844 volume of the *Recherches statistiques de la ville de Paris*, his statisticians spent little time worrying about the possibility of differential mortality. Instead, they made the opposite assumption: they supposed that the absolute figures for deaths by profession they had from the *état civil* were evenly distributed in all groups, and they attempted to use the figures to come up with proportional estimates of the total population in each profession.[47] Such an assumption directly contradicted the evidence from Villermé's earlier study and demonstrated a surprising lack of interest on the part of statisticians in the one social aggregate that should have been of paramount importance: class.

Villermé's 1829 study notwithstanding, the most important area of government-sponsored work on mortality during this period was not in differential mortality between rich and poor but in the analysis of the causes of death. This work produced different aggregates—not populations of workers, bourgeois, and aristocrat, but populations of the contagious, the feverish, and the bilious, populations with broken limbs and cancerous tumors lumped together with the victims of accident, murder, and execution. In the first half of the nineteenth century, an enormous amount of administrative energy was devoted to standardizing this list of the causes of death, and the ensuing debates saw the reemergence of a split between the clinicians and the statisticians in the Académie de médecine in 1857. If the continued mistrust of statistics on the part of the clinicians in the medical community had an effect on official population research it was that between approximately 1830 and 1860 work on the differential mortality between classes was postponed in favor of the attempt to collect information on mortality which emphasized the seat of illness on the body of the individual patient. One effect of this research was to assemble a wide body of data on the causes of death, organized according to categories that reflected the current consensus among doctors on the fatal effects of disease and aging. Another effect, of course, was to preserve a realm for clinicians within the newly emergent population sciences, for it was up to them to provide their assent to the causes of death on the *état civil*.

The tension between the clinical and the statistical reemerged in 1857

47. *RSVP*, 1844, pp. vii–x and table 120.

when the minister of agriculture, commerce, and public works asked the Académie de médecine to approve a standardized nomenclature for the causes of death. In this debate, doctors who had been clinically trained according to Pinel's narrowly empirical definition of "observation" insisted on their right to use whatever language they saw fit to assign the causes of death on the official bulletins demanded by the *état civil*. On the other side, statisticians in the employ of the state expressed their frustration with the many complexities of the clinical vocabulary, which made comparisons and tabulation difficult, if not impossible. The difficulty lay in a simple fact: "populations" were subject to mortality, but only "individuals" died. Statisticians wanted to generalize about the former while doctors prided themselves on the care they took in observing the latter. Unlike their medical colleagues, statisticians cared little about what made any given death unique—they sought only to understand what each death might have in common with other deaths. At the same time, however, under the procedures of the *état civil*, municipal statisticians needed the cooperation of doctors to collect their data. The medical statistician Marc d'Espine of Geneva put it simply: "Place an individual in the most disadvantageous conditions with regard to sex, season, place, habitation, even age, and something else must occur for him to die: what is necessary? An accident or an illness." [48] Only the doctor could fill in the blank on the death certificate.

There was no obvious solution to this problem. How to summarize the many factors that might have led to a single death? How to reconcile the mechanistic causality that determined the fate of individual bodies with the collective understanding of frequencies and tendencies in the population at large? A nosological treatment of causes of death could not be the same as the standard nosologies of disease because not all illnesses were fatal.[49] Furthermore, every generation of doctors emerged from medical training with a different classification, specific to the theories that were prevalent at the time and place of instruction.

As early as 1808, the Prefecture of Police in Paris attempted to solve this problem with its "Tableau des maladies considérées comme causes de mort." This list followed quite closely the categories first put forth by the influential clinician Philippe Pinel in his *Nosographie philosophique* (1798). Pinel had named five classes of illness: fevers, phlegmasias (inflammations), hemorrhages, neuroses, and organic lesions. The 1808 "Tableau" followed this system exactly and added a sixth classification to the

48. Marc d'Espine, "Essai statistique sur la mortalité du canton de Genève pendant l'année 1838," *Annales d'hygiène publique et de médecine légale* 23 (1840): 32–33.
49. Ibid., p. 33.

causes of death, the somewhat confusingly titled *Maladies chirurgicales*, which included contusions, wounds, gangrenous infections, hernias and other displacements of soft and hard tissues, deformities, the effects of childbirth, and finally, death following surgical operations.[50] In 1821 and 1833 the Prefecture's Conseil de salubrité published successive revisions of the original list, reflecting the challenge to Pinel's classifications by François Broussais's *Examen des doctrines médicales et des systèmes de nosologie* (1816). Accordingly, the 1821 and 1833 lists paid more attention to Broussais's inflammations and organic lesions and devoted less space to Pinel's many categories of fever. These changes, although significant, did not depart from the clinician's overall goal: a complete and systematic classification of all diseases that might lead to death.[51]

The potential for confusion in these lists was great. On the 1808 list, the very first order of "inflammatory fever" could be either "continuous," "ardent," "intermittent," or "remittant." "Mucous fevers" could be either "intermittent," "remittent," "continuous," or "verminous." "Putrid fevers" (class 1, order 4) were "simple," "bilious-putrid," "yellow fever," "remittent," or "intermittent," unless they were "putrid malignant," in which case they were classified as "pestilential" (class 1, order 6). Several well-known diseases, such as smallpox, measles, scarlet fever, red and white military fever, scurvy, scabies, and ringworm, were classified as "cutaneous phlegmasias" (class 2, order 1) along with "malignant gangrenous pustules." "Dentition" was classified as a "local nervous affection" (class 4, order 4) along with "aphrodisiac neuroses" ("effects of masturbation," "hysteria," "uterine furor"). Sufferers of "melancholia" (class 4, order 2) may have been frightened to learn that "hypochondria" was a potential cause of death. Doctors uncertain in their diagnosis were left little room to fudge; in the interest of completeness, there was no place for "other causes."[52]

These lists were relatively useless to statisticians because they did not lend themselves to the construction of coherent aggregates. The most innovative and detailed official studies of population during the first half of the nineteenth century—the *Recherches statistiques sur la ville de Paris*, published by the Prefecture of the Seine covering the years 1816–36— did not attempt an account of the causes of death, even though raw data were available on the death certificates filled out by doctors for the *état*

50. AdP, VD4 0011, no. 3103, "Tableau des maladies considérées comme causes de mort." This list was drawn up first in 1808 and reprinted in 1820 in preparation of the revisions made in 1821.
51. AdP, VD4 0011, no. 3104 (1821) and no. 3107 *bis* (1833).
52. AdP, VD4 0011, no. 3103, *Tableau des maladies considérées comme causes de mort.*

civil. Instead, the authors of these studies contented themselves with regular accounts of deaths by age and by district, with separate tables for only a few causes: stillbirths, accidents, smallpox, and, after 1832, cholera.[53] Not until Baron Georges Haussman's 1860 volume of the *Recherches statistiques* (the last in the series) did the Parisian statisticians attempt a complete account of the causes of death in Paris, and even then only for the years 1854–56, the last three years covered by the volume.

The categories used by Haussman's statisticians became the basis for the official list published by the Ministry of Agriculture, Commerce, and Public Works in 1859, following consultation with the Académie de médecine in 1857.[54] The twenty-one classes in this list had little in common with the clinical system used by French doctors earlier in the century. Though the first three classes of disease owed much to the previous classifications (fevers, eruptive fevers, and virulent or contagious illnesses— including snakebite!) classes 4 through 18 pertained to diseases of specific parts of the body—brain, circulatory system, respiratory system, digestive organs, kidneys, urinary tract, genital organs, breasts, bones, muscles, nervous system, and skin. The remaining three classes look like afterthoughts. Class 19 ("diverse illnesses") included contusions, burns, and wounds, as well as "general cancer," while class 20 ("other causes of death") served as the statistician's catch-all: childbirth, old age, suicide, murders, executions, and stillbirths. Class 21 ("unknown causes") stood as an admission that ignorance was possible. The inclusion of these more open-ended categories marked a retreat from the clinical goal of completeness in favor of the more pragmatic approach of the statistician. In

53. *RSVP*, 1821, 1823, 1826, 1829, 1844. The tables in these volumes did not offer mortality rates but merely reproduced the raw data in the form of absolute numbers. Nevertheless, these studies were the most concerted attempt to keep regular accounts of deaths in a large population before the creation of the Statistique Générale de la France.

54. The question of a standardized list for the causes of death received renewed impetus when Adolphe Quetelet organized the first International Congresses of Statistics in Brussels (1853) and Paris (1855). In 1853, the congress passed a motion stating the necessity of forming a "uniform nomenclature for causes of death which will be applicable to all countries." The individual members of the congress pledged to lobby for the adoption of an internationally uniform system of official and medical verification of deaths. A revised death certificate would henceforth become part of the standard equipment of all doctors, and in principle, the collection of these certificates would be centralized and the subject of weekly reports published by each city's municipal office of statistics. Major figures from the statistical and medical communities of Europe attended both conferences, including Farr from London, d'Espine from Geneva, and Villermé and Louis-Adolphe Bertillon of France. The Ministry of Agriculture, Commerce, and Public Works in France undertook its reform of mortality statistics as a result of these international meetings. See *Compte-rendu des travaux du Congrès international de statistique dans ses séances tenues à Bruxelles, 1853, Paris, 1855, Vienne, 1857, et Londres, 1860* (Berlin, 1863), pp. 5, 7. On the international statistical congresses, see Schweber, "Assertion of Disciplinary Claims," pp. 494–523.

their haste to recognize this fact, the compilers of the 1859 list included a row marked "Other" for each of the twenty general categories of cause, even for "other causes of death." This meant that the last row in Class 20 was reserved for the most mysterious category of all: "*Other* other [*sic*] causes of death."[55]

In its general outline, the new system reflected the influence of William Farr, a doctor and expert in vital statistics who had been employed at the English General Register Office since its founding in 1839. Farr's system divided diseases into two general categories: those that were more or less epidemic and those that were sporadic in their effects and distribution. The first category included smallpox, measles, scarlet fever, cholera, typhoid, syphilis, mumps, hydrophobia, and various fevers. The second, much larger, category was organized according to their location in the body, in a manner similar to the list eventually adopted by the French in the 1850s. Farr listed separately the accidental or violent forms of death, including suicide, murder, and industrial accidents, and a final subdivision for old age.[56] His list reflected the bias of the administrator. The distinction between epidemic and sporadic diseases was explicitly made to maximize the attention paid to outbreaks of illness that threatened the public order. The second and largest category, divided according to the seat of the disease in the body, was clearly designed to simplify the terminology used to describe the causes of death.[57]

The two systems for classifying the causes of death thus referred to very different organizing principles. The scrupulous attention to detail exhibited by the early French tables reflected the clinician's desire for an all-embracing view into the workings of pathological essences as they manifested themselves throughout the body. The list served a mimetic function—the goal was to reproduce each and every variation of all the many possible forms of illness, treating them all as if they belonged to separate species of disease. As in the animal kingdom, every species of ailment had its genus, its family of related species, its own niche in the great

55. AdP, VD4 0011, no. 3119, "Commission d'hygiène publique et de salubrité. Prefecture de Police. *Nomenclature des causes de décès.* Tableau jointe à la circulaire du Ministre d'Agriculture du Commerce et des Travaux publics, en date du 7 décembre 1859."

56. For a discussion of William Farr's career and his classification for the causes of death, see John M. Eyler, *Victorian Social Medicine: The Ideas and Methods of William Farr* (Baltimore, 1979), pp. 36–65.

57. Many doctors who published in France, including Marc d'Espine of Geneva, insisted that the list for the causes of death should more accurately reflect the various species of diseases listed in standard nosologies. In a series of articles published in the *Annales d'hygiène publique,* d'Espine quarreled with the distinction between epidemic and sporadic diseases, saying that many diseases occurred occasionally in epidemic form and at other times in more sporadic distributions. As for the division of sporadic diseases according to their seat in the individual body, d'Espine protested

chain of being. The excruciating level of specificity had a purpose as well; the list was meant primarily as a complement to the standard nosologies of disease, guides for doctors who sought to cure individual patients. There was no need for a line marked "other" in such a list; every individual had to die of something.

The French statisticians who came up with the 1859 list, like William Farr before them, had no intention of describing every form and variation of the known causes of death. Their chart was meant for the administrator who was less concerned with doctrinal debates about different species of disease than with their effects on the body's functional mechanisms. Significantly, the prefect's list of 1859 was the first to be presented in the form of a blank statistical table, a grid ready to be filled with numbers. The left-hand column organized the possible causes of death according to their location in the body, with several sections for contagious or virulent diseases such as measles, scarlet fever, and smallpox. The top row broke down the population according to age and sex. The previous lists of 1808, 1821, 1833, and 1848 had no place for numbers—they were clearly intended only as guides to the verbal diagnosis given by the *vérificateur*.

The quest for a uniform nomenclature for the causes of death thus forced a wedge between the purported alliance of medicine and the administration. Doctors who sought to retain their liberty to speak of illness according to the constraints of their own scientific vocabulary found themselves confronted with the administrative bureaucracy's need to restrict the field of language used to describe the possible deaths suffered by the population. The dissonance between the French clinician's earlier nosological system and the statistician's more utilitarian approach mark the boundaries between a clinical vision of disease and a statistical imperative to describe the distribution of possible deaths in the social body. In both cases, the doctor assigned a cause of death in the hopes of finding a way of preventing it from occurring. But for clinicians, the causal nexus that they sought to understand was embedded in an individual body, and the standard of success was absolute: either the patient lived or died. For the statistician, on the other hand, the causal nexus was social, and the standard of success was actuarial. Only the relative proportion of

that certain illnesses, such as tuberculosis, had "a much greater etiological importance than the consideration of the apparatus that they invade." D'Espine went so far as to question the notion of a uniform vocabulary and suggested that statisticians should allow each doctor to follow his own system, observe the results, and classify the causes retroactively. See Marc d'Espine, "Influence de l'aisance et de la misère sur la mortalité," *Annales d'hygiène publique et de médecine légale* 38 (1847): 11; and "Essai statistique," p. 125.

good effects mattered. For clinicians, it was important that the catalog of causes conform exactly to their understanding of the workings of particular diseases, whereas for statisticians, the catalog of death could be incomplete. In fact, it need not reflect any previously conceived order but merely be agreed upon beforehand and followed assiduously by each individual practitioner.

The Académie de médecine ultimately acquiesced to the ministry's wishes and accepted the administration's standardized nomenclature, but the clinicians used the occasion to reaffirm the medical community's independence from the purely utilitarian requirements of the statistical bureaucracy.[58] Their discomfort evidently persisted for some time. Although the academy paid lip service to the minister of agriculture and commerce's proposal, the Second Empire's statisticians never succeeded in establishing a regular account of the causes of death.[59] In 1867, the director of the Statistique Génerale de la France, Alfred Legoyt, complained that although London, Brussels, Vienna, St. Petersburg, and several cities in the United States had already established centralized services to monitor the causes of death, officials in Paris had failed in their attempts to do so. Legoyt blamed French doctors for their lack of cooperation, noting that in other countries statisticians had enlisted the help of family physicians while in France the more perfunctory *médecins vérificateurs* completed the bulletins.[60] Despite these initial difficulties, however, a list similar to that published by the Ministry of Agriculture, Commerce, and Public Works in 1859 eventually became the rule in France. When in 1891 Jacques Bertillon was charged by the International Institute of Statistics with reorganizing the classification of causes of death to reflect advances in medicine, he expressed his general satisfaction with the French adaptation of Farr's system, saying that "the important thing is not that the classification be perfect, but that the morbid unities counted by statistics be the same everywhere."[61] Bertillon asserted that it was unnecessary for mortality tables to conform to a nosological classification of diseases and their species because such classifications changed with advances in med-

58. Jacques-Alphonse Guérard, "Rapport de M. Guérard sur les statistiques, des causes de décès," *Bulletin de l'Académie impériale de médecine* 23 (1857–58): 32.
59. Louis-Adolphe Bertillon, who had attended the International Statistical Congress of 1853 in Brussels, waged a campaign in the French medical press to increase the precision of medical statistics and to eliminate the confusion present in studies of mortality in France. See, for example, "Statistique des causes de décès," *Union médicale*, 4, 6, 8 November 1856; and "Des diverses manières de mesurer la durée de la vie humaine," *Journal de la Société de statistique de Paris* 7 (1866): 45–64.
60. Alfred Legoyt, "De la mortalité à Paris, à Londres, à Vienne et à New York en 1865," *Journal de la Société de statistique de Paris* 8 (1867): 158–59.
61. Jacques Bertillon, *Cours élémentaire de statistique administrative, élaboration des statistiques— organisation des bureaux de statistique—éléments de démographie* (Paris, 1895), p. 262.

icine. Since statisticians could not anticipate such developments, it was preferable to restrict the causes of death to an abridged list of principal maladies organized according to their seat in the body.[62]

In the late eighteenth century, Enlightenment thinkers, armed with a determinist vision of both nature and society, suggested that statistics could be used to discover universal laws of population. An understanding of these laws would allow administrators to predict the annual number of births and deaths, as well as the number of marriages, the number and type of crimes, the quantity of goods that they would produce and consume, and the toll taken by disease. The early social scientists who championed these new techniques for understanding population shared certain mechanistic assumptions about causality, and these assumptions led them to draw several conclusions from the information they began to collect on the population. At the simplest level, they hoped that a better understanding of the causes of social problems would allow the state to find effective legislative or administrative solutions. Initially, this mechanistic notion of causality led French social scientists to adopt a subjective understanding of probability when addressing the mathematical basis of their predictions and measurements. In other words, they believed that statements of probability—such as the anticipated morbidity of a given disease—were not descriptions of objective frequencies that existed in the world but merely statements about what humans did not understand about how particular events occurred. Such a characterization of their methods had the advantage of not contradicting the sensationalist psychology of early empiricists, which held that all scientific knowledge had its basis in the observation of particular events.

By the 1820s, however, population researchers had discovered an unsuspected complexity at the heart of social phenomena, leading them to back away from their initial goal of universal explanations. The postrevolutionary generation of population scientists sought instead to understand the significance of statistical regularity and variation among aggregate groups such as rich and poor, male and female, urban and rural. This interest in aggregate groups would not have been possible without the massive amounts of statistical data collected by government officials in the first decades of the nineteenth century, and as these researchers began to analyze this information, their assumptions about causality and probability began to shift. Fascinated by the patterns they observed among large groups over time, figures such as Adolphe Quetelet

62. Ibid., p. 263.

began to place less emphasis on explanations of mechanistic cause and effect at the level of the particular event. They looked instead for larger, broader causes whose effects were measurable only on the population as a whole, rather than on individual members. Understanding the significance of such causes did not require mechanistic explanations at the level of the individual, nor did they imply that the government could predict with confidence the life chances of any particular citizen. But taken collectively, as members of aggregate groups whose habits, occupation, health, and vulnerability could be analyzed quantitatively, the lives of individual citizens could be shown to be linked in specific ways to the life of the population as a whole and thus to the health of the nation.

This shift toward aggregate analysis nevertheless met with some resistance. In the 1830s, doctors in the Académie de médecine protested against the use of statistics in medicine because of their commitment to a vision of empirical research that emphasized the careful observation of each event. Even those who did most to demonstrate the advantages of quantitative analysis, such as Louis-René Villermé, showed some ambivalence about the implication that aggregate markers of social differentiation might be more important than the behavior of individuals in determining the prosperity and well-being of the population. This anxiety betrayed itself in different ways during the academy debate: in seemingly irrelevant references to political problems ("the tyranny of majority facts"), in a strident defense of established clinical definitions of observation, and in an angry rejection of the most ambitious defender of quantification, Adolphe Quetelet.

Villermé's work on variations in mortality between wealthy and poor neighborhoods in Paris should have led to more nuanced accounts of the effects of socioeconomic status on life chances, but they did not. Not until 1892, over sixty years after the publication of Villermé's pathbreaking work, did anyone in France publish a mortality table that demonstrated the different survival rates of various professions. Instead, studies of mortality at mid-century concentrated on ascertaining with more precision the causes of death. This discussion had the effect of perpetuating the negotiations between clinicians in the medical community and statisticians as the two groups debated the language to be used to describe mortality. At the same time, it allowed population research to focus on aggregates created by the effects of diseases on individual bodies, rather than on aggregates organized according to socioeconomic status or class.

Why did the French wait so long to begin studying in detail the variations in mortality between different professions? Historians of demography Jacques Dupâquier and René Le Mée attributed this failure to an "error" made by Alfred Legoyt, who replaced Moreau de Jonnès as director of the Statistique Générale de la France in 1852. While preparing the procedures for the quinquennial census in 1856, Legoyt insisted that his officials use the household as the basis for the actual count, rather than the nominative lists of individuals that had been used in 1851. When compiling information on the profession of each individual, Legoyt instructed the census agents to "include in each profession not only the head of the family, but also every person directly or indirectly supported by his profession, that is to say, his family, his workers, his various agents, and even his servants." [63] This decision made it impossible to come up with an accurate count of the individuals actually exercising each profession, and without knowledge of this number statisticians could not calculate or compare their various mortality rates. Furthermore, because the original documents created at the communal level were not preserved, it has been impossible for demographic historians to reconstruct these lists.

Legoyt's decision, however, was an "error" only from the perspective of present-day demographic practice. At the time he wrote the circular, he knew exactly what he wanted to know, and it was not a mortality table by profession. Legoyt's circular almost certainly had its origins in the comte de Rambuteau's 1844 volume of the *Recherches statistiques sur la ville de Paris et le département de la Seine*. The authors of this volume at the prefecture produced the first tables listing the number of deaths by profession in the Parisian population, and like Legoyt in 1856, they included dependents as well as heads of households in their lists of the dead. In the introduction to their tables, the authors noted: "At the present moment, we have not been able to determine in a satisfactory manner the natural complement of this work, that is, the knowledge of the number of persons of every age and sex who find their means of existence in the direct or indirect exercise of each of the indicated professions." [64] Legoyt's "error" was an attempt to remedy the perceived shortcomings of the prefecture's earlier work on the Paris population—to establish in an actual census the number of people whose lives were supported by the earnings of every occupation.

Neither the comte de Rambuteau's statisticians at the prefecture of the Seine nor Alfred Legoyt pursued a table of mortality by profession.

63. Circular of 25 June 1856, quoted by Dupâquier and Le Mée, "La Connaissance des faits démographiques," p. 39.
64. *RSVP*, 1844, pp. vii and table 120. Legoyt himself repeated much the same sentiment in his 1848 work, *La France statistique*, where he expressed his wish that the administration follow up on Villermé's and Benoiston de Chateauneuf's research on the influence of profession and social status on mortality. See Legoyt, *La France statistique*, pp. xcii–xciii.

Instead, they chose to see "profession" as an attribute of households rather than individuals, the implication being that the social significance of an individual's professional life was best measured in terms of its effects on that person's family and dependents. But why should this have been the case? Legoyt's decision made sense because of widely shared assumptions in the 1840s and 1850s about the place of the household in the economy and the different roles that men and women played in these household arrangements. Men participated in the economy actively, they believed, while the proper role of women was one of dependency. As we shall see in the next chapter, these assumptions had little to do with the reality of male and female participation in the French economy. They had everything to do, however, with attempts by liberal political economists to talk about collective social aggregates while simultaneously preserving a privileged space for individual agency. In other words, when political economists and statisticians in mid-nineteenth-century France looked for a way to talk about wealth and poverty without surrendering their vision of a society of autonomous individuals, they found their answer in talk about the family.

CHAPTER 4

WORKING WOMEN
AND MARKET INDIVIDUALISM

MARKETS AND FAMILIES

In the 1840s and 1850s, a small, loosely organized group of thinkers and writers in the field of political economy exercised a great deal of influence over population debates in France. They had no official title, but they were unified by a common faith in free trade and Malthusian ideas concerning population growth. Their most significant forerunner was Jean-Baptiste Say, a political economist of an earlier generation who was an enthusiastic promoter of Adam Smith's writings in France. Say had been an early supporter of Napoleon, but he spent the most important part of his career holding the chair of political economy at the Conservatoire des arts et métiers in Paris. Later, perhaps in imitation of the English entrepreneurs he so much admired, Say retired from public life to run a cotton mill at Pas-de-Calais. Say's followers, who included his son Horace Say and the economists Adolphe Blanqui, Frédéric Bastiat, and Joseph Garnier, received public attention first in the 1840s when they defended the principle of laissez-faire against the protectionist policies supported by members of the French business community. After 1851, the free traders and Malthusians became more active and prominent because many of their ideas were compatible with the industrial policy of Napoleon III. Their main bases of institutional support were the Académie des sciences morales et politiques and several intellectual associations, including the Société d'économie politique, the Association pour la liberté des échanges, and the Société de statistique de Paris. They published their works in the *Revue des deux mondes*, the *Journal des débats*, and the *Journal des économistes*, which also published the monthly debates of the Société d'économie politique.[1]

---

1. The best treatment of the political economists and their relationship to Malthus is Charbit, *Du malthusianisme au populationisme*. See especially the overview of his argument, pp. 211–24. See also

As these liberal economists watched the effects of industrialization on patterns of employment, migration, marriage rates, and family structure in France, they attempted to defend the emerging market society by describing its workings as a perfect and naturally self-regulating mechanism. In this endeavor they were opposed by at least three traditions in French economic thought: social Catholicism, "moral" economy, and utopian socialism. The social Catholics, following the work of Alban de Villeneuve-Bargement, had much less faith in the ability of markets to distribute society's resources effectively, and they sought to encourage the development of voluntary charity organizations to deal with the problem of working-class poverty. Villeneuve-Bargement's followers, such as Frédéric Ozanam, the founder of the Société-Saint-Vincent-de-Paul, worked to establish better relations between workers and bourgeois through charitable visits to the homes of the poor, hoping to encourage personal attachments of sympathy and trust in place of the cold bonds linking employer and employee.[2]

The so-called moral economists were not opposed to the development of an industrial society in France, but they believed that a degree of active state intervention was necessary to preserve the family as the foundation of the social order. Led by such political figures as Baron Charles Dupin of the Chamber of Peers, the moral economists believed that economic development and revolutionary conflict had weakened the family and its place in society, and they debated the most effective use of administrative resources to protect working-class families. In 1841, Dupin and several prominent social Catholics successfully pushed the government of the July Monarchy to pass the first important child labor legislation in France, a law regulating the participation and working hours of children in industrial establishments.[3]

The final group opposed to free-market political economists was the

Yves Charbit, "Les Economistes libéraux et la population (1840–1870)," in *Histoire de la population française*, ed. Jacques Dupâquier, vol. 3 (Paris, 1988), pp. 467–81.

2. On social Catholicism, see Jean-Baptiste Duroselle, *Les Débuts du catholicisme social en France, 1822–1870* (Paris, 1951); and especially Lynch, *Family, Class, and Ideology*. Lynch's work is particularly illuminating on the ways in which the moral economists and social Catholics structured official responses to the problems of working-class concubinage, abandoned children, and child labor between 1825 and 1848. My goals in this chapter are somewhat narrower: I focus on the texts of writers who self-consciously wrote in the liberal, laissez-faire tradition of political economy. These authors had less influence over social policy before 1848, as Lynch argued (see p. 228), but their connection to Malthus made them especially important in establishing a mid-century consensus about the significance of the population question.

3. Lynch, *Family, Class, and Ideology*, pp. 168–223. See also Lee Shai Weissbach, *Child Labor Reform in Nineteenth-Century France: Assuring the Future Harvest* (Baton Rouge, 1989).

utopian socialists, whose work is less easily summarized because of their sometimes contradictory commitments. Most utopian socialists combined a fervent religious idealism with a commitment to worker solidarity and active state protection for those made vulnerable by industrial development. This latter tradition included the work of Charles Fourier and Etienne Cabet and was influenced by the earlier writings of Henri de Saint-Simon and Simonde de Sismondi. With the possible exception of Saint-Simon, whose support for a technocratic elite won him favor with many business leaders under Napoleon III, the utopian socialists had few converts among official circles in France.[4]

Like the social Catholics and the moral economists, the laissez-faire political economists assumed that the family was a naturally perfect social institution, but they differed from these groups in their attempts to prove that the family was not threatened by an unrestricted market economy. As a result of their double commitment to both the family and free markets, their arguments moved back and forth between two different registers. First, they sought to describe market society and the place of individuals within it in terms of an abstract economic rationality of supply and demand. When this economic rationality failed to account fully for the society they encountered in their investigations, however, they invoked a moral line of reasoning that placed the family at the center of the social order. Their vision of the family was also an abstraction, but it was one in which there were no individuals without gender and no household without a division of labor based on sex.

These laissez-faire political economists found it difficult to assimilate families into their market model of society without running into contradictions. The market model depended not on families but on allegedly rational (and in principle ungendered) individuals who made decisions about their labor, production, and consumption that would maximize their self-interest. Early investigations into working-class life revealed that stable families did not always emerge from such choices, and they did not always survive once such choices were made. During the early years of industrial development in France, for example, laborers began to move with increasing frequency from the countryside to centers of employment. Both male and female migrant workers often lacked the documentation that could prove their residency in a particular town, and they thus found it difficult to get permission to marry. Many simply formed common law unions as a result. Some of these unions produced children who

4. Jacqueline Hecht, "French Utopian Socialists and the Population Question: 'Seeking the Future City,'" in *Population and Resources in Western Intellectual Traditions*, ed. Michael Teitelbaum and Jay Winter (Cambridge, 1989), pp. 49–73.

were legitimated by a later marriage; others led to the birth of infants who were never officially recognized by their fathers. Single women with children, often recently arrived from the countryside, faced a depressing set of options. They could try to survive on the low wages paid to women workers while consigning their infants to wet-nurses. If this failed, they could put themselves at the mercy of local bureaux de charité or resort to prostitution to survive. Political economists could not accept such situations as the inevitable result of structural transformations in the economy, nor could they conceive of a way to interpret such behavior as the result of rational choices made under difficult circumstances, so they looked elsewhere for explanations. As they did so, however, they left their purely economic reasoning behind them and resorted to arguments based on less utilitarian and more qualitative considerations of the place of the family in the social order.

Caught between an economic rationality based on individual choice and a moralistic political rationality that sought to preserve a privileged place for the family in the name of social harmony, these writers struggled to find a way of writing about the economy that avoided overt contradiction. They did so by emphasizing that the allegedly ungendered abstract individual of liberal economic theory had a sex. The rational individual became the rational man, the head of the household, the protector of the wife, the provider for the children, the laborer, the producer, the entrepreneur, the citizen. By reducing the interest of families to the interest of the father, these liberal political economists avoided the conflicts created by an economic rationality that seemed to offer at least the possibility of wealth and personal fulfillment to both men and women. In France this gendering of the economic and political individual found expression in Napoleon's Civil Code of 1804, which recognized society as an association of individuals and granted the freedom of contracts in the economic realm, while simultaneously giving absolute authority in the family to the husband and father. The code denied women any political voice, restricted their ability to own property in their own name, made divorce (legalized during the Revolution) more difficult for women to obtain, and gave them inferior rights in cases of adultery.

The Civil Code's exclusion of women from active participation in the political and economic life of the nation found its theoretical counterpart in the writings of those political economists who were so influential on the generation of the 1840s and 1850s. From Thomas Malthus, French laissez-faire economists adopted the "principle of population," which saw economic inequalities and poverty as the result of population's tendency to increase beyond its capacity to support itself. Malthus found the solution to overpopulation in the voluntary limitation of family size, which he euphemistically termed "moral restraint." Despite the obvious fact that family limitation was possible in a wide variety of domestic relationships, Malthus went to great lengths to demonstrate that his idea of "moral restraint" did not contradict conventional morality regarding the family. The best way to prevent unwanted population growth, he argued, was to delay marriages until every man could responsibly support his wife and children; he thus linked sexual restraint and male authority in the family to the health of the population as a whole. From Jean-Baptiste Say, the mid-century liberal political economists adopted the "iron law of wages," which attributed the relatively low wages earned by women to their dependent condition in the family. Say argued that since most women were supported by the earnings of a husband, father, or son and very few women lived completely from their own wages, there were always women who were willing to work for less, simply to augment the income of their household.

Neither Say nor Malthus overtly addressed the contradictions between their defense of market individualism and their insistence that men and women had different roles both in the family and in the labor force. For Malthus to admit that his defense of the family was simply cobbled on to his population principle would be to admit that his economic theory was potentially amoral and irrelevant to deeply held convictions about the place of the family in the social order. Likewise, Say never addressed the broader implication of his account of women's low wages, the fact that a dual labor market had developed in France with one set of rules for female laborers and another for male. In the strict logic of economic individualism, the existence of a dual labor market could only mean that assumptions about women and familial relationships were obstructing the workings of the market mechanism and preventing the price of women's labor from reaching its true value. Unwilling or perhaps unable to contemplate challenging widely shared assumptions about male and female roles in the family, however, Say contented himself with an explanation that took both families and markets for granted, as if a contradiction between their respective functions was unimaginable.

By the early 1850s this logic had been incorporated into the statistical tables that purported to represent the functioning of the economy. The heirs of Malthus and Say were so successful at suppressing the contradiction between abstract market individualism and the gendered division of labor in the family and the workplace that their statistics confirmed it in their very structure. This can be seen most clearly in the statistics for women's labor. The statistician's and the economist's unwillingness to treat female laborers as equal participants in the market economy revealed both their conception of the economic individual and their commitment to a familial vision of society based on a division of labor within the household.

In the 1820s, women's labor commanded little attention and was certainly not posed by official statisticians as a problem that needed to be solved. By 1848, in contrast, the form and structure of labor statistics were motivated and determined by a clear impulse to define women's labor as an anomalous and undesirable part of the emerging economic order. Why should this change have occurred? This chapter argues that the intensification of interest in gender, the family, and women's labor during this period was driven by the political economists' concern with the implications of work on statistical aggregates. To avoid concluding that aggregate groups such as "workers" or "poor" were adversely affected by the market economy they sought to defend, liberal political economists reached for explanations for poverty and exploitation that could be resolved in individualist terms. They found such explanations in the sexual division of labor: the poverty of male wage earners could be explained by the inability of working men to limit the size of their families, and the poverty of women could be explained by their inability to conform to the dependent position allotted to them in a market economy. In other words, as the century progressed, the unwillingness of liberal political economists to recognize the force and power of class relationships led them to focus on gender.

MALTHUSIAN FAMILY VALUES

Malthus published his influential *Essay on the Principle of Population* in Britain in 1798. Following the outbreak of a great public debate, he published a much expanded form of the *Essay* in 1803.[5] The first French edition appeared in 1809, translated by Pierre Prévost, a philosophy professor from Geneva who also translated the works of Adam Smith and

5. In this chapter I will be referring to both the 1798 and the 1803 editions of the *Essay*. For the 1798 version I have relied on the Norton edition: *An Essay on the Principle of Population* (New York, 1976), henceforth Malthus, *Essay*, 1976. For the 1803 edition, I have used the most recent (and slightly abridged) Cambridge edition: *An Essay on the Principle of Population* (Cambridge, 1992), henceforth Malthus, *Essay*, 1992. On the debate itself, see Kenneth Smith, *The Malthusian Controversy* (New York, 1978); William Petersen, *Malthus* (Cambridge, Mass., 1979), esp. pp. 58–81; and Donald Winch, *Riches and Poverty: An Intellectual History of Political Economy in Britain, 1750–1834* (Cambridge, 1996). For biographical information on Malthus, see Patricia James, *Population Malthus: His Life and Times* (London, 1979).

Dugald Stewart.[6] In France, as in Britain, the work earned immediate notoriety for its forceful argument about the effects of uncontrolled population growth and the causes of poverty among the working classes. When Malthus subsequently published his *Principles of Political Economy* in 1820, his reputation was high enough to merit an immediate response from Jean-Baptiste Say, who became Malthus's principal interlocutor in France during the 1820s. But it was not until the period of the July Monarchy that Malthus's influence reached its apex, and between 1840 and 1860 his work became the essential reference for any social observer commenting on the troubling relationship between economic development, population growth, and poverty.[7]

Malthus sought to examine the means by which the equilibrium between subsistence and population was maintained, beginning with two postulates: "First, that food is necessary to the existence of man. Secondly, that the passion between the sexes is necessary and will remain nearly in its present state."[8] From the very beginning, therefore, Malthus explicitly linked the sexual behavior of gendered individuals to the fate of the larger community, and in doing so, he attributed a fatal dynamic to all societies, with only two possible outcomes: survival or extinction.

Arguing on the basis of these two assumptions, Malthus concluded that the balance between number and subsistence could be maintained in one of two ways: either by an increase in hunger, illness, and early death or by a delay in the age of reproduction. For the bulk of living creatures on the planet, only the former limits to growth had any effect. Plant and animal populations, he noted, flourished wherever resources were abundant; when resources were lacking, they died. Human beings, in contrast, could react to shortages by adapting their customs and marital practices to their material circumstances before the limits to growth were reached.[9] Malthus euphemistically called such adaptation "moral restraint," a voluntary abstention from sexual relations until the couple could guarantee support for their offspring. To awaken this capacity for adaptation, however, humans needed either to see the results of improvident behavior in others or to suffer its consequences themselves. In other words, Malthus

6. Thomas Malthus, *Essai sur le principe de population ou Exposé des effets passés et présents de l'action de cette cause sur le bonheur du genre humain; suivi de quelques recherches relative à l'espérance de guérir ou d'adoucir les maux qu'elle entraine* (Geneva, 1809). Prévost had been a student of theology, law, and medicine in Paris, where he met Rousseau. After further studies of philology and chemistry in Berlin, he became professor of philosophy and physics in Geneva in 1784. See James, *Population Malthus*, p. 362–63.

7. Charbit, "Les Economistes libéraux et la population," p. 468.

8. Malthus, *Essay*, 1976, p. 19.

9. Ibid., pp. 23–24.

believed that human reason originated in a competitive struggle arising from scarcity, and its first lesson was the control of desire. All subsequent developments in civilization had their origins in this primal inequality, which acted as a constant incentive to labor, a check to the passions, and a spur to self-awareness and self-sufficiency among individuals.

Malthus's skepticism about equality, therefore, was based on his most fundamental assumptions about the origins of society, and he devoted a considerable part of the early chapters of the *Essay* to arguing against those liberals who championed egalitarian positions. "In a state of equality," Malthus wrote, predicting one's future resources and one's ability to provide for a family "would be the simple question." [10] In such a world, by definition, if one child could be fed, so could they all. In his 1803 edition of the *Essay*, however, he amended the sentence to read: "In a state of equality, *if such can exist*, this would be the simple question [emphasis added]." [11] In fact, according to Malthus's argument, such an egalitarian society could not exist, for it would not be recognizably human. Its members could not be constituted as self-aware individuals because such awareness was predicated on visible differences in wealth, rank, and status. Reason could not be born under such circumstances. In an egalitarian society, the relative prosperity or poverty of the individual household would be indistinguishable from the resources available to the society as a whole. The very distinction between public and private property, so important to the liberal tradition that Malthus was very consciously a part of, could have no meaning under such egalitarian conditions.

At this point in his argument, Malthus played on a culturally specific set of assumptions about gender to further support his contention that inequality was a natural and necessary part of the social order. Before having children, Malthus thought, the father (not the mother or the parents acting together) must stop and ask himself: "Will he not lower his rank in life? Will he not subject himself to greater difficulties than he at present feels? Will he not be obliged to labor harder? And if he has a large family, will his utmost exertions enable him to support them? May he not see his offspring in rags and misery, and clamoring for bread that he cannot give them? And may he not be reduced to the grating necessity of forfeiting his independence and of being obliged to the sparing hand of charity for support?" [12] Malthus's language made clear that the recipient of nature's moral lesson about scarcity and the control of desire could only be male, and this internal monologue of the would-be father linked the

10. Ibid., p. 27.
11. Ibid., p. 22.
12. Ibid., p. 24.

patriarchal order of families with the spirit of utility and calculation demanded by the principle of population. The forethought that distinguished humans from animals was possible only in a society of families where men bore primary responsibility for the care and provision of their dependent women and children.

The intrusion of gender into his reasoning at this point makes clear that Malthus was not merely attempting to describe the effects of population pressure on food supply. On the contrary, as his later discussion demonstrated, he wished to use the principle of population to explain a wide range of social phenomena. These included not only property relations and oscillations in the price of labor but also the organization of families and the establishment of different social roles for men and women. Only this ambition can explain Malthus's inclusion of seemingly irrelevant material in the *Essay* of which his long digressions on the family and the domestic ideal and his confusing defense of the double standard regarding women's adultery are only the most notable examples. These sections have little to do with his argument concerning the connection between population growth and inadequate levels of subsistence, but they all demonstrate the sincerity of his commitment to late eighteenth-century standards of heterosexual monogamy within marriage. That Malthus used his account of the awakening of human reason to make assertions about active male subjectivity and implied female passivity further reinforced this commitment: his work was not only about the origins and necessity of inequalities of wealth, it was also about the social obligations attendant on one's sex.

Why would Malthus devote so much time to defending his commitment to conventional standards of family morality if they had little to do with his argument concerning the threat of overpopulation?[13] He did so precisely because his argument about moral restraint came uncomfortably close to admitting that conventional marriage practices were not

13. One might answer this question by pointing out that English marriage rates were at an all-time high when Malthus was writing the *Essay*, and the average age at marriage had fallen considerably in the preceding generations. It would not have been unreasonable for Malthus to assume in 1798 that this would lead to population growth and increased poverty because he could not have foreseen the increases in wages and standards of living that occurred in the coming decades. His call for prudential restraint may have simply expressed a desire to return to the more cautious marital practices of earlier generations. I suggest, however, that this argument cannot account for the particular tone of Malthus's anxiety in the *Essay*. Malthus is clearly concerned about the catastrophic effects of population growth; he also seems deeply disturbed by the implication of his own argument, that a prudent heterosexual monogamy is only one among many possible domestic arrangements that could lead to smaller numbers of offspring. The evidence for this anxiety is the length of his digressions on the family, the role of men and women, and the double standard for adultery, none of which are central to his argument about population. Of course, these digressions did not save him from being accused of "immorality" after his book was published, and he found

enough to guarantee a healthy society. A domestic ideal founded on heterosexual monogamy whereby the male wage earner guaranteed material support to his family was only one among many possible social arrangements that would permit a voluntary limitation of family size. In other words, Malthus's argument about economic rationality did not require any specific conclusions about the role of men and women in the family. That he felt obligated to state loudly and clearly his commitment to conventional moral beliefs only demonstrated his own sense of vulnerability to charges of immorality.

JEAN-BAPTISTE SAY AND THE "DEPENDENT CONDITION"

Jean-Baptiste Say's writings also placed the family at the center of his theory of political economy, and like Malthus, Say's vision of the family was determined above all by the interests and activities of the male provider. Like Malthus, Say refused to see that the gendered language he used to talk about the place of women and men in the family contradicted the neutral language he used to talk about the abstract individuals who made rational decisions in the marketplace. "In political economy," he wrote, "one can consider families as individuals, since they have tastes, resources and interests in common."[14] So long as Say limited himself to a discussion of male breadwinners, this position did not lead him into contradiction, since the individual interest that contained the family's interest was none other than the male breadwinner himself.

As soon as Say addressed the undeniable fact that women also worked in large numbers, however, he admitted that there was more than one kind of individual participating in the French economy. The question of women's labor forced Say to recognize that society's expectations with regard to familial relations played an important role in the workings of the labor market, specifically in setting the low price paid for women's work. Political economists had long assumed that wages for working men could never go below the subsistence level for long, though they might hover at or near this level for unskilled work. Women workers, however, often earned significantly less than a subsistence wage. Economists were troubled by this category of workers because of the difficulty of accounting for their situation in purely market terms.

---

it difficult to convince people that he was not indifferent to the traditional marital practices of his time and place. On marriage rates in Britain at the time of Malthus's *Essay*, see E. A. Wrigley, R. S. Davies, J. E. Oeppen, and R. S. Schofield, *English Population History from Family Reconstitution, 1580–1837* (Cambridge, 1997), pp. 121–39.

14. Jean-Baptiste Say, *Traité d'économie politique* (1841; rpt. Osnabrück, 1966), p. 317.

Say explained women's low wages with an argument that was often repeated in the nineteenth century: women were paid less than men because many of them did not need to survive completely on their own earnings.[15] Women who were partially supported by the wages of men in their families were willing to work for very meager sums to augment the income of their families. Competition among these women for work kept the price of female labor at levels far below subsistence. Several assumptions lay behind this argument. First, it assumed that women competed in the labor market only against other women, for it was this competition that kept wages down. Once lower wages for women were established, of course, they gained a competitive advantage against men in the labor market. Fear of this competition with women caused many male laborers and some economists to call for a family wage, whereby men would earn enough to dissuade the women in their family from working.

Such arguments conformed nicely to Say's second assumption, that a woman's essential social identity arose not from her occupation, as was normally the case for men, but from her place in the family and her relationship to a male worker. In Say's revealing words:

It is not hard to find a seamstress in certain villages who earns less than half of what she spends, though she spends very little; she is a mother, or daughter, sister, aunt or mother-in-law of a worker who would feed her even if she earned nothing at all. If she only had her work to live on, it is obvious that she would have to double the price or die of hunger; in other words, the work would be paid double or it would not take place.[16]

Say's account of women's labor undermined his assertion that families could be considered simply as individuals because it forced him to admit that social preconceptions about gender differences created two distinct kinds of individuals in families, each with a different relation to the market economy. In fact, Say's account revealed how expectations of familial support actually disrupted the delicate mechanism of supply and demand. According to his logic, these expectations distorted the price of women's labor on the open market as well as the value that women themselves attributed to their own earnings relative to the costs or benefits of not working.

Of course, Say could not openly admit that the family "disrupted" or "distorted" the functioning of the labor market without revealing the ex-

15. See Joan Scott's discussion of the justification for lower wages paid to women in "A Statistical Representation of Work: 'Le Statistique de l'industrie à Paris, 1847–1848,'" in Scott, *Gender and the Politics of History* (New York, 1988), p. 129.
16. Say, *Traité*, p. 374.

Table 4.1.   Parisians receiving assistance in the home from the Bureaux de charité in Paris, 1818–25

	Men	Women	Children	Total	% Women	% Women + children	% Men	Ratio of women to men
1818	20,565	31,923	33,927	86,415	36.94	76.20	23.80	1.55
1819	20,427	32,012	32,711	85,150	37.59	76.01	23.99	1.57
1820	20,495	32,615	33,760	86,870	37.54	76.41	23.59	1.59
1821	18,299	31,463	27,430	78,192	40.76	76.29	23.71	1.72
1822	13,834	25,127	15,410	54,371	46.21	74.56	25.44	1.82
1823	15,012	27,107	18,019	60,138	45.07	75.04	24.96	1.81
1824	15,038	27,051	18,454	60,543	44.68	75.16	24.84	1.80
1825	15,949	28,683	20,661	65,293	43.93	75.57	24.43	1.80

Source: RSVP, 1821, table 41; RSVP, 1823, table 58; RSVP, 1826, table 75; RSVP, 1829, table 91.

tent of the tension between his commitment to the family as the basis of all social organization and his faith in the benefits of the market economy. At the same time, however, he could not ignore the question of sexual difference and the labor market because the information generated by new statistical research showed that women and men were affected very differently by the market economy that both Malthus and Say defended.

The very same statistical studies of the Parisian population that Villermé used to determine the differential mortality of rich and poor also clearly showed that women were more likely to be poor in Paris than men. During the years 1818–25—a period of relative economic stabilization between the postwar boom of 1815 and the onset of a recession in 1826–29—the Recherches statistiques sur la ville de Paris showed that the proportion of women among the indigent receiving assistance in Paris was increasing. In 1818, when records showed 86,415 people receiving assistance, the ratio of adult women to adult men was three to two. Seven years later, despite overall declines in the total assisted, the ratio of women to men was closer to two to one. In other words, the figures in the Recherches suggested that by 1825, women in Paris were nearly twice as likely to find themselves without resources as men. Such differences certainly lent weight to the assumption that poor women and poor men were statistically distinct populations, and one might have expected these figures to lead to more studies of the different places occupied by women and men in the Parisian economy[17] (see Table 4.1). According to the strict logic of laissez-faire economics, this information could have been interpreted as evidence of a disruption of the market mechanism: women were becom-

17. RSVP, 1821, table 41; RSVP, 1823, table 58; RSVP, 1826, table 75; RSVP, 1829, table 91.

ing poorer because of low wages, restrictions on their property rights, and limits to the occupations they were permitted to exercise. Women's labor was never seen from the standpoint of such a logic, however, but was always seen through the filter of familial relations.

When political economists discussed the poverty of male workers, they inevitably claimed that prosperity depended on a free market for labor. The most famous example, cited often by the French political economists, was Malthus's criticism of the English poor laws, which guaranteed a level of assistance to the poor. These laws, said Malthus, bound indigent workers to their parish, prevented them from seeking employment elsewhere, and encouraged the creation of families that could not survive without public assistance. Thus the poor laws were an unwelcome intervention in the workings of the labor market, which depended on perfect mobility of workers. The mobility of *female* labor was unimaginable to political economists, however, for they remained committed, as did Malthus, to a notion of the male breadwinner whose social and political identity resided in his ability to care for his dependent wife and children.

Say could not overtly recognize such a contradiction —indeed, he would never have thought of it as a contradiction because it never would have occurred to him to think of a woman's place in the economy as equivalent to a man's. He did, however, offer a revised interpretation of the proper place of women in the economy, one that effectively papered over the dissonances between his views on the family and his views on the market. He had already presented women's labor outside of the home as problematic and anomalous because of its deleterious effect on the wages of both men and other women. Now, he also sought to redefine the work that women did in the home, in caring for the household, raising the children, and providing food for the family. Both Adam Smith and Malthus had discussed this kind of work, and Smith had used such a discussion to distinguish between "productive" and "unproductive" labor. Malthus had rendered this distinction in terms of "productive labor" and "personal services." Say went over some of the same ground but instead of classifying domestic labor in the home as "unproductive labor" or "personal services," he attempted to show that women's work was properly conceived not as labor at all but as a form of consumption.[18]

Say connected women to consumption almost immediately once he broached the subject, in the course of distinguishing between *dépenser* (to spend) and *consommer* (to consume). The distinction turned on the point

18. For Malthus's ideas concerning productive and unproductive labor and his discussion of Adam Smith's views of the same subject, see Thomas Malthus, *Principles of Political Economy* (London, 1836), pp. 35–45.

at which the value of the object was diminished, which occurred not at the point of purchase but only when the object was consumed. Say's example? A housewife. In an apparent non sequitur, Say used the occasion to make an unconnected point about the power of women to determine the purchases a family makes and the products it consumes. "A bad housewife [*ménagère*] quickly destroys limited fortunes. It is the wife, and not the husband, who ordinarily makes the decisions about everyday consumption, those which are so often repeated under a multitude of forms."[19] This gendering of consumption was reinforced in subsequent chapters of the *Treatise*, when Say distinguished between "productive" and "unproductive" consumption.

Using the masculine form of the relevant nouns, Say defined "productive consumption" in terms of (male) commercial activities: "A merchant, a manufacturer, a cultivator, buys raw materials, or productive services, and consumes them in order to produce new products."[20] Say defined "unproductive or sterile consumption" as "consumption whose goal is the satisfaction of a need."[21] Say's gendering of these activities was subtle, but his choice of examples makes the significance clear enough: "By unproductive consumption, man satisfies his most noble desires as well as his most vulgar tastes. He extends his knowledge, his intellectual faculties, he raises his children, sweetens the existence of his family, renders himself useful to his friends, his fatherland, and humanity."[22] In translation, the language retains only its overtly masculine coloring, but the French original contains a much more suggestive set of gendered constructions. "*Par elles* [feminine plural pronoun for "*consommations improductives*"], *il étend ses connaissances, ses facultés intellectuelles; il élève ses enfants, adoucit l'existence de sa famille, se rend utile à ses amis, à sa patrie, à l'humanité.*" It is not necessary to exaggerate the unconscious effects of grammatical gender to see something else at work here. Who else would raise his children, sweeten his family life, entertain his friends, or bear children for the fatherland? Wife and mother.[23]

Both Malthus and Say glossed over the apparent contradiction between families and economic individualism by a series of arguments that proclaimed their allegiance to separate roles for men and women, both in

19. Say, *Traité*, p. 442.
20. Ibid., p. 443.
21. Ibid., p. 446.
22. Ibid.
23. The close linkage of women with consumption in a market society has been the subject of much historical research. See, for example, the essays in Victoria de Grazia with Ellen Furlough, eds., *The Sex of Things: Gender and Consumption in Historical Perspective* (Berkeley, 1996). This work contains a large and useful subject bibliography on gender and consumption.

the family and in the workplace. During the 1830s and 1840s in France similar arguments were repeated by liberal political economists as part of their efforts to defend the emerging market economy against challenges from both the left and the right. In these debates, Malthus's and Say's arguments proved to be useful touchstones because they seemed to show that an optimistic program of economic growth could be compatible with a stable society organized around the family.

THE OPTIMISM OF THE FRENCH MALTHUSIANS

Malthus's "principle of population" found its widest and most responsive audience in France during the July Monarchy. Say's influence, however, endured throughout the century, supported by the further work of his son Horace Say and his grandson Léon Say, both of whom became prominent political economists in their own right. These men, along with Adolphe Blanqui, Charles Dunnoyer, Joseph Droz, Joseph Garnier, Frédéric Bastiat, and other liberal members of the Société d'économie politique and the Académie des sciences morales et politiques used their influence and public stature to educate the reading public and political elites about the economy.

In these years, the concentration of workers in France's newly emerging industrial centers began to expand markedly, although never as rapidly as in Britain. As these populations grew, so too did the problems associated with them: increased burdens on local offices of public assistance, lack of clean water, poor housing, and dangerous outbreaks of contagious disease. The cholera epidemics of 1832 and 1849, each coming on the heels of revolutionary unrest in 1830 and 1848, were only extreme examples of what social investigators perceived to be an ongoing crisis. Malthus's arguments about the limits to growth seemed particularly relevant to economists and officials who had become well-versed in the destabilizing effects of urban expansion, industrial development, high mortality, high fertility, and high illegitimacy rates among the poor.

Malthus's doctrines appealed to these political economists at least in part because they provided useful arguments against some of their main ideological opponents, above all the growing body of socialist critics who sought more radical solutions to the problems caused by industrialization and economic development. When figures such as the early communist leader Etienne Cabet claimed that all citizens possessed a natural "right to work," Malthusian economists could fall back on the harsh lesson of the population principle. According to the standard argument, poverty and unemployment were the fault of the poor themselves for not exercising a prudent restraint on the size of their families.[24] In addition, the liberal economists could use Malthus's analysis of the English poor laws to counter the charitable reforms of social Catholics such as Pierre Leroux, Villeneuve de Bargement, and the members of the Société-Saint-Vincent-de-Paul, all of whom proposed paternalist and philanthropic solutions to poverty among the working classes. Liberal political economists in France may have found Malthus less helpful in their struggle with protectionists who sought tariffs and import restrictions to protect national markets from foreign competition, but here too Malthus offered arguments that may have helped their cause.[25]

Adolphe Blanqui, Jean-Baptiste Say's successor in the chair of economics at the Conservatoire des arts et métiers, wrote in his *Histoire de l'économie politique en Europe depuis les anciens jusqu'à nos jours* (1837) that Malthus's most important contribution to human understanding was his analysis of social and economic inequality. After Adam Smith had published his *Wealth of Nations*, wrote Blanqui, one primary question remained to be answered: "Why are riches so unequally distributed throughout the social body? Why are there always unfortunate ones?"[26] According to Blanqui, Malthus's population principle provided a convincing answer to this question by demonstrating that inequality was an inevitable and even necessary part of the natural order. In Malthus's work, inequalities of wealth served as examples and incentive to self-improvement among the less well-off and were thus a precondition for economic development.

Blanqui went on, however, to criticize the English author for presenting his doctrine in such inflexible and fatalistic terms. As an alternative, Blanqui supported a more moderate version of Malthus's relationship between subsistence and population, suggesting that as a population approached the limits of its food supply, a free market would create new incentives to production and open up new areas for economic growth. Blanqui's more moderate version of Malthus's population principle was

24. On French socialists and Malthus, see Hecht, "French Utopian Socialists," pp. 49–73.
25. Malthus's 1803 edition of the *Essay* criticized the English Corn Laws for producing unnaturally high prices at the expense of domestic consumers, but by 1815 he had come out in favor of a measure of protection for English agriculture. See Malthus, *Essay*, 1992, bk. III, chaps. xi and xii, pp. 151–80. On Malthus's Corn Law pamphlets, see Petersen, *Malthus*, pp. 169–172, and James, *Population Malthus*, pp. 259–69.
26. Adolphe Blanqui, *Histoire de l'économie politique en Europe depuis les anciens jusqu'à nos jours* (Paris, 1837), p. 150. Malthus's explanation for the origins of inequality appealed to a wide variety of social commentators in France before 1848, including the early proponent of social medicine C. G. Prunelle and the moral economist Baron Charles Dupin. See Prunelle, *De l'action de la médecine*, p. 3; and Charles Dupin, *Bien-être et concorde des classes du peuple français* (Paris, 1840), p. 9.

widely shared by economists and officials during the July Monarchy. When the Statistique Générale de la France published its first volumes of national population statistics in 1837, Martin du Nord, the minister of public works, agriculture, and commerce noted that the population continued to increase although the number of births had diminished since the Revolution. Taking this as a sign that the French population had kept its rate of expansion well within the limits of subsistence, he concluded, "This increase in population by diminished mortality is a certain sign of the progress that France has made since 1789. It is the fruit of civilization and peace."[27] Alfred Legoyt, who became the director of the Statistique Générale in 1852, went even further, asserting that Malthusian imbalances between population and subsistence were ultimately short in duration and limited to particular areas. These momentary disturbances, he argued, though possibly severe in their immediate effects, would ultimately disappear as the economy adjusted to changes in the demand for labor and goods. "No doubt, [increases in population] unceasingly tend to surpass the limits of subsistence," he wrote, "but only that subsistence which is immediately available. Soon, new products are created by the stimulus of need, re-establishing the equilibrium."[28]

A key element in the development of a more moderate Malthusian position in France was the discussion of "well-being" or *bien-être*, a subject that received much attention in the years leading up to the revolution of 1848.[29] On the surface, the discussion of well-being and standard of living was an attempt to counter socialist demands for shorter hours, higher pay, and improved working conditions with the now familiar argument that a rising tide raises all ships. In response to continued labor unrest during the July Monarchy, liberal political economists argued that the best cure for poverty and related social ills would come from the increase in general prosperity that would accompany economic development, the spread of innovative technologies, and the opening up of new markets. Baron Charles Dupin, a moral economist who was less committed to unrestricted market freedom, was nevertheless in agreement with this faith in the benefits of economic development. In his *Bien-être et concorde des*

27. *Statistique de la France. Territoire, population* (Paris, 1837), pp. x–xi.
28. Legoyt, *La France statistique*, p. civ. Malthus would have disagreed with this more optimistic assessment of his work.
29. Among the many works of political economy that treated this question under the influence of Malthus, see Dupin, *Bien-être et concorde des classes*; Jean-Baptiste Say, *Cours complet d'économie politique pratique* (Paris, 1840); Villermé, *Tableau*; Legoyt, *La France statistique*; Joseph Droz, *Economie politique, ou Principes de la science des richesses* (Paris, 1846); Hippolyte Passy, *Des causes de l'inégalité des richesses* (Paris, 1848); Victor Cousin, *Justice et charité* (Paris, 1848); Joseph Garnier, *Du principe de population* (Paris, 1857).

classes du peuple français (1840), Dupin argued that poverty was simply a stage in the development of human society, one that was rapidly retreating into the past. The "half-naked *lazzaronis*" of Italy, the Spanish poor "whose proud indolence cannot hide the poverty revealed in their tattered clothing," and the Irish "dressed in rags sent from England by the boatload," he wrote, were rapidly becoming a part of Europe's past. In France, he concluded, "this social condition no longer belongs to our age."[30] Dupin argued that the most deserving members of the French laboring classes had progressed beyond this stage of "apathy and degradation" by virtue of their thrift and hard work, and by exercising a prudent control over the size of their families. In other words, they had approached the wealth and standard of living of the bourgeoisie by acting more like the bourgeoisie.

When French writers imported Malthus's treatment of inequality into their own work, they emphasized the extent to which social distinctions had their origins in natural differences of ability and persistence in the face of scarcity. Furthermore, like Malthus, they posed the question in terms of individuals and families. This allowed them to avoid considering the inequalities that emerged from the analysis of social aggregates, such as those discovered by Villermé in his analysis of differential mortality in the various neighborhoods of Paris. An early example of such Malthusian logic appeared in C. G. Prunelle's work of public hygiene, in which he lent legitimacy to the social hierarchies that separated the propertied from the poor. "As soon as the desire for reproduction created the family," wrote Prunelle, "it encountered needs which it could only satisfy by the products of labor . . . which each individual executed with a zeal proportional to their desires, their capacity, and consequently, with unequal success: some obtained a surplus, and others lacked necessities. Society, which at first consisted of strong and weak men, divided itself soon into rich and poor and this new inequality increased in proportion to the population and the multiplication of desires."[31]

Malthusian assumptions also lay behind the often-quoted investigations into the moral habits of workers during the July Monarchy. Villermé famously observed that workers in industry exhibited a "lack of sobriety, economy, thrift [*prévoyance*], and morals" and that "very often their misery is their own fault."[32] This situation, he claimed, "results primarily from the habitual gathering of workers in large workshops, which are nothing but great harems, where sexes and ages find themselves mixed

30. Dupin, *Bien-être et concorde des classes*, p. 18.
31. Prunelle, *De l'action de la médecine*, pp. 3–4.
32. Villermé, *Tableau*, 2:351.

together . . . above all in large cities, where manufactures multiply and create large agglomerations of population."[33] Villermé's warning was much more than an expression of moral outrage; his alarm at the situation in factories was the direct result of his Malthusian assumptions about uncontrolled sexuality and population increase. The solution to this problem was to remove women from the workforce, and during the 1840s the social investigators followed Villermé's lead in drawing attention to the large number of women who worked outside the home. H. A. Frégier, a prominent police official in Paris, complained of women workers that "the depravity in this part of the population, though more hidden, is no less real, and its broad scope escapes statistical appreciation."[34]

Adopting Malthusian arguments in this fashion allowed French political economists during the 1830s and 1840s to hold potentially contradictory positions. On the one hand, they argued along with Malthus that inequalities of wealth had their origins in natural distinctions of ability. They rejected the arguments of influential anti-Malthusians such as Simonde de Sismondi, who argued that poverty was systemic and determined by fluctuations in the labor market that workers could not control.[35] At the same time, however, liberal political economists argued that the poor could eliminate their poverty through family limitation and sexual restraint.[36] Placing the discussion of poverty in these terms had the clear advantage of allowing liberal political economists to broach the disturbing question of social hierarchies without conceding that a market economy could itself produce class divisions and leaving the solution to the problem of poverty to the poor themselves.

After the violence of the 1848 revolution, it became increasingly difficult for these political economists to claim that improvements in "well-being" for workers were a self-evident proposition, let alone a solution to Malthusian warnings of overpopulation. Nevertheless, many economists continued to echo the moral lessons arising from Malthus's views on the family, even when they began to depart from his analysis of the popula-

33. Ibid.
34. Frégier, *Des classes dangereuses*, p. 33.
35. J.-C. L. Simonde de Sismondi, *Nouveaux principes d'économie politique ou de la richesse dans ses rapports avec la population* 2 vols. (Paris, 1819), 2:252–53, 259–60. For other examples of French liberals who argued that inequality was based on natural differences of ability, see Dupin, *Bien-être et concorde des classes*, p. 9; Blanqui, *Histoire de l'économie politique*, p. 150.
36. See, for example, M.-T. Duchâtel's comments, written in 1829, before he served as minister of the interior under the July Monarchy: "The laboring classes hold the key to their circumstances in their own hands. Their standard of living [*aisance*] depends on their wages, their wages are determined by the ratio of capital to the number of workers. It is not possible for the laboring classes to increase the amount of capital according to their needs, but they can, by acting prudently in their marriages, limit the population" (*De la charité dans ses rapports avec l'état moral et le bien-être des classes inférieures de la société* [Paris, 1829], p. 112).

tion principle. Joseph Garnier, a tireless publicist for Malthus in France, noted that improvements in well-being acted to slow population growth by "strengthening morality, forethought, and the dignity of the family father, rendering him more able to exercise his reason, and more capable of prudence in his marriage." [37] Of course, this was precisely the opposite of what Malthus had originally argued in the *Essay*, when he claimed that it was scarcity, not improvements in well-being, that incited the development of a masculine rationality and a prudent heterosexual monogamy. Garnier seemed unaware of the extent to which his economic argument contradicted Malthus at this point, so convinced was he that he agreed with the English economist on what was most important—the necessity of paternal authority and moral restraint within the family. By this time, Malthus's and Say's assumptions about the place of the family in the liberal economic order had become so automatic as to make them virtually inseparable from one another. Nowhere is this more clear than in the *Statistique de l'industrie* of 1848.

THE *Statistique de l'industrie* OF 1848

In 1851, the Paris Chamber of Commerce published a large statistical study of industry and labor in the capital, the *Statistique de l'industrie à Paris*, covering the years 1847–48.[38] This study took great pains to distinguish between men and women in its tables on the laboring populations of Paris. Based on data from 64,916 enterprises, the *Statistique* found 334,389 workers residing and working in the city: 112,884 adult women, 197,184 adult men, and 24,321 children of both sexes. These figures were further broken down in a series of detailed tables, giving the number of men, women, and children working in each trade, their wages, level of education, place of employment, and residence. Furthermore, the discussion of this information made clear that the authors of the study saw these workers not only as free agents in a network of market relations but also as members of families with specific obligations that depended on gender. The *Statistique de l'industrie* thus embodied the logic of political economists who wished to show that a commitment to economic individualism need not conflict with a vision of the social order centered on the family.

The attention paid to the gender of the workforce in the 1848 *Statis-*

37. Garnier, *Du principe de population*, p. 42.
38. Chambre de Commerce de Paris, *Statistique de l'industrie à Paris résultant de l'enquête faite par la Chambre de Commerce pour les années 1847–1848* (Paris, 1851).

tique was relatively new. As late as the 1820s, statistical work on the Parisian economy paid little attention to the question of women's labor. Statisticians remained preoccupied with gender in other areas — the figures for people receiving public assistance in Paris between 1818 and 1825 in the *Recherches statistiques sur la ville de Paris* carefully distinguished between male and female indigent populations[39] — but this zeal to distinguish between male and female populations came later to the study of the workforce. For example, the volumes of the *Recherches statistiques sur la ville de Paris* contained the most detailed studies of individual industries available at that time, yet none of these volumes directly addressed the question of women workers. In only a few instances did the editors even note distinctions between male and female workers. In the 1823 volume, a detailed table on the manufacture of *gazes, barèges, tissus et schals soie et laine* carefully noted the number of women who worked as *tisseurs* (818 out of 3,270) and as *dévideurs* (2,861 out of 3,270). The table even went so far as to note the number of boys and girls among the 4,716 children who worked in the industry (3,537 and 1,179 respectively). The same volume's table on the cotton spinning industry made no distinctions between its male and female workers, however, despite the large number of women employed in the cotton trades. Instead, the table simply noted the "number of workers of all ages and both sexes" in the designated column. The 1826 volume in the same series contained the results of a detailed investigation into thirty different industries in Paris, with no indication of workers' gender.[40] The editors of the *Recherches* may have simply lacked reliable figures. Nevertheless, given the wide range of information that these tables do contain — production figures, cost of raw materials, gross from sales of finished goods, number of workers in Paris, number of workers employed outside of the city — one can only conclude that the editors did not view women's labor as a pressing problem but

39. *RSVP*, 1821, table 41; *RSVP*, 1823, table 58; *RSVP*, 1826, table 75; *RSVP*, 1829, table 91. The careful attention paid to the composition of the indigent population was especially evident in the 1817 census, which produced a table describing the 15,910 people housed in the capital's civil hospices and hospitals according to their profession. This table did not distinguish by sex, although in cases such as *blanchisseuses, fileuses*, and *brodeuses* the distinction is clear. See *RSVP*, 1821, table 37.

40. *RSVP*, 1823, tables 83 and 84; *RSVP*, 1826, tables 77–91; *RSVP*, 1829. The survey of Parisian trades and manufactures in the 1829 volume of the *Recherches* showed signs of an increased attention to the question of women workers, although the treatment was by no means systematic. A table on production at the royal tobacco works contained a detailed breakdown of the workforce, distinguishing between male and female employees in each occupation and giving average daily wages for each group. Nearly one-quarter of the factory's 1,054 workers were women, and they were limited to two occupations: *écotage* and *fabrication des cigarres*. The average daily wages of these two groups (1.80 F and 2.10 F respectively) were roughly comparable to the wages earned by the bulk of the male employees, but women were excluded from the more highly paid jobs in the factory. The same volume also distinguished the gender of workers in its survey of fan production, colored

simply as a natural part of certain trades. Put more abstractly, at a time when statisticians were careful to distinguish between the male and female poor, the social aggregate called "workers" had not yet been fully dissociated into male and female groups.[41]

The *Statistique de l'industrie* was produced by the Paris Chamber of Commerce immediately following an episode of intense social violence, the 1848 revolution. In February 1848, a popular uprising in the capital put an end to the July Monarchy and brought a loose coalition of centrists, republicans, and socialists together in a provisional government. As the members of this government debated the procedures for establishing permanent republican institutions in France, large numbers of unemployed workers gathered in Paris. Louis Blanc, a prominent socialist and member of the provisional government, called on his colleagues to respond to the demands of workers to show gratitude for their support during the revolutionary days of February. The government made Blanc director of the Luxembourg Commission, a body devoted to resolving disputes between workers and their employers. In this capacity Blanc also began an ambitious program of public works, the National Workshops, to deal with the problem of unemployment. In the meantime, he pushed for the creation of a Ministry of Labor, a cabinet-level office that would make economic policy and recognize the rights of labor and their representatives to negotiate freely with management. In the face of large demonstrations of support for the new ministry, the newly elected conservative assembly rejected Blanc's proposal as an unwarranted violation of the freedom of trade. As a compromise, however, the assembly voted on 25 May to undertake a broad statistical investigation into the condition of labor and industry throughout France. One week later, the assembly abolished the National Workshops, and the workers of Paris once more took to the streets to protest. In the ensuing fighting, perhaps as many as five thousand people were killed.[42]

Because of its timing and its origins, the *Statistique de l'industrie à Paris*

---

paper, and jewelry, as well as the lithographic trades. In tables dealing with other trades, however, the gender of the employees remained undetermined. See *RSVP*, 1829, tables 117–29.

41. This willingness to see women as a natural part of the working population had support from high places in the 1820s. Baron Charles Dupin, a member of the Chamber of Peers whose views were highly respected under both the Restoration and the July Monarchy, went so far as to claim that women's place in society would benefit from the mechanization of production because the precise and repetitive nature of mechanical labor was well suited to women's abilities (*Des forces productives et commerciales de la France* [Paris, 1827], p. 97).

42. On the circumstances leading to the establishment of the *Statistique de l'industrie*, see Scott, "Statistical Representation of Work," pp. 120–21, and H. Rigaudias-Weiss, *Les Enquêtes ouvrières en France entre 1830 et 1848* (Paris, 1936).

could not help but reflect the views and prejudices of Paris's business and governing elites. The Paris Chamber of Commerce consisted of a board of between fifteen and twenty prominent figures from the world of business and manufacture in the capital and had been in existence since 1803. Their regular meetings permitted a considerable degree of cooperation between business and government during this period, and they reported their activities to the minister of the interior. This body observed that Paris was being neglected in the larger national project mandated by the National Assembly in May 1848, and they undertook their own investigation into the conditions of labor and production in Parisian industries, appointing Horace Say, the son of Jean-Baptiste Say, as director of the project. Horace Say was himself a member of the Paris Chamber of Commerce and had wide connections in both the business community and government circles.

Appropriately, given the extremely politicized and tense atmosphere in Paris in 1848, the *Statistique* was made possible by the military. After the repression of the June revolt, the capital remained under the dictatorial authority of General Eugène Cavaignac, who divided the city's twelve districts into military circumscriptions. Every district came under the authority of a legion, each legion was divided into four battalions, and each battalion was divided into four or eight companies, depending on the density of the population. As Say put it, "Paris was thus divided into 362 circumscriptions . . . and this framework lent itself marvelously to the work of the investigation."[43] Each of these districts became the target of a house-by-house census, performed by paid investigators, who came armed with preprinted bulletins. Eventually, these researchers visited more than thirty-two thousand buildings. They wrote the names of those interviewed, filled in the responses to the questions that had been determined beforehand, and reported these results to Say's office. Say and his colleagues then divided the information according to thirteen different categories of manufacture and compared the raw data from each industry for inconsistencies. If they found that information from similar establishments diverged widely, they revisited each one and double-checked their reported figures. Only after careful checking did Say's office compile the final tables.

The quantitative work was certainly impressive, but the *Statistique de l'industrie* contained far more than statistical tables. Say's precedents, such as the *Recherches statistiques sur la ville de Paris* volumes from the 1820s and 1844, contained only brief introductory essays and allowed the numbers

43. *Statistique de l'industrie*, p. 19.

to stand on their own. This spartan presentation implied that statistics needed no support from the indeterminate realm of words and narrative description. Say's *Statistique*, in contrast, contained accompanying chapters that explained the procedures by which the investigation was completed. They also prepared the reader to accept the author's conclusions regarding the situation of industrial production and labor in Paris.

Horace Say and his colleagues at the Chamber of Commerce wanted the *Statistique de l'industrie* to provide a factual assessment of Parisian industry and labor that could be used as a counterargument to the socialist claims made by Louis Blanc and his supporters. The tone of the explanatory texts, therefore, was relentlessly optimistic, in spite of the overt tensions in the city. "One fact can be established at the outset," wrote Say in his introduction to the chapter on the morality of workers, "in ordinary and normal times, the working population in Paris is in satisfactory condition in all respects."[44] The vision of the Paris economy that emerged from the *Statistique*, therefore, did not place the interests of workers against those of their employers. Say's goal was to illustrate the vitality of industry in the nation's capital; the *Statistique* thus represented Paris as a happily buzzing hive of *petites entreprises*, individually led small firms, whose employers and employees shared in the general prosperity.[45]

The census method used for gathering the information confirmed this individualist orientation. The key to avoiding uncomfortable talk of social aggregates such as class lay in the definitions of each statistical category. Say admitted that the description of an economy as complex as that of Paris entailed a great number of difficult decisions regarding the classifications of such key terms as "enterprise," "manufacture," and "worker." At what point should a worker working alone in his house be treated as an independent operator? At what point should a merchant who provided this worker with raw materials be treated as an agent of industry rather than a simple commercial entrepreneur? Should women and children who were related to the "patron" be considered "workers"?

Say and his colleagues decided to classify as industrial manufacturers [*industriels*] "all entrepreneurs performing manual labor or having manual labor performed," so long as they fit one of four categories. Say defined his criteria for *industriel* as follows:

1) All individuals manufacturing for their own account.
2) All individuals in the putting-out trades employing one or more workers.

44. Ibid., p. 61.
45. Scott, "Statistical Representation of Work," pp. 126–27.

3) All individuals in the putting-out trades working alone, when this work is destined for a bourgeois clientele. Even though these individuals could be considered as simple homeworkers, it was impossible not to count them as entrepreneurs because without this consideration, they would not figure in the investigation.

4) All individuals in the putting-out trades working alone, who are employed by diverse entrepreneurs without having a special relationship with any one of them.[46]

By this definition seamstresses and out-workers in the clothing trades who obtained raw materials from others and sold the finished products back at piece rates were classified as *industriels* along with master artisans with several employees and the owners of large enterprises. Such procedures facilitated the collection of information because they absolved the census takers from any responsibility for making difficult distinctions between dependent workers and independent operators. As the historian Joan Scott pointed out, however, Say's definitions forced the authors of the *Statistique* to remind the reader repeatedly that certain categories of entrepreneurs were "really workers." [47] The classification was particularly distorting in the case of workers in the putting-out industries, whom the *Statistique* classified as *petites entreprises*. Meanwhile, the merchants in these trades who directed production, set prices both for raw materials and the finished products, and gleaned most of the profit were excluded from the *Statistique* because their occupation was deemed purely "commercial." The intent of the *Statistique*, needless to say, was to count as many workers as possible as independent, autonomous agents, capable of benefiting from the fruits of their own labor and thrift.

In the *Statistique*'s tables, therefore, *petites entrepreneurs* did not appear under the heading "*population ouvrière*" but under the label "*fabricant*." *Fabricants* were divided into three categories: those employing more than ten workers, those employing two to ten workers, and those working alone or employing only one other worker. Unlike the columns for "*population ouvrière*," the columns for *fabricants* were not subdivided by sex, presumably because the authors of the *Statistique* assumed that few women could be considered employers or masters of industrial establishments. By the *Statistique*'s own definitions of *petites entrepreneurs*, however, many women workers were included as *fabricants*. In the table on employment in the clothing industries, for example, 104 *blanchisseuses*

46. *Statistique de l'industrie*, p. 17.
47. Scott, "Statistical Representation of Work," p. 127.

Table 4.2.   Industrial employment in Paris according to place of work, 1848

	Workshop/ factory (No.)	Work- shop/ factory (%)	Building site (No.)	Building site (%)	Home (No.)	Home (%)	Total
Men	150,953	73.7	22,519	11.0	31,453	15.3	204,925
Women	63,929	56.6	157	0.1	48,805	43.2	112,891
Children	24,036	97.3	678	2.7	na	na	24,714
Total	238,918	69.8	23,354	6.8	80,258	23.4	342,530

Source: Statistique de l'industrie, p. 48.

employed more than ten workers, 1,521 employed two to ten workers, and 3,222 laundresses were listed as *fabricants* who either worked alone or employed only one worker. The only indication that these *fabricants* were primarily women lay in the feminine ending to the label *blanchisseuses*. Even such grammatical hints were missing in the case of the 6,898 *tailleurs d'habits*, who were listed as *fabricants* working alone or employing only one other worker. Presumably many of these solitary "tailors" were women, given that about half of the workers in this trade were female. There is no way of knowing how many, however, for the table did not enumerate the number of women who qualified as *petites entrepreneurs*, that is, women who did not conform to Horace Say's notion of the "dependent condition."[48]

In contrast, the men and women of the *population ouvrière* were the subject of very careful accounting. (These figures are summarized in Tables 4.2 and 4.3.) Here, the *Statistique's* table distinguished between male and female workers, as well as residents and nonresidents. Furthermore, the table divided each of these subgroups according to the location of their work, whether it be in a large workshop, in an open site in the city, or in a private home. Unsurprisingly, many women workers were included in this last category, especially in the clothing and textile trades. Throughout the text that accompanied these statistical tables, Horace Say and his colleagues confirmed that women's labor could not be separated from their place in the family. This was most clear in the section on needlework, where Say repeated the justification for women's low wages first given by his father. "In this type of work," wrote Horace Say in the *Statistique*, "woman habitually submits to that law of her nature that places her in a constant state of dependence, in both the family and in so-

48. *Statistique de l'industrie*, table 27.

Table 4.3.   Industrial employment by sector in Paris, 1848

Sector	Men (No.)	Men (%)	Women (No.)	Women (%)	Children (No.)	Children (%)	Total
Food	7,951	76.2	1,394	13.4	1,083	10.4	10,428
Building	40,083	96.3	135	0.3	1,385	3.3	41,603
Furnishing	28,745	79.4	3,845	10.6	3,594	9.9	36,184
Clothing	30,274	33.6	54,398	60.4	5,392	6.0	90,064
Thread and textile	11,028	30.1	21,874	59.6	3,783	10.3	36,685
Skin and leather	4,241	92.7	234	5.1	98	2.1	4,573
Carriages and military	10,625	77.3	2,694	19.6	435	3.2	13,754
Chemicals and ceramics	6,572	67.5	2,727	28.0	438	4.5	9,737
Metals and mechanics	22,081	88.7	1,269	5.1	1,544	6.2	24,894
Precious metals	10,835	64.4	3,739	22.2	2,245	13.3	16,819
Barrels and baskets	4,021	74.4	632	11.7	752	13.9	5,405
Articles of Paris	17,583	49.3	15,540	43.6	2,556	7.2	35,679
Printing, engraving, paper	10,886	65.2	4,410	26.4	1,409	8.4	16,705
Total	204,925	59.8	112,891	33.0	24,714	7.2	342,530

Source: Statistique de l'industrie, p. 48.

ciety. In effect, woman has a special mission: the work of the household and the care of the children. In return she has a right to count on a part of the product of her father's labor, or that of her brother, husband, or son."[49] When this same woman accepted a small sum for piecework that she could do in addition to her housework, she remained ignorant of her "fatal competition with women whose unhappy lot it is to live without a family." Say noted that this competition was most common in the embroidering trades because "women belonging to honorable families, and whose husbands earn regular wages" often chose such work.[50]

The distinction made between "sedentary" and "mobile" laboring populations in Paris also worked to confirm the political economists'

49. Ibid., p. 52.
50. Ibid.

Table 4.4.   Laboring population in Paris by
sex and residence, 1848

	Sedentary population	Mobile population	Total
Men	197,184	7,741	204,925
Women	112,884	7	112,891
Children	24,321	393	24,714
Total	334,389	8,141	342,530

Source: Statistique de l'industrie, p. 48.

notion of women's "dependent condition." Out of 342,530 workers in
Paris, the *Statistique* classified 334,389 as "sedentary," that is, as permanent residents of the city (see Table 4.4). The "mobile" remainder, some
8,141 people, consisted of workers who maintained a residence elsewhere.
Many of this latter group were masons and carpenters who migrated to
the city during the warmer months of the year to take jobs in the building trades, finding lodging in the many furnished rooms of the capital.
Even this fact cannot fully account for the astonishing discrepancy between male and female members of the "mobile" population: 7,741 men
versus 7 women. Out of a total workforce of almost 343,000 individuals,
the *Statistique* concluded that only seven women were part of the float-
ing population. Say admitted that "everything leads one to think that the
declarations regarding the mobile population remain incomplete."[51] But
the discrepancy in the printed statistics also points to the significant differences in how the labor of men and women was treated by statisticians.
Only men were presumed to be fully in control of their economic activity, and only men, therefore, could exercise the autonomy required to
maintain one residence for their family while temporarily occupying another. Both single women and women in families could only be classified
as sedentary, the former because by definition they could have no family
ties to another location, the latter because the location of her household
determined her residence.[52]

In passages recounting the situation of women in other branches of
manufacture, Horace Say made haste to reassure his readers that the unhappy women who lived outside of the "dependent condition" were in
fact anomalous cases whose situation was by no means typical. At this
point, Say's account broke off from its recitation of aggregate figures and

51. Ibid., p. 48.
52. Ibid., table 1.

resorted instead to anecdotal stories to account for the extremely low salaries reported in certain trades. Say noted that some women reported earning as little as 15 centimes per day (the average female wage in Paris was 1.63 francs per day). This alarming poverty, however, was "always exceptional, and earned only by women in the putting-out trades, who have very little ability, and who spend very little time on the work. Thus, the minimum of 15 c. is the result of declarations made by two infirm and very poor women, one aged sixty-eight years and the other seventy-one, who lived from charity, and yet who sometimes sewed trousers for soldiers."[53] These women, who lived outside of any relationships of familial dependency and obligation, could only be seen as aberrant or abnormal.

Individual female workers thus appeared in the *Statistique* as marginal figures, what statisticians today would refer to as "outliers"—points on a graph that lie far from the normal curve. Say offered no corresponding anecdotal evidence for male workers, but in drawing conclusions on the moral life of the Parisian labor force, he revealed that what distinguished good workers from bad was precisely their success in establishing themselves as autonomous individuals. The good worker saved his earnings, lived in his own apartment, and owned his own furniture. He knew how to read and write, cared for the well-being of his family and the education of his children, and was impervious to the temptations of the bistro, the street, and the utopian promises of political propagandists. The bad worker lived in furnished rooms, owned no more than the clothes on his back, was illiterate, lived with women to whom he was not married, abandoned them when they had children, and was all too willing to succumb to drink, sensual pleasures, and radical politics. The former was capable of citizenship; the latter exhibited his true personality only when acting as a member of a crowd.[54]

"One can represent the totality of the population," wrote Horace Say, "as formed of successive social levels, the most elevated of which is composed of those who have succeeded in placing themselves in a position of ease and whose level of self-respect is most developed."[55] The people who

---

53. Ibid., p. 51.
54. "In all professions, almost without exception, one finds two categories of workers: the first composed of well-behaved economical men and women who have a family life; the other includes those who lack all foresight, who madly spend the highest wages and who subsequently find themselves without resources during times of scarcity. . . . Unfortunately, certain individuals are caught in a fatal bind. They are born in bad conditions, and they possess a kind of congenital malformation, a bad point of departure. Few possess the elite characteristics necessary to transcend this handicap" (ibid., p. 62).
55. Ibid., p. 67.

occupied these higher levels were distinguished by their ability to transcend the power of class, circumstance, upbringing, and the temptations of material and sexual desires. Of course, there is nothing surprising about this moral judgment—other historians have well documented the middle-class bias of mid-nineteenth-century social investigators. What is significant is the extent to which Say's description of good and bad workers is structured by a set of assumptions about the relationship between the general and particular, between the collective and the individual, between a quantitatively realized aggregate mass and the fully autonomous *père de famille*. The authors of the *Statistique de l'industrie* wanted to prove that workers could, in fact, become more than just statistics.

This is the essential tension between the moral message of the *Statistique de l'industrie* and the epistemological foundation that propped up its statistical conclusions. Horace Say the liberal political economist was intent on demonstrating to workers that they need not be mere cogs in a productive system that was beyond their control. On the contrary, they could determine their own existence and their relative state of well-being by modifying their behavior, exercising their reason, and moderating their desires. Horace Say the statistician, on the other hand, sought to show that his aggregate figures for the size of the workforce, their wages, their level of education, and their moral qualities had objective force and value as statements about the truth of workers' existence, taken en masse.

A paradox? Only apparently. The very notion of the autonomous individual could take on its fullest meaning only against the background of some aggregate body. For the individual male worker, this background was not necessarily his more unfortunate fellows (who remained at least potentially redeemable no matter how degraded) but the figure of his wife. Again and again, the *Statistique* demonstrated that women workers could not be individualized as men were. They existed only in a network of kinship relations, and their participation in the economy was always either a simple supplement to a household income or an anomalous act of desperation by an aberrant and solitary female who had somehow eluded her familial obligations.

The laissez-faire political economists' gendered vision of the market economy served as an antidote to their fear that the laws producing social aggregates had more objective force and reality than individual decisions in the marketplace. Following this theory, they concluded that poverty was the result of a multitude of individual failures, a failure of men to provide adequately for their families and a failure of women to live in the "dependent condition." Nowhere, however, did these writers betray any aware-

ness of the contradiction between their assumptions about male and female social roles and the rhetoric of individual autonomy that pervaded
their writings.

Seen in this light, Malthus's and Jean-Baptiste Say's works on political
economy were attractive not so much for the clarity of their logic as for
their ambiguities, which allowed French political economists to persist
with some of their own inconsistencies in a period of bewildering political turmoil and socioeconomic change. But even if Malthus and Jean-
Baptiste Say were unsuccessful in assimilating families into their vision of
a market economy without contradicting themselves, their persistent
blindness to this fact indicates that there may have been certain political
benefits to be gained from learning to live with these contradictions.
Both Malthus and Say reaffirmed the necessity of separate social roles for
men and women and never gave up on their commitment to gendered
hierarchies. Nevertheless, their own ideas exposed the potential for contradiction between the interest of families and the population as a whole
or between the desires of individuals and the workings of the market.

The convolutions of this thinking had a profound effect on the ways
in which political economists and government administrators in France
interpreted and organized the data from early empirical studies of the population. Since their vision of the economic individual excluded women
by definition, they found it difficult to see female laborers as anything
but an anomaly, despite the fact that their own studies revealed large numbers of women working for wages in many different occupations. Presented with the opportunity to explore the connection between female
poverty and differential wage rates, political economists and social statisticians chose instead to explore those aspects of a woman's life which were
more closely related to motherhood and the family. When early statistical studies of the Parisian population revealed in the 1820s that indigent
women outnumbered indigent men by a ratio of three to two, nobody
called for an end to restrictions on female labor. Instead, they chose to examine in excruciating detail the plight of working-class families, captured
most clearly in high levels of illegitimacy, abandonment, and infanticide.

By linking the health of the population to the most intimate actions of
individual men and women, Malthus's population principle destabilized
the neatness of liberalism's distinction between public and private, revealing the two realms to be intimately connected. After the publication
of Malthus's *Essay*, it became much easier to claim that the public had an
interest in matters that were part of the private, domestic sphere: childbearing, the care of infants, the labor of wives and children. Such claims
threatened the stability of patriarchal families by opening up the possi-

bility of legislation that might challenge the authority of the father within his family. An awareness of this fact led Malthus and his supporters to promote such solutions as "moral restraint," which would leave control of family matters in the hands of individual family members. As we shall see in the next chapter, however, when working men and women found other solutions and strategies for coping with the difficult circumstances they found themselves in, many reformers concluded that family matters could not be left up to families themselves.

CHAPTER 5

"A SUDDEN AND TERRIBLE REVELATION"

REINTERPRETING INFANT MORTALITY

In 1858, a young doctor named Louis-Adolphe Bertillon presented a paper to the Académie de médecine with the unassuming title "Etude statistique sur les nouveau-nés." Bertillon did not publish the paper at the time, but when he died in 1883, his heirs discovered the manuscript in his private papers. Believing it to be "assuredly one of the most celebrated works of M. Bertillon," they published it in the *Annales de démographie internationale*, an important forum for the new science of demography.[1] At the time of his death, Bertillon was without question the most distinguished and respected French demographer of his generation, but it is somewhat curious to see this short piece on the health of newborn infants touted as one of his "most celebrated works." In fact, the paper seemed important only retroactively—the connection he made in 1858 between infant mortality and wet-nursing led eventually to the passage of the Roussel Law of 1874, which established strict regulations for wet-nursing in France. Bertillon's paper turned out to be the first in a series of papers on infant mortality that converted first the Académie de médecine and later the government of the Third Republic (1870–1940) to an enthusiastic campaign for infant welfare reform. Coming as it did on the heels of the academy's debate concerning the standardization of the causes of death, Bertillon's paper and its reception marked an important moment in the wider acceptance of aggregate analysis in population research.

In 1858, Bertillon was not yet a prominent demographer, but he was already a member of a politically active group of academicians in the capital's Latin Quarter. As a medical student in Paris during the 1848 revo-

1. Louis-Adolphe Bertillon, "Etude statistique sur les nouveau-nés," *Annales de démographie internationale* 7 (1883): 169–78.

lution, Bertillon had openly proclaimed his sympathy for the republican cause, and during the uprising in June 1848 he attended to the wounded on both sides of the barricades. Bertillon was arrested and briefly imprisoned after Louis-Napoleon's coup-d'état in December 1851. His earliest population studies were heavily influenced by the work of both Quetelet and his father-in-law, Achille Guillard, an educator and social theorist who coined the term *démographie* in 1854. Bertillon's thesis on vaccination and his paper on infant mortality brought him to the attention of Paul Broca at the Faculté de médecine, and Broca offered Bertillon a chair in demography when he founded the Ecole d'Anthropologie in 1859. During the 1850s and 1860s Bertillon published widely, including seminal articles for the *Dictionnaire encyclopédique des sciences médicales* on natality, mortality, and marriage. The fall of the Empire and the establishment of the Third Republic made it possible for Bertillon to take more public roles near the end of his life: he served as mayor of the fifth arrondissement in Paris when the city was besieged by Prussian troops in 1870, and he later became the first director of the city's municipal statistics office when it was reorganized in the late 1870s. Under Bertillon's leadership, and that of his son and successor Jacques Bertillon after 1883, the Paris statistical office surpassed the Statistique Générale de la France in its innovative and ambitious research on population questions.[2] Louis-Adolphe Bertillon thus was an active member of the educated class of republican notables who were ready to serve the Third Republic in the first decades after its founding in 1870.

When Bertillon first appeared before the academy in 1858, he was certainly aware of this august body's history of skepticism toward statistics, and he knew his paper's success depended on his ability to avoid offending the strictly clinical sensibilities of many academy members. Careful to eschew the grandiose claims that had made Quetelet so suspect to the academy earlier in the century, Bertillon made his case for the necessity of aggregate analysis in plain and simple terms. Statistics revealed new facts about the population that were not apparent from clinical observations. This was not a tyranny of "majority facts" but a method for seeing what had previously been invisible.

2. Jacques Bertillon later founded the Association nationale pour l'acroissement de la population française in 1896. A second son, Alphonse Bertillon, later headed the office of Judiciary Identification at the Prefecture of Police in Paris, in which capacity he (incorrectly) identified the handwriting of the famous *bordereau* used to convict Alfred Dreyfus of treason. See Jacques Bertillon, *La Vie et les oeuvres du Docteur L.-A. Bertillon* (Paris, 1883). On Guillard and Louis-Adolphe Bertillon's role in the creation of demography as an independent discipline, see Schweber, "Assertion of Disciplinary Claims," chaps. 1 and 2.

The story that Bertillon wanted to tell about the power of statistics depended on their ability to unleash an outpouring of moral outrage, and the vulnerability of French infants provided him with the necessary focus. Simple lists of averages were insufficient. Bertillon dismissed these as "nothing but relations between numbers," effectively preempting the kinds of criticism that had earlier been leveled at Quetelet.[3] His statistics for infant mortality constructed a wider web of significance, connecting numbers to widely shared and deeply held notions of maternal obligation and the place of the family in the social order. Identifying the cause of high infant mortality in the region around Paris as the widespread practice of wet-nursing, Bertillon decried this "immoral and barbarous practice whereby mothers abandon their infants to foreign hands."[4] He blamed French mothers for abandoning their children to mercenary wet-nurses "at a time when they require for survival a care so assiduous, so tiring, and often so painful and repugnant that only mothers could be expected to do it."[5] Bertillon's defense of statistical aggregates thus went beyond a celebration of their ability to reveal facts about society that had hitherto been poorly understood. He wanted to show that these facts were the first step to active intervention, and he found no better topic than mothers and infants to make this connection.

Using figures from the period 1840–49, Bertillon observed that the statistics for deaths in infancy were highest in the thirteen departments that surrounded the Paris region. Noting that these departments supplied most of the nurses for Parisian babies and finding as well that the statistics reproduced themselves in a fairly consistent fashion from year to year, Bertillon concluded: "These ratios cannot be the effect of chance. . . . In these departments a *constant and intense cause* is showing its effects, aggravating the natural mortality of infants."[6] Clinical observations of individual deaths, he pointed out, could not have revealed such a fact because the "natural mortality" of infants could be measured only in aggregates.[7] Positing a "natural" equilibrium between life and death that could be measured statistically, Bertillon's argument created a set of objective normative standards for evaluating the success or failure of families in caring for their children.

3. Bertillon, "Etude statistique des nouveau-nés," p. 170.
4. Ibid., p. 172.
5. Ibid.
6. Ibid., p. 171. Emphasis in original.
7. Other demographers wrote of the notion of a "natural mortality" in this period. Alfred Legoyt, the director of the Statistique Générale de la France and an active member of the Société de statistique, wrote that a figure for the "true mortality, or more exactly the real vitality" of the country

In the years that followed, Bertillon's statistical analysis of infant mortality was cited by a wide range of doctors and social reformers who used both his data and those of subsequent studies to support legislation regulating the practice of wet-nursing. The supporters of this campaign faced a long-standing and well-entrenched official reluctance to intervene in the lives of French families, and they found the statistical support offered by Bertillon's paper to be an indispensable part of this effort. In 1874, the reformers achieved their goal. A scant four years after the founding of the Third Republic, Senator Théophile Roussel sponsored a law in the National Assembly which placed wet-nurses and their charges under state supervision and required all women employing wet-nurses to register this act with the police.[8] In other words, the moment at which the study of statistical aggregates finally overcame the methodological reservations of the clinicians was also the founding moment of what would become a new republican initiative on family law.

Bertillon's attention to age cohorts allowed him to develop new justifications for official intervention in the lives of French families. According to Bertillon, the deaths of children and young people, "so precious to the family and to the nation,"[9] were much more likely to be the result of environmental circumstances extrinsic to the individual than deaths of those over the age of sixty. Assuming that scientific experts could identify the environmental factors that contributed to increased infant mortality, Bertillon reasoned that early deaths could be eliminated by well-informed state action to counter these causes. This emphasis on environmental conditions also lent a new dimension to the study of infant morality. No longer seen as a simple measure of the number of infants who died, infant mortality became an important indicator of social health. Children were valuable as sensitive gauges, much like the canaries kept by miners to de-

---

could be determined by "subtracting from the category all violent deaths (suicides, accidents, duels, executions, murders and assassinations, deaths on the field of battle)." The resulting figure, consisting only of "deaths by old age or illness . . . could give a reasonable idea of the morality rate [chiffre mortuaire] . . . and notably of the average life span" ("Les Accidents en Europe," Journal de la Société de statistique de Paris 6 [1865]: 249). It is ironic that Legoyt insisted on retaining the particularly undemographic notion of death by old age as an indicator of "true mortality." "Death by old age" has a questionable status as a demographic and medical concept because it abstains from pinpointing the event that led to death—it is a noncausal "cause." For a related discussion, see Hervé Le Bras, "Malthus and the Two Mortalities," in Malthus Past and Present, ed. Jacques Dupâquier and A. Fauve-Chamoux (London, 1983), pp. 31–42.

8. Théophile Roussel, "Proposition de loi ayant pour objet la protection des enfants du premier âge et en particulier des nourrissons," Assemblé nationale, no. 1707 (1873).

9. L.-A. Bertillon, La Démographie figurée de la France (Paris, 1874), p. liv.

tect gas leaks: "Early childhood is very vulnerable, because of the weakness inherent in this age, it is the period of life where the surrounding environment acts with the most energy [on children]. Their mortality, is therefore . . . a very sensitive *reactant*, which forcefully indicates the quality of the milieu." [10]

Such a conception of infant mortality did not, of course, replace earlier forms of condemnation that had characterized discussions of the wet-nursing industry since the eighteenth century. It did, however, expand the horizons of the potential threat represented in the figures Bertillon produced in support of his argument. Because mothers bore the primary responsibility for the nursing infant's environment, Bertillon's argument made it possible to see the infant mortality figures as a gauge not only of social health in general but of motherhood in particular.

Bertillon's connection between infant mortality and maternal responsibility proved decisive in transforming public attitudes toward the possibility of official intervention in the family to protect children. Parents and municipal authorities had tolerated high levels of infant mortality for much of the century, and few had looked to the state to remedy the situation. The Chamber of Deputies had even voted down a previous attempt to regulate the wet-nursing industry in 1846.[11] This resistance to intervention had its roots in the Civil Code of 1804, which held the interest of the family to be indivisible, embodied in the interest of the male head of the household, as husband, father, and citizen.[12] The doctors, hygienists, and reformers who campaigned against the wet-nursing industry challenged this inviolate sphere by finding and defending other interests within the family: the interest of the child and the interest of society in the production of future generations of productive citizens. By claiming that French women were no longer fulfilling their "natural" maternal obligations, Bertillon and the reformers who followed his lead succeeded in targeting infant welfare as a new and legitimate concern of government

10. Bertillon, "Etude statistique sur les nouveau-nés," p. 170. Emphasis in original.
11. Jacques Bonzon, *La Législation de l'enfance* (Paris, 1899), p. 40.
12. Paternal authority was the subject of a long-standing debate in French legal circles during the nineteenth century. For a detailed examination of the Roussel Law's relation to the legal tradition of *puissance paternelle* see especially Schafer, *Children in Moral Danger*, pp. 19–86. Schafer's book is particularly compelling in its attention to the wide range of legislation that encroached on paternal authority during this period, above all laws that dealt with the perceived moral failings of parents with regard to their children. See also Louis Coirard, *La Famille dans le Code Civil* (Aix, 1907), pp. 153–55; Esther Kanipe, "The Family, Private Property and the State in France, 1870–1914" (Ph.D. dissertation, University of Wisconsin, Madison, 1976), pp. 212–22; and Claudia S. Kselman, "The Modernization of Family Law: The Politics and Ideology of Family Reform in Third Republic France" (Ph.D. dissertation, University of Michigan, 1980), chap. 4.

while simultaneously sidestepping the charge of tampering with paternal authority.[13]

This shift began in the 1830s and 1840s when economists and Catholic social reformers initiated a debate about child abandonment and the state's responsibilities for foundlings. Katherine Lynch and Rachel Fuchs have shown that the work of "moral economists" on abandoned foundlings served to focus public attention on parental responsibilities during the July Monarchy, and these discussions provided later reformers with an important precedent for their attacks on the wet-nursing industry.[14] The moral economists argued that industrialization had produced a new source for abandonment: urban female workers, whose participation in the market economy had perverted their "natural" maternal instincts, making them unfit to raise their own children. Lynch argued, however, that these pejorative views had more to do with changing perceptions among middle-class social observers than with any underlying deterioration of maternal feelings among French women. Lynch suggested an alternative interpretation. Increasingly, working women attempted to adapt foundling hospitals to their own needs by taking advantage of the free placement of infants with wet-nurses that these public offices provided.[15] Lynch supported this conclusion with evidence that many women attempted to maintain contact with their infants even after "abandoning" them to the public welfare system. In other words, work-

13. Historians have tended to present the targeting of infant death by demographers and the promulgation of laws designed to lower its cost to society as the results of a happy conjuncture between medical know-how and political will. George Sussman, for example, argued that doctors and legislators paid more attention to the wet-nursing industry in the 1860s and 1870s simply because the problem was getting worse. He pointed out that a current of reform had targeted the nursing business as a source of great suffering and harm to society since the eighteenth century. These arguments for reform, wrote Sussman, simply became more relevant as the nursing industry expanded to accommodate the needs of larger urban populations. After the 1840s, the development of the railway made it feasible to send children further away from their homes, effectively making the nursing business a national industry. Sussman pointed out that the mortality rates for children sent to nurse had risen since the early part of the century and even risen sharply in the late 1860s and early 1870s because of the necessity of using "dry nurses" who bottle-fed their charges as the supply of good wet-nurses became more and more scarce. In Sussman's view, then, the structural evolution of the industry itself, which created an "internal crisis" in the wet-nursing business just as "public tolerance for such high levels of infant mortality was declining" accounts for the increased discussion of the problem and the ensuing legislation (*Selling Mother's Milk: The Wet Nursing Business in France, 1715–1914* [Urbana, 1982], pp. 38–43, 120–12). See also M. F. Morel, "Théories et pratiques de l'allaitement en France au XVIIIe siècle," *Annales de démographie historique* (1976): 393–426.
14. Lynch, *Family, Class, and Ideology*, pp. 114–167; Fuchs, *Abandoned Children*, pp. 34–43.
15. Lynch, *Family, Class, and Ideology*, p. 165. For more evidence on working women who resorted to wet-nursing, see Accampo, *Industrialization, Family Life, and Class Relations*, pp. 63–65, 125–26.

ing women in France preserved their wage-earning capacity by resorting to wet-nurses, and when they could not afford to pay for one themselves, they used the foundling hospitals to place their infants for them.

Bertillon's 1858 paper on infant mortality made no connection between women's labor and the wet-nursing industry, and the issue could not be addressed overtly by Senator Roussel and the supporters of his 1874 law. The republican establishment remained committed in principle to a liberal free trade policy, even if that meant allowing women to enter freely into the labor market. Nevertheless, as Joan Scott has demonstrated, the figure of the female laborer was the subject of a profound and destabilizing anxiety during this period, repeatedly condemned in print with the most vitriolic expressions of disapproval, fear, and disgust.[16] In such a context, Roussel's proposed regulation of the wet-nursing industry provided republican legislators with an avenue for supervising the very institution that allowed working-class women to seek jobs, even after bearing children. Defining the problem in terms of women who abdicated their natural function as mothers provided legislators with the opening they needed. They could then justify their intervention as a moral defense of the family and a medical defense of the child's own health, without ever mentioning the troubling issue of women's labor.

Bertillon's statistical treatment of infant mortality thus lay at the root of a turn toward motherhood in republican social policy at the end of the nineteenth century.[17] Historians have already made clear that the development of the welfare state in France had much to do with anxiety about the declining birthrate, a concern that brought a great deal of attention to the problems of maternity and childbearing by the end of the nine-

16. Joan Scott, "'L'ouvrière! Mot impie, sordide . . .': Women Workers in the Discourse of French Political Economy," in Scott, *Gender and the Politics of History* (New York, 1988), pp. 139–63. On the long debates concerning women's labor, regulations for night work, and maternity leaves in the Third Republic, see Stewart, *Women, Work, and the French State*, chaps. 6–8.

17. Recent research into the origins of the welfare state in Europe and the United States has demonstrated that both male and female reformers were often motivated by a concern to reward women who chose to become mothers. Some feminists cooperated in these efforts, in the hopes of gaining wider societal recognition of the special contributions women made to society by virtue of their role as mothers. See, for example, Ann Cova, "French Feminism and Maternity: Theories and Policies, 1890–1918," in *Maternity and Gender Policies: Women and the Rise of the European Welfare States, 1880s–1950s*, ed. Gisela Bock and Pat Thane (New York, 1991), pp. 119–37; Karen Offen, "Body Politics: Women, Work and the Politics of Motherhood," ibid., pp. 138–59; Alisa Klaus, "Depopulation and Race Suicide: Maternalism and Pronatalist Ideologies in France and the United States," in *Mothers of a New World: Maternalist Politics and the Origins of Welfare States*, ed. Seth Koven and Sonya Michel (London, 1993), pp. 188–212; and Susan Pedersen, *Family, Dependence, and the Origins of the Welfare State: Britain and France, 1914–1945* (Cambridge, 1993). For the most detailed overview of infant welfare policies in France, see Catherine Rollet-Echalier, *La Politique à l'égard de la petite enfance sous la IIIe République* (Paris, 1990).

teenth century.[18] The desire to find a remedy for high levels of infant mortality preceded the depopulation debate by almost a generation, however, and the passage of the Roussel Law cannot be attributed solely to an intensification of natalist concern following the French defeat in the Franco-Prussian War. Rather, reformers and legislators in the 1860s and early 1870s had already firmly established a concern for maternity and infant health before the fear of depopulation found a wide audience.

Once the foundations of the Third Republic had been firmly established in the late 1870s, anticlerical republican legislators increasingly used family policy to distinguish themselves from their conservative Catholic opponents. Mobilizing behind such issues as Naquet's divorce law, Ferry's proposals on education, and the 1889 measure on the "moral abandonment" of children, they sought to emphasize their continued respect for the "traditional" French patriarchal order, even while passing laws that substantially changed the relationship between families and the state. When Roussel's law regulating the wet-nursing industry came before the National Assembly in 1874, republican control over the government was far from complete. In this uncertain political context, the supporters of wet-nursing reform found it in their interest to downplay any obstacles and setbacks their efforts faced from the defenders of paternal authority so that their reforms might seem to be the product of common sense and advances in medical understanding.

WET-NURSING AND INFANT MORTALITY

Parents throughout Europe resorted to wet-nurses, but the French had developed this practice into a much more highly organized business than their European neighbors. Elites sent their children away to nurse throughout recorded history, and historians agree that the French experience did not differ markedly from that of the rest of Europe until the seventeenth century. From the eighteenth century until just before World War I, however, large numbers of French mothers, from different social milieus and in all parts of the country, preferred not to nurse their babies themselves and had recourse to paid nurses.[19]

18. On the fears of population decline, see Spengler, *France Faces Depopulation*; Angus McLaren, *Sexuality and Social Order: The Debate over the Fertility of Women and Workers in France, 1770–1920* (New York, 1983); Karen Offen, "Depopulation, Nationalism and Feminism in Fin-de-Siècle France," *American Historical Review* 89 (1984): 648–76; and Chapter 6 of this book.
19. On the wet-nursing industry in France, see Sussman, *Selling Mother's Milk*, and Fuchs, *Poor and Pregnant in Paris*, pp. 152–55. For regional studies, see A. Fine-Sauriac, "Mortalité infantile et allaitement dans le sud-ouest de la France au XIXe siècle," *Annales de démographie historique* (1978):

Paris provided wet-nurses with most of their paying customers, although other urban centers also possessed their *bureaux des nourrices*. Young women from outlying rural areas who had recently borne a child of their own would register at these offices, hoping to obtain an additional child to nurse in return for a monthly allowance.[20] Before passage of the Roussel Law, two municipal offices in Paris excercised minimal control over wet-nurses and their charges. The Direction des nourrices on the rue des Tournelles acted as a referral service for families and nurses and provided some guarantees of medical inspection for the Paris region. The Hospice des enfants-assistés, or Foundling Hospital, on the rue d'Enfer took in abandoned children and orphans and placed them with rural nurses. Most families, however, avoided the municipal offices and made their own arrangements with rural women, either through a private nursing bureau or through the services of a midwife. In many areas the nursing bureaus employed special agents, called *meneurs*, who ferried the babies back and forth from the city to the countryside, making it unnecessary for the parents to meet their child's nurse. In making his case for the necessity of regulating this activity at the national level, Roussel claimed that out of an annual birth contingent of nearly fifty-four thousand infants in Paris, more than twenty thousand were sent to nurses in the countryside. Of these, perhaps a third died while still in their infancy.[21]

The accuracy of infant mortality statistics in nineteenth-century France is difficult to gauge. Many infant deaths went unreported. Nevertheless, beginning in the 1830s, when reliable figures first became available at the national level, the figures for infant death demonstrated a remarkable stability (see Figure 5.1). A slight tendency to increase during the years 1850–70 is the only exception to this stability, and the first signs of marked decline do not appear until the late 1890s, over twenty years

---

81–103; Paul Galliano, "La Mortalité infantile dans le banlieue sud de Paris à la fin du XVIIIe siècle (1774–1794)," *Annales de démographie historique* (1966): 139–77; and André Armengaud, "Les Nourrices du Morvan au XIXe siècle," *Etudes et chronique de démographie historique* (1964): 131–39.
20. Sussman, *Selling Mother's Milk*, pp. 38–43. See also Bonzon, *Législation de l'enfance*, pp. 12–13, 35–46.
21. Théophile Roussel, "Rapport au nom de la commission chargée d'examiner la proposition de loi de M. Théophile Roussel relative à la protection des enfants du premier âge, et en particulier des nourrissons," *Assemblé nationale*, annex no. 2446 (9 June 1874), p. 10. Roussel's figures came from Armand Husson, *Note sur la mortalité des enfants du premier âge, nés dans la ville de Paris* (Paris, 1870). Estimates on infant mortality in the wet-nursing industry varied enormously by region and whether the child had been placed with the nurse by parents, by a private bureau, or by the office of public assistance. See discussion in Rollet-Echalier, *La Politique à l'égard de la petite enfance*, pp. 37–48.

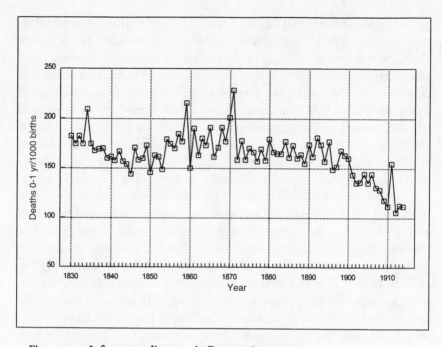

Figure 5.1.   Infant mortality rates in France, 1830–1914
  Source: Brian Mitchell, *European Historical Statistics* (New York, 1978), 39–46.

after the Roussel Law went into effect. Peaks in 1834, 1859, and 1911 were
the result of extremely hot summers, which increased the risk of infant
mortality from gastrointestinal ailments and contaminated milk. The extreme peak in 1870–71, of course, was caused by the dislocation resulting
from the Franco-Prussian War, the siege of Paris, and the repression of
the Commune.

Certain infant populations were particularly vulnerable, and officials
knew this long before Roussel began his campaign to regulate the wet-
nursing industry. In 1835, the Statistique Générale published a table on
abandoned children in the state's care, clearly showing how many infants
did not survive their consignment to a wet-nurse. To cite a few examples
taken from the table: out of 7,953 foundlings or orphans admitted to the
hospice system in the Dordogne between 1824 and 1833, 1,256 (16 percent) reached the age at which they were allowed to leave on their own,
2,445 (31 percent) were released into the custody of their parents or a
benefactor, and 2,586 (33 percent) died while in the care of a nurse. In
Calvados, out of a total of 7,649 children admitted, 1,002 (13 percent) at-
tained the exit age, 1,157 (15 percent) were released to the care of their parents or a guardian, and 2,842 (37 percent) died while in the custody of a

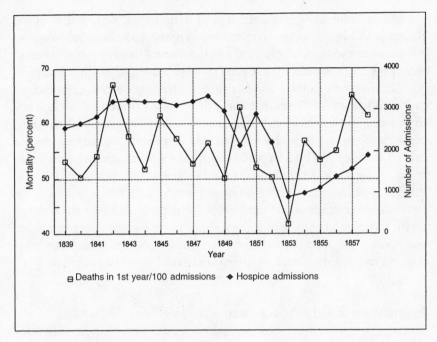

Figure 5.2. Mortality of Parisian Foundlings, 1839–58 (registered by the Foundling Hospital and subsequently wet-nursed)

Source: Catherine Rollet-Echalier, *La Politique a l'égard de la petite enfance sous la IIIe République* (Paris, 1990), 46.

Note: The decline in admissions from 1853 to 1858 resulted from a reform aimed at reducing abandonments.

nurse.[22] Figures from the Paris Foundling Hospital revealed that mortality rates for infants in their first year dipped below 50 percent only once between 1839 and 1858, and then only because of an administrative reform that temporarily reduced the number of admissions to the hospital (see Figure 5.2). The Foundling Hospital generally sent these babies to paid wet-nurses in the countryside, and their high mortality demonstrated the vulnerability of this marginalized group in French society, the "illegitimate" children of unmarried mothers and the poor. It was statistics similar to these that led Louis-René Villermé to write in 1838 of the foundling hospitals, "Here we allow abandoned children to die at public expense."[23]

22. *Documents statistiques sur la France, publiés par le Ministre du Commerce* (Paris, 1835), p. 36.
23. Louis-René Villermé, "De la mortalité des enfants trouvés considérée dans ses rapports avec le mode d'allaitement, et sur l'accroissement de leur nombre en France," *Annales d'hygiène publique et de médecine légale* 19 (1838), p. 39, cited by Rollet-Echalier, *La politique à l'égard de la petite enfance*, p. 45.

Despite these well-publicized figures dating back almost fifty years, Roussel and his supporters in the 1870s were successful in presenting the reform of the wet-nursing industry as the natural outcome of a new and recent spirit of cooperation between the legislature and medical researchers. According to Roussel and his supporters, only official ignorance of the insufficiency of "maternal surveillance" had prevented such a law from being enacted before. In fact, administrative awareness of the dangers of wet-nursing dated back to the mid-eighteenth century and in the case of abandoned children placed with nurses by municipal authorities at least as far back as the 1830s. Roussel was certainly correct in claiming that his law marked a turning point in French protective legislation, but he was disingenuous about the level of public awareness on the issue of infant mortality. People had known about these statistics for some time, but because of enduring beliefs in familial autonomy, it had not been possible to imagine official intervention to deal with the problem.

Preserving Family Autonomy

Examples of official indifference to the plight of infants are not difficult to find in the literature of public administration in early nineteenth-century France. In fact, some writers went so far as to justify this indifference as purposeful, claiming that the lives of infants were actually worth less than the lives of productive adults. By the 1860s and 1870s, however, this indifference to vulnerable infants had turned into its opposite—an overwhelming imperative to administer to the special needs of this particular group in the population. For this transformation to take place, the private sphere of paternal authority had to become an object of public scrutiny.

In the early years of the Restoration, Dr. Clément Gabriel Prunelle cited the work of Jean-Baptiste Say, who suggested that each adult represented the sum of all the capital invested for his or her upbringing. Following this logic, Prunelle claimed that "the loss of an infant is hardly detectable, while the death of a man who has achieved the age of sixteen simultaneously destroys the capital accumulated on his head, and the profit that this capital was on the verge of producing."[24] The official attitude among members of the administration accorded well with such opinions. In 1823, for example, a circular from the Administration générale des hôpitaux, hospices civils et secours in Paris stated that the primary goal of the municipal Bureaux des nourrices was to "procure nurses

---

24. Prunelle, *De l'action de la médecine*, pp. 22–23.

for the bourgeois and artisans of the city of Paris at a moderate price" and "to assure the payment of [the nurse's] salary." Only as an afterthought did the official add to the list the necessity of supervising "the choice of nurses and the preservation of the infants." The circular never addressed the problem of infant mortality specifically, and the health of the children was mentioned only in connection with the means of transporting babies to and from the countryside.[25]

As late as 1845 the prefect of the Seine actively intervened to prevent amending the laws in the interest of infant health. In that year, Dr. Joseph-Napoléon Loir submitted a proposal that would allow the declaration of birth to take place in the home in the presence of a municipal official, claiming that the obligatory trip to the registrar's office constituted an unacceptable threat to the newborn child's health.[26] The prefect of the Seine adamantly expressed his disapproval of Loir's proposal after consulting with the mayors in his jurisdiction, explicitly citing the autonomy of the family as his reason:

> The moral side of the question . . . concerns the effect produced by the inspector's presence in the home of women recovering from childbirth. The mayors are unanimous in pointing out the difficulties and trouble that would ensue following the application of this measure; to apply it, they claim, would be to violate both the spirit and letter of the law. Those whom the law is called upon to protect would be exposed to a dangerous abuse of privacy. Families would be troubled by the sight of a municipal official, and his presence alone would be enough to unveil certain facts that one might have great interest in keeping hidden from public view; finally, it might awaken a great deal of anxiety [*favoriser peut-être une sorte de perturbation*], and give birth to an evil no less great than that which one sought to avoid.[27]

25. AAP: Fossoyeux, Liasse 709(1), circular entitled "Instruction sur le service des préposés à la service des enfans placés dans les départmens par l'intermédiaire de la direction des nourrices," dated 1823. The only mention of infant mortality in this circular, which included six pages of instructions, stemmed from a complaint that the carts used to transport the babies were often encumbered with merchandise and baggage. The official commented, "As a consequence, a very great number of infants are brought back in a bad condition [*mauvais état*] and the number of deceased infants has been out of all proportion" (ibid., p. 6).
26. Joseph-Napoleon Loir's books and pamphlets concerning the *état civil* include *Du service des actes de naissance en France et à l'étranger, nécessité d'améliorer ce service* (Paris, 1845); *De l'exécution de l'Article 55 du Code Civil relatif à la constatation des naissances* (Paris, 1846); *Des sexes en matière d'état civil, comment prévenir les erreurs resultant de leurs anomalies* (Paris, 1854); and *De l'état civil des nouveau-nés au point de vue de l'hygiène et de la loi* (Paris, 1854). The first two pamphlets listed above can be found in AdP: ser. VD6 0015, n. 2.
27. "Observations du Préfet de la Seine, présentées au Conseil général du département dans sa session de 1846," copy included in a letter from the Prefect to the Mayor of the 1st Arrondissement of Paris, dated 4 September 1847, AdP: VD6 0015, no. 2.

The prefect then ridiculed Loir's plan, suggesting ironically that a service for home baptisms should be established because churches were even more damp and chilly than the municipal registrar's office.

Neither the prefect nor the mayors of Paris's twelve districts opposed measures that addressed infant health in principle—he even cited wet-nursing as a more pressing problem than the registering of births at the Hotel de Ville. He chose instead to point to a "moral" dimension of the question, in which the interest of the child had little significance separate from the interest of the family itself. The presence of an observer could not "protect" the child if it threatened the autonomy of the household. In matters of such domestic intimacy, the intrusion of the state could only be unseemly and give rise to uncomfortable ambiguities in the role of the state as the guardian of paternal authority. The embarrassment of the administration in the presence of the mother was underscored by the almost inevitable turn of phrase that concluded the prefect's opinion— his concern that an ill-advised administrative invasion of the home might "give birth to an evil no less large than that one had sought to avoid." It is as if the prefect imagined a sordid ménage à trois, substituting the state for the father in the conjugal bed, with monstrous consequences.[28]

For the prefect, the danger lay in crossing the boundaries between the public interest and what needed to remain private, the domestic scene, the site of the birth, the pain of the mother. The prefect's opposition to Loir's proposal rested on a gendered conception of state power, which saw itself as congruent with the paternal authority of the husband over his wife and family. Precisely because of their structural similarities, there could be no question of allowing one to impose on the other. Protection of the child by the state would supplant the duty to protect that fathers possessed under the Civil Code, thus threatening the integrity of the family as a social institution.

To win support for his cause, Loir refused to engage the issue of paternal authority directly. He concentrated instead on the urgent need for state action to protect newborn infants. Citing recent developments in hygiene which emphasized the infant's vulnerability to environmental

28. The allusion to the "monstrous" is not as fortuitous as it may seem. Loir himself, in his pursuit of precision and perfection for the administration of the *état civil*, wrote extensively on the problem of identifying the sex of the hermaphrodite for the purposes of the birth certificate. For example: "It would be sufficient that the mayors be advised to be on the alert for exceptional cases, and to identify them in the birth certificate . . . by the denomination "Doubtful Sex" [*Sexe Douteuse*], and to place in the margins of the register the initials S.D. . . . If from this formality there must result some slight prejudice for the individual who is its object, there would be at least the immense advantage of preventing much more serious circumstances." It is left to the reader to wonder just what these more serious circumstances could be. See Loir, *Des sexes en matière d'état civil*, p. 28.

factors, he wrote that newborn infants in cities did better than in the countryside because they were "generally less exposed, and better protected against the effects of the air" when taken to church for their baptisms.[29] Loir also elaborated on an idea that was to have great resonance in the work of early demographers concerned with infant mortality: the progressively smaller and smaller periods of life that were held to be of utmost importance in understanding the vulnerability of newborn children. In his major work, published in 1854, Loir wrote, "Existence in a newborn is counted by hour, by day. For them hours have an importance just as large as months and years for other ages."[30]

Loir's work was soon reinforced by Bertillon's research, and Villermé lent the prestige of his position at the Académie de médecine to the campaign.[31] By the 1860s, Bertillon's, Villermé's, and Loir's opinions had won adherents both among the administration and from Alexandre Mayer's Société protectrice de l'enfance, a private charity organization founded in 1866. In the spring of 1867 Mayer's society addressed a petition to the Senate, and in December another was sent to the prefect of the Seine; both supported Loir's proposal to allow for the declaration of births in the home.[32] These petitions were followed in January 1868 by similar opinions from the Académie de médecine.

On 12 November 1868 the mayor of the seventh arrondissement of Paris wrote in a letter to the prefect that "the arguments long put forth in order to demonstrate the necessity of declaring births in the home no longer seem contestable."[33] The prefect agreed, and his decree combined the old administration of death certificates with the new service of declaring births in the home into one bureau: the *médecins de l'état civil*. These doctors, as municipal employees, were charged with the dual responsibility of verifying deaths and witnessing the declarations of birth in the home on the parent's request. Charles Monot, a doctor who wrote extensively on the problem of infant mortality, noted that the minister of interior's instructions on the matter did not even mention the question of privacy or paternal authority. As if to complete the symmetry involved

29. Loir, *Du service des actes de naissance*, pp. 17–18.
30. Loir, *De l'état civil des nouveau-nés*, p. 60.
31. Louis-René Villermé wrote that it was impossible to exaggerate the importance of focusing "the attention of public functionaries and legislators on the irregularities which exist in the administration of birth certificates, and the necessity of protecting with greater efficacy the lives of newborns." See Villermé's "Notice," appended to Loir, *Du service des actes de naissance*, p. 23.
32. The Senate petition was sent on 24 May 1867 and that of the prefect of the Seine on 9 December 1867. See discussion in Charles Monot, *De la mortalité excessive des enfants pendant la première année de leur existence, ses causes, et des moyens de la restreindre* (Paris, 1872), p. 29.
33. Letter from mayor of the seventh arrondissement to prefect of the Seine, 12 November 1868, AdP: VD6 1503, no. 12.

in this reversal of opinion, Monot pointed to church baptisms as an "incontestable cause of mortality" and sincerely expressed the wish that this unfortunate practice would also come to the attention of the administration.[34] Armand Husson, the director of the administration of public assistance in Paris, gave Monot reason to hope, writing in 1866, "The question of infant mortality is not only a humanitarian question; it is a veritable question of state."[35] By the 1860s, then, Loir's campaign had succeeded. The priorities of government on the issue of the health and welfare of infants had changed, and the state was no longer seen as a threat to the private realm of the family. Simultaneously, regulating the wet-nursing industry became a central question for French doctors, hygienists, and local officials.

MATERNAL RESPONSIBILITY

As the Parisian administration changed its mind about the wisdom of Loir's proposals, a new current of medical literature focused on the problem of infant health. Two themes in this literature seem to have been particularly well-received by Roussel and his supporters in 1874, and both had their origins in Bertillon's 1858 paper in the Académie de médecine: first, a meticulous and empirically based attention to the environmental factors that influenced infant health and mortality; and second, the failure of French women to breast-feed their own children. These two themes were intricately connected, for as the medical experts paid more and more attention to the environmental factors that caused high mortality, they placed an increasing emphasis on the maternal body as the key element in a healthy infant's environment. The discussion, therefore, imperceptibly blended a scrupulous practice of empirical observation with an equally careful idealization of the good mother. Such a formulation made it unnecessary to probe the complex web of social and economic practices that might have driven a woman to put her infant out to nurse or become a nurse herself. On the contrary, Roussel and his supporters posed the question of infant mortality almost entirely in the context of maternal responsibility and maternal failure.

In the literature that followed Bertillon's 1858 paper, wet-nursing represented only one point in a wide spectrum of maternal neglect, encom-

34. Monot, *De la mortalité excessive des enfants*, pp. 32–33.
35. Armand Husson, *Discours sur la mortalité des jeunes enfants* (Paris, 1866), p. 6. The phrase became a catchword for reformers writing on infant mortality. See the identical wording used by Monot in *De la mortalité excessives des enfants*, p. 13.

passing common practices such as bottle-feeding and the substitution of broth for milk, as well as the extremes of abandonment and infanticide. André-Théodore Brochard, a medical inspector for the Direction des nourrices, published two studies of the effects of wet-nursing on the health of infants in 1866 and 1867 and followed them soon after with a study of maternal breast-feeding and its importance to the child's survival.[36] Brochard claimed that for some categories of children, especially those placed through private nursing bureaus, the mortality figures approached 90 percent, and he recommended the abolition of all such private bureaus, which he held responsible for the worst abuses. Dr. Charles Monot sent a report to the Académie de médecine in 1866 on infant mortality in the Morvan region of Burgundy.[37] He too pointed to astonishingly high rates of infant mortality in rural areas.

Both Brochard and Monot stressed the role of maternal neglect in contributing to high infant mortality rates and extolled the virtues of breast-feeding by the mother. In a piece that appeared in 1868, Brochard, for example, attempted to demonstrate that "maternal breast-feeding [was] a natural law which results from the structure of women [*l'organisation même de la femme*]."[38] He wrote that "lactation is the physiological complement of parturition; the mother must, in consequence, nurse [her child] in the interest of her own health."[39] For Brochard, the mother's body testified to her own biological destiny:

In the woman, the breasts are situated in the anterior and superior section of the chest. The result of this is that a mother cannot give suck to her child without taking him in her arms, without giving him an attentive eye; she senses in this way his needs. In nursing, she converses with him through the gaze, and by this mute and loving language she excites and develops his intelligence. Thus placed, the newborn searches the maternal breast with his little hands, and by these slight and soft frictions he simultaneously aids the flow of milk and the suction. Finally, one of the breasts is located in the precordial [*sic*] region so that the mother cannot nurse her

36. Dr. André-Théodore Brochard made his reputation for his work during the cholera epidemic of 1849. Subsequently he became a doctor for the administration supervising the wet-nursing industry in Paris and an inspector of *crèches*, small centers for child care in urban areas. His published works included *De la mortalité des nourrissons en France* (Paris, 1866), which won the Montyon prize; *De l'industrie des nourrices dans la ville de Bordeaux* (Bordeaux, 1867); and *De l'allaitement maternel étudié aux points de vue de la mère, de l'enfant et de la société* (Paris, 1868). In addition to his publications on the problem of infant mortality, he edited a journal entitled *La Jeune Mère ou l'éducation du premier âge.*
37. Charles Monot, *De l'industrie des nourrices et de la mortalité des petits enfants* (Paris, 1867).
38. Brochard, *De l'allaitement maternel*, p. 4.
39. Ibid., p. 4.

child without pressing him to her heart and without teaching him, smiling, to know and love her.[40]

Of course, such sentimental depictions of breast-feeding served a specific function in a work devoted to depicting the terrible effects of the wet-nursing industry on French society. The child's earliest education occurred at the breast, and the abdication of this moral responsibility by the mother not only threatened the child's life but loosened the bonds that held the family together.

The mother was not only the constituent element of the child's physical environment, she was also the vehicle for transmitting the physiological traits that marked the infant as a member of the family. Brochard contended that milk was "modified blood . . . a humor." [41] Wet-nursing thus interrupted and distorted the exchange of hereditary material, tainting the child and diluting the bloodline. "How many families in the world whose blood, pure until that moment, is thus altered forever!" exclaimed Brochard, adding, "This fear alone should make all those women who confide their newborn to a mercenary nurse tremble." [42] In his 1872 work, *De la mortalité exessive des enfants*, Monot exploited the same anxieties, writing, "Do not forget, Madame, that the first caresses of your child, the first words that he mouths [*bégaye*] are not for you, but for another. It is only by the force of time and labor that you will transplant, or graft onto his soul, this love that he should have drawn from your breast." [43]

Brochard's depiction of mother's milk as blood, and much of the rhetoric of his *De l'allaitement maternel étudié aux points de vue de la mère, de l'enfant, et de la société*, clearly served to exploit a very masculine set of fa-

40. Ibid., p. 13. Brochard's depiction of maternal breast-feeding was duplicated by Dr. Pierre-Auguste Despaulx-Ader, president of the medical committee of the Crèche of the Madeleine in Paris. Despaulx-Ader wrote that "woman . . . carries on her chest the secreting organs of milk, which nature has given her less as ornaments, less as embellishments of her body, than for utility. . . . In placing the organs of lactation on the front of a woman's chest, God wanted the child to begin his apprenticeship for life in the arms of his mother, cheered and reassured by her benevolent and encouraging smile; he wanted this little newborn being to be raised under the caressing and joyful gaze of she who has fulfilled the highest and sublime function for which she has been made" (*De l'allaitement maternel au point de vue de la mère, de l'enfant, de la société* [Paris, 1868], pp. 8–9).
41. Brochard, *De l'allaitement maternel*, p. 23.
42. Ibid., p. 23. Brochard's anxiety over this issue led him to recommend that a child of a consanguineous marriage should never be breast-fed. Because these children were nearly always "scrofulous, deaf-mutes, or idiots," Brochard believed that one must "diminish as much as possible the hereditary influence of the mother with a foreign milk, instead of increasing it to a greater power with lactation" (ibid., p. 126).
43. Monot, *De la mortalité excessive des enfants*, p. 23. Monot explicitly made the connection to degeneration in his claim that nurslings "will transmit by heredity the bad germ which circulates in their veins, they will spawn in turn only feeble rejects, without force and vigor" (ibid., p. 44).

milial concerns.[44] His choice of title appears ironic—the book had very little to do with mothers' and children's points of view, revolving instead around paternal anxieties of family purity, inheritance, and class contamination, even hinting at castration, as in the following horror story recounted by Brochard:

> An inhabitant of M . . . had a son which he confided to a nurse from the country. Several months later, he gathered together at his table his relatives and friends, and in order that the party be complete, he had the nurse come with his child. The happy family was ecstatic about the healthy glow of the latter, and at their request, the father ordered the nurse to remove his wrappings in order that they might judge the beauty of his body. The nurse accomplished this with some embarrassment, but she had to acquiesce. What a surprise for the unhappy father! His son . . . was a girl![45]

Brochard claimed that in his work as an inspector for the Direction des nourrices he had often witnessed nurses who, after arriving together in their villages from the trip to Paris, became momentarily confused as to which baby was theirs. To his consternation, they merely took the closest one, saying, "Bah! If I am mistaken, his father will accept him anyway."[46]

The discussion of Brochard's and Monot's work in the Académie de médecine further publicized the issue of infant mortality in the wet-nursing industry, although at least one member claimed that the academy was only responding to increased awareness of the issue among the general public.[47] Some of the credit for increasing public awareness must also go to Alexandre Mayer, the infant health activist whose Société protectrice de l'enfance had been so helpful to Loir's campaign to declare births in the home.[48] At the time of its first meeting in Paris in 1866, Mayer's

---

44. Michel Foucault pointed out that the bourgeoisie in the nineteenth century made biological notions of heredity into a means for drawing social hierarchies in much the same way that the aristocracy used genealogical tables in earlier periods (*History of Sexuality*, pp. 124–25). Robert Nye developed this idea into an argument concerning notions of familial honor and "normal marital sexuality" as they were represented in French medical literature of the period. See Nye, "Honor, Impotence, and Male Sexuality in Nineteenth-Century French Medicine," *French Historical Studies* 16 (1989): 51. See also Nye, *Masculinity and Male Codes of Honor in Modern France* (New York, 1993).
45. Brochard, *De l'allaitement maternel*, p. 88.
46. Ibid., p. 86.
47. Brochard quoted the surgeon and obstetrician Alfred Velpeau, who remarked: "The question of wet-nurses and the mortality of nurslings is in the air at the moment; public opinion is preoccupied with it; it is urgent that the academy discuss it in depth and draw the attention and solicitude of the higher administration" (*De l'allaitement maternel*, p. ix).
48. Alexandre Mayer, *Des rapports conjugaux considérés sous le triple point de vue de la population, de la santé, et de la morale publique*, 4th ed. (Paris, 1860); *De la création d'une société protectrice de*

society numbered 228 members. In the next few years his associates established similar groups in Brussels, Lyon, Metz, Bordeaux, Beauvais, and Le Havre, with membership nearing one thousand.[49] According to a notice circulated in 1869, the goals of the society were

1. To honor and to propagate [the spread of] maternal breast-feeding, which is so imperiously demanded by the voice of nature and by the interest of the mother, the child and the social order.

2. To preserve children at the moment of their birth from the many dangers that menace them when they are abandoned to nurses who carry them so far away that their parents cannot exercise sufficient surveillance on them.

3. To protect children in any circumstances against abandonment, negligence, ill treatment, or the immoral examples that they may be exposed to by those persons charged with watching them; in a word, all circumstances where they have need of protection.

4. To disseminate to families the most useful precepts of the physical and moral hygiene of children, and to favor their application in order to prepare future generations that are healthy in both body and mind.[50]

To fulfill these goals, Mayer's society set up a free service of medical inspection for parents who had sent their children to the countryside to nurse. Parents had only to register the address of the nurse at the society's office to receive every month a regular report on the health of their child.[51]

Mayer's society thus aimed to monitor the nursing child's physical environment, and in doing so its program conformed well with Bertillon's emphasis on causes of death that were extrinsic to the individual. Mayer's contribution was to make the mother's own milk the most important component of this environment. In his conception of the mother-infant relationship, the body of the mother had no integrity of its own; it existed

---

l'enfance pour l'amélioration de l'espèce humaine par l'éducation du premier âge (Paris, 1865); and *De la mortalité excessive du premier âge considérée comme cause de dépopulation et des moyens d'y remédier* (Paris, 1873).

49. Sussman, *Selling Mother's Milk*, p. 122.

50. "Notice," Société protectrice de l'enfance, 1869, AdP: VD6 1575, no. 3.

51. "Avis," Société protectrice de l'enfance, 1869, AdP: VD6 1575, no. 3. See also a similar "Avis" in VD6 1388, no. 3. Although it is unclear how many parents availed themselves of Mayer's service, the above dossiers contain complaints by members of the society that many parents did not seem to care enough to enlist the help of the inspection service.

for the child, not for itself. He had written of a woman's body that "atmospheric influences, temperature, and electricity act more powerfully on women than on men; woman has a more intimate relation with nature, *she belongs more to all; she is less distinct*." [52] This curious construction revealed how far reformers were willing to push the functionalist arguments for the "utility" of women's bodies: they would quite literally disappear as independent agents and dissolve into the realm of the social.

Invoking as they did the themes of maternal neglect, indifferent and uncaring nurses, and a woman's obligation to breast-feed her own children, the reformers' calls for action struck a deep chord among the assembly of doctors at the Académie de médecine. Dr. Félix Boudet, a member of the academy, recalled the galvanizing effect of Monot's work on infant mortality in Burgundy: "It burst on the scene like a sudden and terrible revelation, it provoked an explosion of pity and indignation and soon had conquered its place among the most pressing preoccupations of public opinion and the counsels of government." [53] Boudet's words convey the extent to which legislators conceived of infant mortality as a new problem, despite the long history of wet-nursing and a general awareness that large numbers of children had been dying for many years. The sudden revelation had nothing to do with knowledge about infant death, however. Boudet's shock was at the "discovery" that the problem could be blamed on French mothers. On his list of the causes of infant mortality, Boudet began with the weakening of "the sense of the primary duty of motherhood." "Maternal breast-feeding," he wrote, "has fallen into neglect: mercenary feeding, artificial feeding, and premature weaning [*l'alimentation prématurée*] have taken its place." [54]

In accordance with this new and belated sense of purpose, the academy proclaimed its conviction that infant mortality possessed an undeniable social dimension that justified a concerted response by the government. The doctors set up a permanent committee to discuss infant hygiene and issues related to the protection of children, and this body

52. Mayer, *Des rapports conjugaux*, p. 191. Emphasis added. Mayer explained this proximity which women bore to nature: "Woman is created and placed in the world, in order to perpetuate the species above all, and then to contribute, in the sphere determined by nature, to social life. She has qualities and faults that are proper to her; her instincts are more certain and her intelligence is less developed. Above all, she is mastered by her genital apparatus which means that she is not in full possession of herself—and is subject to a periodic function capable of modifying her moral being completely" (ibid., p. 253).
53. Félix Boudet, *Discussion sur la mortalité des jeunes enfants* (Paris, 1870), p. 5, cited by Monot, *De la mortalité excessive des enfants*, p. 6.
54. Boudet, *Discussion*, p. 32.

eventually presented a report containing its recommendations to the minister of the interior, Adolphe Forcade de Roquette, on 16 March 1869.[55] Although the work of this committee was interrupted by the Franco-Prussian War in 1870, its report provided Senator Théophile Roussel with a framework for the regulatory measures contained in the 1874 law.

To minimize the threat posed to the family by medical intervention, the reformers and members of the academy stressed a perceived homologous relationship between parental care and official medical supervision. Boudet declared that the problem of infant mortality was "essentially medical" and "inevitably linked to . . . protection and education."[56] He justified the academy's intervention by stating, "It is the Académie de médecine which, as the representative of the French medical community, must treat all general questions that concern the life and health of the great French family."[57] Dr. Pierre-Auguste Despaulx-Ader, an obstetrician and specialist in pediatrics who was also the president of the medical committee at the Crèche de la Madeleine in Paris, used the metaphoric relation between maternal care and hygiene even more pointedly: "When the first woman saw her firstborn lying naked and shivering on her knees, exposed to the influences of the surrounding airs . . . she was led by her tenderness to protect him and keep him from these dangers. That is the origin of medicine, and of its most important branch, hygiene."[58] In other words, the intercession of doctors and state officials could not be a challenge to families because such intercession was itself fundamentally familial.

The challenge to familial autonomy was very real, however, and reformers aimed this challenge directly at French mothers. In 1872, Alexandre Mayer declared that maternal breast-feeding should be made a legal obligation, writing, "The ideal that we dream of—I know by experience that one must have a certain courage to confess it—is obligatory breast-feeding by the mother [*allaitement maternelle obligatoire*]."[59] Mayer gave a speech to this effect in the National Assembly only one week after the

---

55. See Sussman, *Selling Mother's Milk*, p. 127.
56. Boudet, *Discussion*, p. 6.
57. Ibid., p. 3. Other writers insisted on the medical nature of the problem. Brochard claimed that the responsibility for inspecting nurslings should be confided only to doctors and not to "men foreign to medical science, who, despite their zeal and talent cannot appreciate the pathological facts to which they are a witness" (*De l'allaitement maternel*, p. 148).
58. Pierre-Auguste Despaulx-Ader, *De l'influence de l'hygiène sur le développement physique, moral et intellectuel de la première enfance* (Paris, 1866), p. 2.
59. Mayer, *De la mortalité excessive du premier âge*, p. 23.

suppression of the Commune.[60] Though his proposal never made it past the floor of the assembly, it is remarkable that Mayer was allowed to be heard at all, given the uncertainties of the moment and the tumult surrounding the government in the summer of 1871. In many respects, of course, Mayer's work was simply a rather unoriginal pastiche of a large medical and moral literature that had discussed the dangers of wet-nursing since the mid-eighteenth century.[61] But in the 1870s, against the background of demographic work such as that put forth by Bertillon, Mayer's discourse on breast-feeding focused attention on a new social dimension to infant death. Mayer himself saw no need to humor the "fanatics of individual liberty"[62] who were uncomfortable with the repressive aspect of his proposals. He found a legal justification for the suppression of wet-nursing in the Napoleonic Code, article 203 of which stated: "The spouses contract together, by the fact of their marriage, the obligation to feed, maintain, and raise their children." When he was called before the commission investigating Roussel's proposal for what would become the law regulating the nursing industry, Mayer repeated this point, claiming that the code made the practice of putting babies out to nurse illegal.[63] Despite Mayer's enthusiasm, obligatory maternal breast-feeding was the one aspect of his society's program that was not eventually adopted and taken over by administrators of the Third Republic.

Set against the backdrop of the 1870s, Mayer's seemingly extremist proclamations were in fact quite commonplace. Roussel's proposal came in 1873, less than three years after the defeat at the hands of the Prussian army, and as historians have well documented, in an atmosphere of intense anxiety about the form of France's government, the viability of its national culture, and the quality of its population.[64] The census of 1872, delayed because of the war, revealed that the decline in the birthrate,

60. In his speech, Mayer stated, "Of all European nations, it is France where the greatest number of mothers refuse the mission that nature has assigned them. In my mind this is the origin of our decline . . . I would like therefore that the law oblige the mother, in all cases where reasons of health provide no obstacle, to give her milk to the child she has brought into the world" (ibid., p. 24).
61. In this connection, see Morel, "Théories et pratiques de l'allaitement," pp. 393–427.
62. Mayer, *De la mortalité excessive du premier âge*, p. 26. Monot also attacked the defenders of individual liberty: "We love liberty as much as the next, but we will have none of a liberty that drives us to moral depravation, to the weakening of family bonds, to the physical degradation of our species, and to the death of 126,000 children" (*De la mortalité excessive des enfants*, p. 48).
63. "Extraits des Procès-verbaux des séances de la Commission," appended to Roussel, "Rapport," pp. 97–98, copy in APP: DB/63.
64. On the literature of national decline and anxiety about the working classes, see Susanna Barrows, *Distorting Mirrors: Visions of the Crowd in Late Nineteenth-Century France* (New Haven, 1981); and Robert Nye, *Crime, Madness, and Politics in Modern France: The Medical Concept of National Decline* (Princeton, 1984).

which first received widespread attention after the census of 1866, had continued unabated. When the demographers and public health officials combined these figures with the casualties of war, they painted an alarming portrait of the nation. Eventually, the statistical representation of decline became a common rhetorical device for social critics of many ideological persuasions.[65] Roussel was no exception, and he explicitly linked the question of population decline with a failure on the part of French mothers, asking:

> Can't one see the decline of births and the frightful mortality of certain categories of infants . . . as two related signs? Can one fail to recognize that the movement of *depopulation* is the all-too faithful measure of demoralization, since the effacement of the constitutive sentiments of the family and the weakening of the most vital and essential of these sentiments, maternal love, leads the list of causes of the downward movement of our population?[66]

By placing a failure of maternal love at the head of the list of the causes of depopulation, Roussel helped to lay the foundation for what would become a long and distinguished current of opinion among social reformers who sought to demonstrate that the roots of France's social malaise could be found in the feminine half of the population.

Together, the testimony of Bertillon, Brochard, and Monot in the Académie de médecine, and Mayer's work with the Société protectrice de l'enfance, served to create a crisis of national proportions where previously none had been perceived. Their work focused on and emphasized the mother's responsibility in high rates of infant death while simultaneously minimizing the socioeconomic factors that led mothers to resort to wet-nurses. A more sympathetic observer may have seen two classes of female victims in this economy: on one hand, a group of primarily urban women who were forced to give up their children in order to maintain

65. Armand Husson, an administrator at the office of public assistance, had already connected infant mortality to the question of a stagnating population in 1866, when he wrote: "Today, one cannot deny that the population, the primary strength of powerful nations, is diminishing in France or is remaining approximately stationary. Marriages are stricken in their fecundity: in previous times one counted 5 children for one marriage . . . today, hardly 3 are produced in each marriage for all of France, and in Paris one counts little more than 2 per household. But the danger does not lie in this situation without remedy. Among those children who die soon after birth there are a large number who would live if one could succeed in destroying the bad habits and the bad methods used . . . in the education of newborn infants" (*Discours sur la mortalité des jeunes enfants*, p. 25). On the transition between a concern with high mortality to a concern with declining fertility, see Charbit, *Du malthusianisme au populationnisme*, and Spengler, *France Faces Depopulation*, pp. 111–20.
66. Roussel, "Proposition de loi," p. 3. Emphasis in the original.

their wage-earning potential, and on the other a group of rural women obligated by poverty to neglect their own children while nursing an infant from the city. Instead, the medical observers saw only evidence of corruption and proof that French women had abdicated a role that both biology and society required of them.

An Unspoken Consensus

Given the complexity of the issues raised by the Roussel Law, the state's obligation to protect those unable to protect themselves, the autonomy of the family, and the inviolability of paternal authority, one might well ask why they did not receive more discussion on the floor of the National Assembly. These questions did not arise in the Assembly during the discussion of the Roussel Law,[67] however, because they had already been debated and provisionally resolved in the discussion of another piece of protective legislation, adopted on 19 May 1874, only seven months before the promulgation of the Roussel Law. This law sought to extend the limitations on child labor set by the law of 1841. It aroused a passionate debate about the freedom of industry, the right of the father to the labor of his children, the right of the child to the protection of the state, and, perhaps most important for the ensuing discussion of the wet-nursing industry, the desirability of regulating the employment of women outside of the home.[68] Like the Roussel Law, then, the child labor law contained an implicit confrontation between the state and paternal authority, but whereas the assembly came to a quick consensus as to the legitimacy of regulating commercial wet-nursing, it had a long and at times bitter debate on the question of protecting women's and children's labor.

67. The Roussel Law was passed with little discussion in the assembly (see speech by Chabaud La Tour in support of Roussel and his law, *Journal Officiel*, 16 December 1874, p. 8331). What little controversy existed was dealt with firmly by Roussel in committee. See, for example, his handling of the issue of the freedom of industry as it related to commercial wet-nursing: "If there is one industry which we must circumscribe, restrain, and surround with guarantees it is that of the agents for the placement of nurses and nurslings. . . . I affirm that if we want to make a good law, we must, from this moment, put out of our minds any preoccupation with the freedom of industry. The principle of liberty is dear to me; but there are exceptional situations where the best principles cannot be applied, and this is incontestably the case here" (Roussel, "Rapport," p. 64).
68. Joubert first proposed the law in the spring of 1872, and a report on his proposal appeared in the *Journal Officiel*, 30 May 1872, p. 3605. The first deliberation took place on 25 November 1872 (*Journal Officiel*, 26 November 1872, p. 7295); the second lasted from 22 January to 10 February (*Journal Officiel*, 23 January–11 February, 1873, pp. 475, 511, 538, 650, 668, 810, 835, 868, 908, 933, 961, 997); the third and final discussion was on 18–19 May (*Journal Officiel*, 19–20 May 1873, pp. 3351, 3381). The law was promulgated on 2 June 1874 (*Journal Officiel*, 3 June 1874, p. 3697). For further discussion of this law, see Weissbach, *Child Labor Reform*, pp. 181–204.

The original proposal for a law on child labor came from Ambroise Joubert-Bonnaire, a conservative representative from Maine-et-Loire.[69] Joubert sought to prohibit children from industrial labor until they reached the age of ten, at which time they could begin to work half-time (six hours per day). At thirteen, under the provisions of Joubert's proposal, the child could begin full-time work, but only if he could produce a certificate from a teacher demonstrating that he had completed primary school.[70] The law further stipulated the establishment of a special inspection service to monitor child labor in industry and the formation of local commissions in each department to ensure the application of the law's provisions. Finally, a national commission would report on the law's progress to the Ministry of Commerce. Roussel's Law on the regulation of the wet-nursing industry followed a similar plan in establishing its administrative procedures.

A parliamentary committee convened to discuss the Joubert proposal not only accepted its essential principles and intentions but extended its coverage to include the "protection" of women's employment. It also added a section that sought to prohibit women of all ages from night shifts and from work underground.[71] Joubert noted in a speech to the assembly that the committee was driven "by a natural inclination, to occupy themselves with the question of women's labor." This extension of the law was natural "because woman, too, is a weak creature [*un être faible*] who, in our social situation, is not always master of her destiny."[72] Joubert's characterization of protection contained the same gendered symmetry between the power of the father and the power of the state that the prefect of Paris cited in 1845 when rejecting Loir's proposal to register births in the home. By 1873, however, this symmetry served to reinforce the argument for state intervention. Both Joubert and the prefect claimed to be defending paternal authority, but whereas in 1845 such

69. The grandson of a Bonapartist deputy, Joseph-François Joubert-Bonnaire, Ambroise Joubert was a conservative member of the center-right faction in the National Assembly. He contributed little to the assembly beyond the child labor law under discussion here.
70. The final version of the law amended this age limit from thirteen to twelve, on the insistence of legislators who sought to protect the rights of industry. See "Loi sur le travail des enfants et des filles mineures employés dans l'industrie," Article 2, *Journal Officiel*, 3 June 1874, p. 3697.
71. "Rapport fait au nom de la commission chargée d'examiner la proposition de loi de M. Joubert, relative au travail des enfants dans les manufactures, etc., par M. Eugène Tallon, membre de l'Assemblée nationale," *Journal Officiel*, annex no. 1132, 30 May 1872, pp. 3605–13.
72. Joubert continued: "Whether unmarried or married [*fille ou femme*], [a woman] is always dependent on a father or a husband; and when those whom nature and the law have given her for protectors are lacking in forethought or affection, an oppression results which makes her its victim. If the legislator can come to her aid, he has the right and the duty [to do so], because society owes aid and protection to the weak and oppressed" (*Journal Officiel*, 26 November 1872, p. 7297).

authority was an inalienable right, by 1873 it contained a notion of responsibility. As the socialist Louis Blanc argued during the 1872 debate:
"Paternal authority is the most respectable thing in the world; but it is
precisely because it is worthy of all respect that one cannot consider it as
absolute. Here above all the exercise of a right is inseparable from the ac-
complishment of a duty."[73] In other words, the father's right to non-
interference became dependent on the fulfillment of his wife's maternal
obligations.

Other members of the assembly were more concerned about the ability of employers to fill their factories with workers than with the ideological underpinnings of republican familialism. They criticized the committee's decision to include women in the provisions of the law, claiming
that paternal authority should remain inviolate. A center-right representative from Indre, Pierre-Léon Clément, called it "an extremely grave innovation" that contradicted "very considerable principles: the freedom of
labor, the freedom of industry, and marital authority."[74] Attempting to
counter a familialist argument with one of his own, Clément argued that
seeking to regulate the work of a married woman who had "contracted
with the authorization of her husband" was an unacceptable breach of the
husband's autonomy.[75] Eugène Tallon, also from the center-right but one
of the law's staunchest supporters in the assembly,[76] replied by asserting
that the child's needs necessitated the regulation of the mother's work. "Is
it possble," he asked, "to occupy ourselves with the child for an instant
without thinking of the mother? . . . If you do not protect the mother,
how can you protect the child in this important moment of his existence?"[77] Though both Clément and Tallon could claim to be defending
the rights of the family—the former in the name of the husband as the
sole arbiter of his wife's activity and the latter in the person of the child—
their disagreement underscored the extent to which the family itself was
pictured as a divided sphere of interests, gendered hierarchies, and moral
obligations.

In the debate over the child labor law, Clément's opinion carried the

73. Louis Blanc, *Journal Officiel*, 26 November 1872, p. 7298. Of course, the political resonance of
such a speech extended beyond the family in 1872—there were still many monarchists in the assembly who would see in such arguments an attack on their aspirations for the fledgling national
government.
74. Pierre-Léon Clément, *Journal Officiel*, 24 January 1873, p. 513. Clément later voted against the
divorce law for the same reasons.
75. Ibid.
76. Eugène Tallon, a lawyer and representative of Puy-de-Dôme, sat among the Orléanist group
in the National Assembly. He also wrote the initial committee report on Joubert's proposal.
77. Eugène Tallon, *Journal Officiel*, 24 January 1873, p. 513.

day, at least as far as the issue of regulating women's labor was concerned, and Joubert and Tallon were forced to withdraw the relevant articles "protecting" women.[78] A last attempt by representative Louis Wolowski to reinstate the protection of women through an amendment also failed, despite his attempts to tie women's work outside the home to the disintegration of the family.[79] Among the ninety who voted in favor of Wolowski's amendment were Roussel, Alfred Naquet (who later sponsored the divorce law), Louis Blanc, and Léon Gambetta—the heart of the Republican left. Despite their failure, this group's support of what was essentially a conservative proposal emanating from the center-right demonstrates that a paternalist concern for the protection of women transcended the ideological boundaries that divided members of the assembly.

But if the attempt to subsume the category of women into the category of children failed, neither Joubert's initial supporters nor his republican allies had any problem in convincing the assembly that the interest of the child transcended its immediate family context. As Joubert put it, the question was simple. The "interest of industry and the honorable situation of a father who is obliged to send his child into employment" were both worthy of respect, but he concluded that "there is a more sacred interest, that of the child . . . which is that of society as a whole."[80] Against the value of the child as laborer, Joubert placed the value of the child as symbol of a new generation, of the future, of the progress of civilization itself. Clearly, acceptance of Joubert's argument entailed the acceptance of an ideological vision that transcended a purely economic definition of social or familial prosperity. Eugène Tallon gave voice to this transcendent vision in equally glorified rhetoric when he wrote, "Legislators would seriously misunderstand the duties of social guardianship [tutelle social] . . .

78. The only gender distinction that remained in the final version of the law pertained to night shifts, which were forbidden to all children generally before the age of sixteen, but for girls who worked in factories in particular until the age of twenty-one. See Article 4, Journal Officiel, 3 June 1874, p. 3697.
79. François-Michel-Raymond-Louis Wolowski, a veteran of the Polish struggle for independence, became a naturalized French citizen in 1834 after being sentenced to death in his native country. A professor of industrial legislation at the Conservatoire des arts et métiers and an enthusiastic supporter of General Cavaignac during the revolution of 1848, Wolowski was most notable as a republican economist for his opposition to Louis Blanc's labor reform proposals. Wolowski reentered political life in 1871, when he was elected to the National Assembly from the Seine. He sat on the center-left, and was named senator in perpetuity only eight months before his death. Wolowski explicitly reproduced the gendered conception of tutelle, which formed the basis of protective legislation when he stated in the assembly, "We dispose of woman without consulting woman; we dispose of her without conceding her any rights; we hold ourselves above her as her guardian. Let us exercise this guardianship in a manner that is generous and favorable to the condition of women" (Journal Officiel, 5 February 1873, p. 641).
80. Ambroise Joubert, Journal Officiel, 26 November 1872, p. 7296.

if they do not dream of safeguarding in the person of the child the most sacred interests of humanity."[81]

Roussel capitalized on this point when his law came up for consideration. Representative Jean-Baptiste Godin[82] gave him his opening by protesting that the withdrawal of the articles regulating women's labor left the child insufficiently protected: "It's only at the age of 10 that you begin to exercise your guardianship on the child. . . . What is he going to do before that age? What protection will you accord him?"[83] Significantly, Godin could see the protection of women only as it affected their children, and the protection of women for their own sake seemed not to occur to him. The terms of Roussel's wet-nursing law made this interpretation of protection clear: the state would take it on itself to protect the child where both previous law and the mother had failed.

Roussel was more successful with his law regulating the nursing industry because, although the assembly was divided on the issue of protection and the reach of the state, there existed a wide consensus on the social danger in allowing women, especially women with children, to engage in employment outside the home. Even those who had argued against Wolowski's amendment tended to agree that such practices were destructive to family life. The connection of women's employment to the wet-nursing industry was never openly discussed, but neither was it ever in doubt. Representative André Prétavoine, an outspoken defender of the rights of industry and a holdover from the Bonapartist regime,[84] had posed

81. Eugène Tallon, *Journal Officiel*, 30 May 1872, p. 3605. Even among allies, however, the family proved to be a sticky subject, with all sides struggling to occupy the moral high ground. Roussel, for example, submitted an amendment that indicated how far into the family he would have liked to see his legislation go. Article 1 of the Joubert proposal stipulated that the law sought only to protect those children who worked "outside of the family" ("Projet de loi," *Journal Officiel*, 30 May 1872, p. 3613). Roussel's amendment added the words "or even within the family, when [the child] takes part in work defined by the official nomenclature of industry as insalubrious or dangerous" (*Journal Officiel*, 23 January 1873, p. 485). Tallon himself took the opportunity to protest against Roussel's excessive zeal, saying, "We must not, and we do not want to intervene between father and child; we cannot say to the father that you cannot employ this child in your home. In reality that would be to expel the child from under the paternal roof . . . And as for intervention in the family, allowing inspection to penetrate to its heart, provoking the denunciation of the father to the son, of the mother to the husband, is that possible?" (ibid., p. 486). The assembly shouted out its disapproval, and Roussel's amendment was voted down.
82. Jean-Baptiste André Godin, former mayor of Guise and a left republican representative of Aisne in the National Assembly, had founded a cooperative familistère on Fourierist principles in his hometown. Associated with his extensive ironworks and heating stove factory, Godin's cooperative included six hundred lodgings, stores, a restaurant, library, gardens and fields, both primary and vocational schools, a nursery, and retirement programs.
83. Jean-Baptiste Godin, *Journal Officiel*, 30 January 1873, p. 669.
84. André-Germain-Casimir Prétavoine, representative from Eure in 1871, owed his political career to the Bonapartist administration that had appointed him mayor of Louviers in 1851. He continued to support the cause of the fallen Empire until he retired from politics in 1875.

the problem in somewhat guarded terms. "The truth is," he wrote, "that whenever the wage that enters the house of the worker is not sufficient to allow the wife to devote herself exclusively to the care of its interior, it is a great misfortune. The domestic foyer is troubled, and the peace of the household is menaced."[85] This consensus on the subject of women's labor lay behind the lack of controversy which the Roussel Law raised in the assembly. If paternal authority still stood as an obstacle in the minds of some legislators to the extension of state power, there was little disagreement that maternal responsibility was a different matter altogether.

In late nineteenth-century France, political talk about the family served a specific ideological function: it bound the natural world, with its ineluctable laws of death, reproduction, and renewal, to the social universe of French families. Because the heterosexual union of man and woman was perceived to be both the most "natural" of relationships and the most fundamental unit in the "social" organization of the French nation, the republican defenders of the family could claim nature as an accomplice in their plans for national regeneration. At the same time, however, the accumulated evidence of families in distress, of working women who were forced to send their infants out to nurse, created an anxiety-ridden paradox for republican social reformers. Unable to see the existence of the wet-nursing industry as the result of socioeconomic factors that left working women little choice, Roussel and his supporters could only interpret the evidence for infant mortality as signs of maternal irresponsibility, of nature gone awry.

By focusing on the mother's responsibility in the high rates of infant death, observers such as Brochard, Monot, and Mayer opened the way for Roussel to resolve this anxiety through increased state involvement in the lives of French families. By the 1860s, a growing proportion of lawmakers and reformers had come to expect more from the state in its supervision of commercial wet-nursing than a simple guarantee of the essentially free economic transaction between parents and nurses. No longer primarily concerned with the guardianship of a sphere of paternal authority, the officials at the end of the Second Empire and the beginning of the Third Republic chose to "protect" a different set of relations within an idealized vision of the family, those between the mother and child. Claiming that the nursing industry consisted of a demonstrably "perverse" exchange of money for mother's milk that harmed infants and disrupted the proper relations between mothers and their children, these re-

85. André Prétavoine, *Journal Officiel*, 6 February 1873, p. 869.

formers called on the government to act, even at the cost of diminishing individual liberty and familial autonomy. This imperative motivated the campaign for reform led by Brochard's and Monot's research and Mayer's Société protectrice and ultimately acted as the catalyst for the Roussel Law of 1874.

The Roussel Law became a precedent for the intercession of the state in the interest of the child. It opened the way for later legislation, such as the education laws of the early 1880s, the 1889 law on "moral abandonment," and the 1892 law on assistance to indigent pregnant women which protected the fetus. Having resolved the question of the family's autonomy in favor of state intervention, the champions of the Roussel Law established a principle that would resonate throughout the history of family policy during the Third Republic: "the right of the child to his mother."[86] In the end, however, the paradox of finding the French family's staunchest supporters among those who did the most to weaken any notion of family autonomy is not a paradox at all. Insofar as it was politically significant, the discussion was always weighted toward the collective needs of the social body. The power of republican familialism had little to do with the power of families.

86. Roussel, "Rapport," p. 7.

CHAPTER 6

"THERE ARE ONLY GOOD MOTHERS"

DECEIVING THE ORGANS

"There are good and bad wives," wrote Jules Simon in 1892, "[but] there are only good mothers. A bad mother, if such exists, is against nature. One would not know how to classify her, nor understand her."[1] For Simon, senator for life in the French Third Republic from 1875 to 1896, the connections between women, wives, mothers, and nature were both unambiguous and yet somehow disturbing. Good and bad wives, yes, he seemed to say, but not bad mothers, surely. A bad mother would not be a mother at all, perhaps not really a woman—how would we classify her? Simon's willful lack of comprehension, expressed in the face of the "bad mother, if such exists," can be understood only in light of his evident assumption that maternity defined the essence of womanhood. But Simon's intriguing blend of confident assertion and nagging doubt are signs of what Mary Poovey has termed "ideological work,"[2] an attempt to find soothing solutions to perplexing social problems in a comfortably defined natural realm. Simon's statement was not made entirely in good faith—he and his republican colleagues in the National Assembly had demonstrated their belief in "bad mothers" by supporting a law in 1889 which allowed the Administration de l'assistance publique to take charge of children who had been "morally abandoned" by their parents.[3] Simon's statement operated in another register—it was meant to reassure his readers that motherhood remained an undisputed social obligation in the face of a great deal of evidence that French women were choosing to have children in ever smaller numbers.

In the decades before 1914, the declining birthrate in France became

1. Jules Simon, *La Femme du vingtième siècle* (Paris, 1892), p. 189.
2. Mary Poovey, *Uneven Developments: The Ideological Work of Gender in Mid-Victorian England* (Chicago, 1988).
3. See Schafer, *Children in Moral Danger*, pp. 67–86.

the object of an intense controversy[4] (see Figure 6.1). Few who noticed the declining birthrate at the turn of the century could refrain from commenting on it. By 1910 one writer could observe, "One can hardly open a newspaper or a review without finding an article on depopulation, on its causes and its effects, and on the remedies which must be implemented."[5] Despite the cacophony of conflicting explanations and cures, however, one issue stood at the center of the debate: the relationship between a woman's reproductive capacity and the social and political aspirations of the nation. The good doctor Boutan, a character in Emile Zola's novel *Fécondité* (1899), captured this central theme when he warned the young hero, Mathieu Froment, of the dangers that he and his wife faced if they did not allow her to conceive:

> Think about it! . . . One cannot deceive an organ with impunity. Imagine a stomach which one continually tantalized with an indigestible lure whose presence unceasingly called forth the blood while offering nothing to digest. Every function that is not exercised according to its normal order becomes a permanent source of danger. You stimulate a woman, contenting her only with the spasm, and you have only satisfied her desire, which is simply the enticing stimulant; you have not acceded to fertilization, which is the goal, the necessary and indispensable act. And you are surprised when this betrayed and abused organism, diverted from its proper use, reveals itself to be the seat of terrible disorders, disgraces and perversions! . . . Listen well! My friend, here is the root of the problem. Nature deceived turns against you. The more one deceives, the more one perverts, and the more the population is weakened and degrades itself.[6]

Zola's metaphor of the stomach, coming from the mouth of Dr. Boutan, established a series of relations that carried the prestige of medical truths:

4. In the mid-1850s French economists began to realize that whereas the populations of England, Germany, and Italy were continuing to grow at astonishing speeds, the population of France had begun to slow its rate of growth appreciably. In all, from 1790 to 1914, fertility in France declined 57 percent, translating to an average annual decrease of 6 percent. In England, the crude birthrate reached a maximum of 35 births per 1,000 population during the period 1862–78 before beginning its slow decline. By comparison, the French birthrate peaked at 33 per 1,000 in the early decades of the century and fell continuously thereafter, with only a brief period of stabilization in the period 1860–80. Because of this diminished growth, France lost its predominant position in the ranking of European nations: from 1800 to 1940 the population of France increased by only 50 percent while during the same period Germany's population quadrupled and Britain's tripled in size. See Jean-Pierre Bardet, "La Chute de fécondité: Le constat," in *Histoire de la population française* ed. Jacques Dupâquier (Paris, 1988), 3:355; McLaren, *Sexuality and Social Order*, pp. 2–3; and Theodore Zeldin, *France, 1848–1945: Anxiety and Hypocrisy* (Oxford, 1981), p. 185. The classic work on this question is Spengler, *France Faces Depopulation*.

5. Robert Hertz, *Socialisme et dépopulation* (Paris, 1910), p. 3.

6. Emile Zola, *Fécondité* (1899: rpt. Paris, 1927), pp. 380–81.

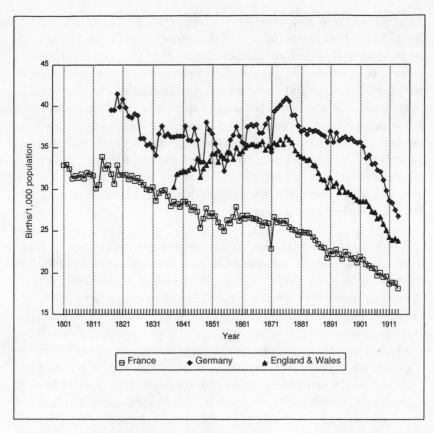

Figure 6.1. Birth rates in Europe, 1801–1914

Source: Brian Mitchell, *European Historical Statistics* (New York, 1978), 18–32.

organ is to function as woman is to reproduction, and hunger is to the maintenance of the body as desire is to the maintenance of the species. These metaphors functioned by way of a subsidiary synecdoche—a tacit substitution of "woman" for "womb" was operative in the phrase "you stimulate a woman, contenting her only with the spasm." The ease with which the doctor moved from the level of organs to organisms and the condensation that this effected on the body of "woman" reduced the figure of "woman" to her sex and provided her life with an essential linearity, summarized in a progress toward fertilization. The move from the level of organisms to populations in the last sentence carried the moral further, establishing the bodies of women as repositories of future generations and linking their individual destinies with that of the species.

To the extent that Dr. Boutan's speech was about the social significance of individual actions, that is, the decision to use contraception, Zola offered the reader a gendered commentary on the question of individual agency in sexual matters. The transitive verbs used by the doctor have men as their subjects; "woman," and feminized terms such as "nature" or "organ," appear only as their objects, except in cases of obvious pathology, as in the sentence "Nature deceived turns against you." Contraception, by eliminating the necessary connection between the satisfaction of feminine desire and reproduction, threatened to disrupt the natural order that constituted men as active subjects and women as passive objects. The "permanent source of danger" alluded to by Dr. Boutan arose from the possibility of a sexual and ultimately social agency for women outside the conventional realm of motherhood.

Dr. Boutan's speech to Mathieu invoked a structural logic that could conceive of a woman's body only in terms of her reproductive capacity. In turn, Zola's doctor could consider reproduction itself only in the context of its significance for the collective population.[7] This series of linkages, which established female bodies as the crucial vehicles for the continued survival of the nation, lay behind much of the writing on fertility decline in late nineteenth-century France. The influence of this thinking can be seen in the wide range of remedies that natalist reformers proposed to stem the process of "depopulation" in the decades leading up to World War I: encouragement of maternal breast-feeding,[8] assistance to mothers (both married and single), the regulation of women's employment, mandatory maternity leaves for pregnant women,[9] abrogation of the divorce law,[10] penalties for unmarried adults, fiscal incentives for large families,[11] and increased penalties for abortion and the sale of contraceptive de-

7. Of course, Zola's *Fécondité* is only one example of a widespread preoccupation with questions of female agency in nineteenth-century French literature. Naomi Shor asserts that "what seals the degradation of the feminine in nineteenth-century French fiction is the devastating fact that the post-revolutionary female protagonist is consistently deprived of the most minimal attribute of subjecthood" ("Unwriting *Lamiel*," in *Breaking the Chain: Women, Theory, and French Realist Fiction* [New York, 1985], p. 135).

8. See, for example, Alfred Legoyt, "L'Infécondité de la France," *Revue scientifique* ser. 2, 19 (1880): 218–27, 278–83, esp. 283.

9. For treatment of maternity assistance programs and aid to poor mothers in relation to anxieties about depopulation, see especially Fuchs, *Poor and Pregnant in Paris*, pp. 56–76. On the regulation of women's employment, see especially Stewart, *Women, Work, and the French State*. For contemporary examples, see Bonzon, *La Législation de l'enfance*, p. 236; and Legoyt, "L'Infécondité de la France," p. 282.

10. Attacks on the divorce law were common in the natalist literature, especially among conservative Catholic writers but also among the disciples of the Catholic sociologist Frédéric Le Play. See, for example, Georges Deherme, *Les Classes moyennes: Etude sur le parasitisme social* (Paris, 1912), p. 316.

11. See Paul Leroy-Beaulieu, *La Question de la population* (Paris, 1913), p. 481; Roger Debury, *Un Pays de célibataires et de fils uniques* (Paris, 1897), pp. 29–30; Emile Cheysson, "L'Affaiblissement de la natalité française—ses causes—ses remèdes," *La Réforme sociale*, 1 June 1891. On the plan submitted by deputy Cochery to treat children as a form of taxation, see the newspaper article "Impots et patentes," *L'Eclair*, 7 February 1897. The senator Edme Piot also described possible legisla-

vices.[12] With the possible exception of the divorce law, which was supported primarily by anticlerical republicans in the Chamber of Deputies, a broad consensus existed among political and civic leaders as to the desirability of such measures, all of which aimed at encouraging French women to produce and nurture more children.

In the decades leading up to World War I in France, therefore, the question of women's fertility became an ideological prism, refracting a multitude of ideas concerning the political order of contemporary society. Facing seemingly irrefutable evidence that the nation was no longer living as if sexuality was automatically linked to reproduction, alarmists echoed the words of Dr. E. Maurel, who in 1896 wrote: "In our epoch, one can say that . . . in legitimate as well as illegitimate sexual relations, fertilization is not the goal but the danger."[13]

Historians have usually seen the attention paid to the threat of "depopulation" as simply the domestic component of a renewed spirit of nationalism that followed the French defeat in the Franco-Prussian War of 1870. This interpretation has tended to accept the definition of the population crisis given by contemporary demographers and has treated the problem in terms of France's geopolitical status in the period leading up to World War I. Seen in this light, the measures put forth by the natalist lobby appear to be a rational response to a national emergency.[14] This refusal to examine the demographic literature for anything more than empirical data on the fertility decline has resulted in a general neglect of the important role played by population experts in connecting the theme of maternal responsibility to that of national decline. As we have seen in earlier chapters, the treatment of population questions for the first sixty years of the nineteenth century was dominated by a Malthusian orthodoxy that focused attention on the threat of excessive growth, precisely the opposite problem decried by the natalists. Given this about-face in the lit-

tive plans in his works *La Question de la dépopulation en France, le mal—ses causes—ses remèdes* (Paris, 1900), p. 45, and *La Dépopulation, enquête personelle sur la dépopulation en France* (Paris, 1902), pp. 19–27, 28–44. See also Victor Turquan, "Contribution à l'étude sur la dépopulation de la France," *Bulletin de la société d'anthropologie de Lyon* 21 (1902): 1–170, esp. 158.

12. Leroy-Beaulieu, *La Question de la population*, pp. 439–41.

13. E. Maurel, *De la dépopulation de la France, étude sur la natalité* (Paris, 1896), p. 12.

14. See Spengler, *France Faces Depopulation*. See also John C. Hunter, "The Problem of the French Birth Rate on the Eve of World War I," *French Historical Studies* 11 (1962): 490–503; and Richard Tomlinson, "The Disappearance of France, 1896–1940: French Politics and the Birthrate," *Historical Journal* 28 (1985): 405–15. Tomlinson points out that the association of a low birthrate with a military threat from Germany was "facile" but widely held. The importance of comparisons with German statistics is treated in Allan Mitchell, *The Divided Path: The German Influence on Social Reform in France after 1870* (Chapel Hill, 1991), esp. pp. 24–43.

erature on population in France, a closer examination of the role played by demographers in diagnosing the threat of fertility decline is warranted.

An alternative line of historical investigation has attempted to place the fertility debate in the larger context of competing ideologies that made up the landscape of social politics in fin-de-siècle France. These historians have pointed to the extent to which the natalist campaigns of the 1890s and 1900s were the result of simultaneous developments: the emergence of a new professional class of medical and population experts, the appearance of an organized feminist movement in France, the spread of knowledge about contraceptive techniques, and a general anxiety produced by the apparent break in the linkage between sexual practice and reproduction.[15] Angus McLaren has pointed out the important role played by doctors in framing the discussion of female sexuality and reproduction throughout the nineteenth century, asserting that "medical science was . . . used to substantiate rather than to challenge old sexual stereotypes."[16] McLaren explained this collusion between social convention and medical practice as a logical tendency of doctors to appeal to established moral standards at a time when their own profession was seeking greater recognition and legitimacy. Likewise, he traced the appearance of similar views on family limitation among Catholic writers and "secular moralists."[17] I would like to carry this discussion further by looking at the way "traditional attitudes" toward the family changed as they were recast in the language of political economy and population research. Did the prescriptions on *individual* behavior that were a part of such traditions carry over unchanged to the new discourses on the *collective* responsibility of mothers to produce children for the nation?

Karen Offen has examined the persistence of such "traditional" attitudes toward motherhood in her important article on the emergence of a family-oriented feminism in late nineteenth-century France, alongside the larger and more heterogenous natalist movement. Offen has argued that the depopulation controversy was inextricably linked to a larger debate concerning the role of women in society, and her work has demonstrated that the "woman question" was not simply an issue broached by feminists but was a preoccupation of a wide range of political and moral commentators, including socialists, republicans, and Catholics. From a wide range of sources, Offen traced the emergence of a moderate feminism in France that based its claims for women's citizenship on their so-

15. See Offen, "Depopulation, Nationalism and Feminism," pp. 648–76; and McLaren, *Sexuality and Social Order*.
16. McLaren, *Sexuality and Social Order*, p. 46.
17. Ibid., pp. 31–43, 65–76.

cial role as mothers. Because of its emphasis on the importance of family and maternity, this domestic ideology won support from many republicans, who saw in this position an effective bulwark against a conservative attempt to frame the "woman question" in terms of a defense of "traditional" patriarchal values.[18]

Ultimately, both the fertility debate and the discussion of feminism in late nineteenth-century France posed the same fundamental questions: What agency should women exercise in society? Should they be allowed to define themselves as citizens and subjects of the nation according to their own volition? Or has nature provided women with a maternal obligation that is independent of their desires and aspirations? That moderate feminists and republican natalists found similar answers to these questions, as Offen has argued, indicates how difficult it was for French feminists to base their claims for political participation on notions of individual right rather than the collective good. But this rapprochement between moderate feminists and natalists must also be seen as part of a widespread consensus in French society that the problem to be solved in the "fertility crisis" was the proper social dimension of motherhood. How did this consensus become so powerful? What possible constellation of ideas placed women's bodies and their relation to reproduction at the center of social debate in France?

The key to answering this question lies first in the literature of the population sciences. From the 1860s on, as the influence of Malthus on French population studies waned, a growing community of demographers, hygienists, and political economists began to examine the problem of natality. Participants in the fertility debate had access to an unprecedented amount of medical and demographic information, which framed the discussion. By examining the demographic literature that brought the fertility decline to public attention and identifying the extent to which these sciences participated in the characterization of motherhood as a woman's "natural" destiny, we can better understand how maternity came to be viewed as a social responsibility in late nineteenth-century France. How did the presentation of this information to the public influ-

18. Offen's view, however, that this familial strategy "became a vehicle not only for improving the status of women but also for subverting the sexual system from within" ("Depopulation, Nationalism and Feminism," p. 675) remains problematic. This argument implies that French feminists were aware of a possible contradiction between accepting their culture's valorization of motherhood and their own aspirations as independent subjects and citizens but were willing to accept this in exchange for short-term gains in the field of social policy. Certainly many women benefited from measures to protect maternity in the first half of the twentieth century such as family allowances and improved access to medical care. Nevertheless, these benefits in no way amounted to a subversion of the "sexual system." In many respects they perpetuated the view that having children was an obligation for all women.

ence the search for political and legislative remedies to the crisis? To what degree did the language of late nineteenth-century French population studies contribute to the inordinate amount of attention paid to the question of women and their reproductive capacity?

GENDER AND THE FERTILITY INDEX

In 1886, the pioneering French demographer Emile Levasseur wrote:

One can read the great facts of history and above all the economic history of France inscribed under the curve of births: natality carries the imprint of politics. The population, which lives off of wealth and prospers from labor and security is a sensitive thermometer, affected by all social, political and commercial crises. . . . Natality carries the imprint of history.[19]

When Levasseur claimed that natality bears the trace of history and politics, he meant of course that the birthrate reflected the social and political organization of the nation. But the statistics for measuring birth bore other traces as well. The statistical description of fertility in late nineteenth-century France carried with it a host of ideas about the place of men and women in the social order. Neither demography nor the demographers themselves were immune to the ideological visions of the family that were the culture's common currency.

Demographers of the period reinforced the presumed connection between womanhood and motherhood by defining the fertility index as a ratio between the number of births and the total population of women of childbearing age. Twentieth-century demography textbooks still find the ratio of births per female population superior to the crude birthrate (a simple ratio between births and total number of inhabitants regardless of sex) because, in the former, "the denominator is more nearly restricted to those actually 'exposed' to the risk of childbearing."[20] Nevertheless, the origins of the fertility index amounted to more than a simple story of rational improvement and greater empirical precision. The very notion of "childbearing age" or "reproductive years" places individuals in a tightly defined life-cycle trajectory that presumes motherhood as the biological destiny of women. Furthermore, the bearing of children could be conceived of as a "risk" to which women alone are "exposed" only in a culture that assumed that women have little or uncertain control over

19. Emile Levasseur, "Histoire de la natalité française," in *25ème anniversaire de la Société statistique de Paris* (Paris, 1886), pp. 103–4.
20. Donald J. Bogue, *Principles of Demography* (New York, 1969), p. 659.

their reproductive lives and that men play no measurably responsible role in the process that produces children for demographic observation. Both of these assumptions were taken for granted by the European statisticians who invented the measures for natality and fertility in the nineteenth century. They should not be accepted, however, as transhistorical and universally applicable descriptions of the objective reality of reproduction. On the contrary, historians should be aware that these empirical conventions for measuring fertility codified into scientific terms an asymmetrical relation of men and women to the process of reproduction that had implications far beyond the relatively limited scope of the population sciences. Understanding the extent to which a demographic conception of fertility contributed to the definition of this asymmetry will help clarify exactly what was at stake in the debate over the declining birthrate in late nineteenth-century France.

Historians of demography agree that the development of precise measures for fertility lagged far behind that of other demographic indices in the nineteenth century. Jacques and Michel Dupâquier have pointed out that the modern conception of the mortality table had been very nearly worked out by the end of the eighteenth century by Per Wargentin in Germany, Richard Price in England, and Emmanuel Duvillard in France.[21] In contrast, well into the nineteenth century, statisticians continued to measure births in relatively crude terms by modern standards: usually as the ratio of baptisms per marriage or alternatively as the number of inhabitants per baptism.[22] Such measures provided only very rough indications for the purposes of comparison because they did not take into account the differences in age structure or sex ratios which demographers now use to determine the differential fertility of given populations. As late as 1856 the Statistique Générale de la France defined the "fertility [*fécondité*] of the population" as the ratio between the number of births and the number of inhabitants, with its only caveat being to subtract stillbirths from the numerator.[23] Later writers would use the term *taux de natalité* for this ratio, reserving the term *fécondité* for figures arrived at by isolating the female population.[24]

21. Dupâquier and Dupâquier, *Histoire de la démographie*, pp. 250, 354.

22. Ibid., p. 365. An example of this tendency in the nineteenth century is Benoiston de Chateauneuf's index of births per marriage, which by modern standards was more precise than the crude birthrate but which did not attempt to limit the denominator to the female population. See L.-F. Benoiston de Chateauneuf, "Notice sur l'intensité de la fécondité en Europe au commencement du dix-neuvième siècle," *Annales des sciences naturelles* 9 (1826): 431–50, esp. p. 449.

23. *Statistique de la France, mouvement de la population en 1851, 1852, et 1853* (Strasbourg, 1856), p. xvii.

24. The Dupâquiers credit the English statistician William Farr for the invention of the natality index in 1870. (Dupâquier and Dupâquier, *Histoire de la démographie*, p. 369). See, however, the discussion of J. Matthews Duncan below.

The historian and demographer Hervé Le Bras has argued that nineteenth-century demographers were unwilling to treat the question of fertility because of "the mystery, the scandal, and the anxiety which surrounded contraception, particularly in a country such as France."[25] The Dupâquiers disagreed with Le Bras, asserting instead that the delay merely reflected "the insufficiencies of descriptive statistics: because no country, with the exception of Sweden, registered the age of the mothers at birth, demographic analysis lacked the materials necessary for its exercise."[26] By claiming that the development of precise measures of fertility was simply dependent on the technical collection of certain data, however, the Dupâquiers have omitted an important historical dimension of the problem: what conceptual change rendered the established procedures obsolete and necessitated the gathering of new information? Le Bras's argument, that developments in the population sciences were related to and obstructed by other protocols is more promising but needs to be pushed farther. The "mystery" surrounding the issue of sexuality, reproduction, and contraception in nineteenth-century France did more than obscure the logic of today's demographic procedures and delay their development. More important, powerfully charged preconceptions of sex, birth, and motherhood permeated the work of social scientists and played an important role in linking the particular circumstances of an individual woman's decision to have children with the needs and requirements of the national community. Ultimately, as the empirical techniques for measuring fertility were "perfected," reproduction came to be seen as a social responsibilty.

French demographers did little to improve the measurement of births in their own country and were forced to wait until J. Matthews Duncan, a Scottish gynecological surgeon, explored the issue in 1868. Duncan's *Fecundity, Fertility, Sterility and Allied Topics* and the series of papers he delivered to the Royal Society of Edinburgh between 1864 and 1867 established the standards for the measurement of fertility that were soon widely accepted across Europe.[27] Taking advantage of a short-lived revision of the Scottish census procedure in 1855 that provided more infor-

25. Hervé Le Bras, "Les Outils de la démographie," *Le Débat*, 8 January 1981, cited in Dupâquier and Dupâquier, *Histoire de la démographie*, p. 355.
26. Dupâquier and Dupâquier, *Histoire de la démographie*, pp. 355, 365. In support of the Dupâquiers one could cite Major Graham, William Farr's patron at the English General Register Office, who complained in 1845 that "the statistics of a country in which the age of a mother at marriage, and at the birth of her children, is not recorded, must always remain imperfect, and leave us without the means of solving some of the most important social questions" (quoted by J. Matthews Duncan, "On the Laws of the Fertility of Women," *Transactions of the Royal Society of Edinburgh* 24 [1867]: 288).
27. J. Matthews Duncan, *Fecundity, Fertility, Sterility and Allied Topics* (Edinburgh, 1868). See the discussion of Duncan in Dupâquier and Dupâquier, *Histoire de la démographie*, pp. 370–72. Dun-

mation than usual, including the age of mothers at the moment of giving birth, Duncan proceeded to measure the "Actual Fertility" of the "Female Population as a whole at Different Ages."[28] In doing so, he made an important distinction between the concept of "fertility" and that of "fecundity," and it was this distinction that explicitly connected the fertility index to a specifically gendered vision of population.

In his 1868 work, Duncan defined the distinction between "fertility" and "fecundity":

> By fertility or productiveness I mean the amount of births as distinguished from the capability to bear. This quality of fertility is interesting chiefly to the statistician or the political economist. When a population is the subject of consideration it does not even involve the capability of every individual considered to bear, nor even the conditions necessary for conception. By fecundity I mean the demonstrated capability to bear children, it implies the conditions necessary for conception in the women of whom its variations are predicated. This quality of fecundity is interesting chiefly to the physiologist and physician. In short, fertility implies fecundity, and also introduces the idea of number of progeny; while fecundity simply indicates quality without any superadded notion of quantity.[29]

In other words, "fertility" was a measurement of the number of children produced by a particular population with no regard to the circumstances attendant to any particular individual birth, whereas "fecundity" was an indicator of capacity, or reproductive potential. The former was useful when looking at populations; the latter was ultimately an attribute of individual women.[30]

Duncan's definition of "fertility" created the possibility of revealing the reproductive power of a given female population, without having to ac-

can's papers included "On the Variations of the Fertility and Fecundity of Women according to Age," *Transactions of the Royal Society of Edinburgh* 23 (1864): 475–90; "On the Laws of the Fertility of Women"; "On Some Laws of the Sterility of Women," *Transactions of the Royal Society of Edinburgh* 24 (1867): 315–25; "On a Lower Limit to the Power Exerted in the Function of Parturition," ibid., pp. 639–51. Later, Duncan examined the relation between female sexual pleasure and sterility, apparently convinced that women needed to experience orgasm, or at least sexual desire, to conceive. His statistical studies did not bear him out. See Laqueur, *Making Sex*, pp. 189–90.
28. Duncan, "On the Variations of the Fertility and Fecundity of Women," p. 476.
29. Duncan, *Fecundity, Fertility, Sterility and Allied Topics*, pp. 3–4.
30. In this respect, Duncan followed the strict delineation that had already been made between sciences of the social body and sciences of the individual body. See Foucault, *History of Sexuality*, p. 139. For comments on Foucault's "great bipolar technology" and its relation to the emergence of demography see Hacking, "Biopower," pp. 279–95.

count for the complicated circumstances under which any individual woman decided to bring a child to term. "Fertility" was a way of measuring the sum effect of these circumstances without having to pinpoint them exactly. Furthermore, his definition of "fecundity" implied that only a particular subset of these complicated circumstances was scientifically important: the physiological or biological conditions that allowed a woman to conceive. In other words, Duncan's distinction effectively effaced the individual woman's social and cultural context from the demographic equation, by default on the one hand, in the definition of fertility, and by exclusion on the other, in the definition of fecundity. At the individual level, Duncan perceived of reproduction as a biological problem. At the level of populations, fertility could be conceived of as the result of complex social and cultural factors, but his method of measurement effectively precluded a consideration of how this cultural context might be of significance to an individual woman's reproductive life. In the absence of an opportunity to discuss why individual women might choose not to have children (for reasons other than involuntary sterility), Duncan's definition was only too easily reversed: fertility implied fecundity, but fecundity also implied a responsibility to be fertile.

Duncan's distinction caused some confusion initially, but it was eventually adopted in some form by most writers on the subject.[31] Significantly, when French demographers adopted Duncan's terminology, they reversed the terms: "*fécondité*" was used to mean "fertility" and "*fertilité*" took the place of the English expression "fecundity." The instability between discussions of individual fecundity and collective fertility can be traced in one of the first French converts to Duncan's methods, Louis-Adolphe Bertillon.[32] In an article for the *Dictionnaire encyclopédique des sciences médicales*, entitled "Natalité" (1876), Bertillon both introduced Duncan's method of calculating fertility according to the female population and reversed his own vestigial Malthusianism. This article, whole-

---

31. Dupâquier and Dupâquier, *Histoire de la démographie*, pp. 372–73. In an earlier work, Duncan himself had been unclear about this distinction: "By fertility or productiveness I mean the amount of births as distinguished from the capability to bear. This quality of fertility or productiveness is interesting chiefly to the statistician or the political economist. It does not involve the capability of every individual considered to bear, nor even the conditions necessary for conception. By fecundity I mean the capability to bear children; it is measured by the number born, and it implies the conditions necessary for conception in the women of whom its variations are predicated. This quality of fecundity is interesting chiefly to the physiologist and physician" ("On the Variations of the Fertility and Fecundity of Women," p. 476). Here Duncan somewhat confusedly asserts that both "fertility" and "fecundity" are quantitative measurements that apply to populations as a whole, while at the same time implying that "fertility" is an attribute of groups but "fecundity" is an attribute of individual women.

32. See discussion of Louis-Adolphe Bertillon in Chapter 5.

heartedly natalist in both its tone and its conclusions, distinguished between "general natality," corresponding to what is now called the "crude birthrate," or the simple ratio of births per 1,000 inhabitants; "special natality," referring to the number of births per 1,000 women aged fifteen to fifty; and finally the "effective fertility of married women."[33]

In defining the fertility index, Bertillon compared it to the figure used for mortality. Each could be stated in terms of "that quotient obtained by dividing the number of times the given physiological act (birth or death) arises from the breast of those living beings which produce them. [*en divisant le nombre de fois les actes physiologiques étudiés (naissance ou mort) sont survenus par le nombre des vivants au sein desquels ils sont produits.*]"[34] My literal translation preserves the peculiar counterpoint set up by Bertillon's turn of phrase. The expression "*au sein de*" can mean "within," "at the heart of," "at the breast of," or even "within the womb of." Applied to mortality, the expression has a purely utilitarian function: deaths occur "within," or "at the heart of," a particular population. In the case of birth, the other "physiological act" in Bertillon's definition, the resonance of "*au sein de*" is clearly more than a simple prepositional phrase. Births occur "at the breast of"—or "in the womb of"—individual women's bodies. Bertillon's description thus served to reinforce a conflation between the language used to describe individual women and that used to characterize the reproductive potential of the nation's female population as a whole.

Later in the article, Bertillon gave a mathematical justification for the attention paid to female populations:

From the mathematical point of view, the probability or frequency of an event arises from the ratio between the number of observed events and the

33. Louis-Adolphe Bertillon, "Natalité," *Dictionnaire encyclopédique des sciences médicales* ser. 2, II (1876): 446–47. Bertillon's terms were *natalité générale, natalité spéciale*, and *fécondité effective des épouses*. Bertillon did not cite Duncan's work, and it is probable that he was introduced to the Scottish doctor's classification system through William Farr of the General Register Office in London. Bertillon's conversion can be dated as occurring between 1874 and 1876. In an 1874 work Bertillon insisted on emphasizing the dangers of high mortality, although he was certainly aware of declining fertility at this date. He wrote: "It is not by chance that I have chosen this subject [mortality]. Our fatherland is in need of workers and defenders; from all sides one hears complaints, not without reason, of our slow and feeble reproduction. But I think that before studying the conditions of increase . . . it is urgent to discover the causes of our devastation, and in a word, that it is better to conserve generations than to renew them" (*La Démographie figurée de la France*, p. 2).
34. Bertillon, "Natalité," p. 444. This definition was often repeated by other writers on the subject, although not always with the same turn of phrase resorted to by Bertillon in this example. See, for example, Alexandre Lacassagne, "La Natalité à Lyon," *Bulletin de la société d'anthropologie de Lyon* 6 (1887): 52–53; and A. Beaujon, "La Fécondité des mariages aux Pays-Bas et les causes de ses variations," *Journal de la Société de statistique de Paris* 29 (1888): 207.

total number of cases that can produce them. Now, the event in question is the bringing to term of a child, and because only women are apt to do so, the indication is to compare births to women alone.[35]

Bertillon chose to model the birthrate in terms of a frequency: a given number of births per women present in the target population. As he did so, however, he also asserted that these women's bodies possessed objective properties that gave meaning to the observed frequencies of births. His claim that "only women are apt to" produce a child became more than a simple statement about the fact that women bear children and men do not. It described a world in which the only measurably interesting fact about birth was the number of potential mothers. Bertillon's definition continued in the same vein, making his point clearer:

> Meanwhile, there is cause to restrict even further the ratio in question; evidently it is not all women regardless of age who are apt to produce newborns; little girls and old women can hardly compete in this matter, only women of childbearing age [*les femmes nubiles*]. Thus, only the latter category should be compared to the annual number of births, and this point is all the more important to the extent that the number of [women] unable to reproduce is highly variable in each collectivity, and their distribution alters in many ways the strict ratio between births and those who contribute to it.[36]

The key point in Bertillon's argument was a slippage between two registers: the level of the individual woman and the "nubile" population. Finding it relatively easy to say that "only women are apt to" produce children on an individual basis, Bertillon assumed by analogy that an equally transparent causal link existed between the collective body of women and the expected annual number of births. This focus on the female population allowed Bertillon and his followers to set aside the entire panoply of social and cultural practices that impinge on the produc-

---

35. Bertillon, "Natalité," pp. 447–48.

36. The power of this logic applied to the measurement of births is made clear in a further example put forth eleven years later by Bertillon's son Jacques, also a prominent demographer and militant natalist. In an 1887 article that defined the proper procedure for measuring the number of illegitimate births, Jacques Bertillon asked: "Who produces an illegitimate birth? An unmarried woman. Thus, one must compare the number of illegitimate births to the number of unmarried women, and not to the total number of births. A legitimate birth can contribute nothing to an illegitimate birth; they are two facts absolutely independent of one another; and there is no reason to compare them than there is to compare the number of illegitimate births to the number of marriages or the number of deaths" (*Les Naissances illégitimes en France et dans quelques pays d'Europe* [Vienna, 1887], p. 1).

tion of children, not to mention the physiological characteristics of the men who were presumably participating in this activity. The strict internal logic of Bertillon's argument should not detract from our understanding of how it resonated in the larger context of the discussion of fertility among his contemporaries. The constitution of reproduction as a cause-and-effect relationship between *les femmes nubiles* (aged fifteen to fifty) and birth could only be benign in an ideal world that allowed individuals who fit this category the free exercise of their reproductive capacity. Since late nineteenth-century France was manifestly not such an ideal world, we must examine the consequences of such a definition of fertility in both the scientific and political realms.[37]

Bertillon claimed that the best indicator for measuring the process by which a society reproduced itself was the *fécondité effective des épouses*, or marital fertility, and subsequent studies by him and other writers made marital fertility an important part of demographic study. Bertillon pointed out that "under the laws of our society, only married women have been granted the privilege, or the duty, of producing children."[38] In later articles, he often cited figures that showed great disparities among European nations in marital fertility, disparities that were often masked in comparisons of the crude birthrate. For example, noting that the natality of the Belgian population was only slightly higher than that of the French, Bertillon pointed out how great the difference between the two nations became when one compared the fertility of married women. In fact, when he compared marital fertility for European countries he came up with the following figures: for every 1,000 married women aged fifteen to fifty, 248 babies were born in England, 275 in Prussia, and 279 in Belgium, but only 173 in France. "Thus, we who have the most wives capable of having children, have the least, because our wives [*épouses*] are the least fertile [*fécondes*]."[39] Bertillon's use of the term *fécondes* to speak of "our wives" provides a further example of the powerful naturalizing tendency inherent in the vocabulary of demographic analysis. An individual woman's marital status had no necessary connection to her bio-

37. Some writers did mention the possibility of calculating the fertility index relative to other groups besides that of "nubile women." See, for example, the argument put forth by A. Beaujon, whose 1888 study of fertility in Holland opened with the assertion that "it would no doubt be more correct to compare legitimate births to the number of married couples, living together, who were of the age to reproduce." Beaujon eventually rejected this as too difficult to measure and beyond the capabilities of any official census office ("La Fécondité des mariages aux Pays-Bas," p. 207).
38. Bertillon, "Natalité," p. 449. Bertillon's unwillingness to discuss the large numbers of illegitimate births only confirms the essential moralism that lay behind his support of high marital fertility.
39. L.-A. Bertillon, "De la natalité française," *Journal de la Société de statistique de Paris* 18 (1877): 200.

logical capacity to bear children, nor did it make sense to assume that the collective body of French wives were alone to blame for the declining birthrate. But by speaking as if such terms as *fécondité* were naturally applicable to the population of "our wives," Bertillon implied that reproductive capacity meant reproductive duty. Being "fecund" implied an obligation to be "fertile."

The index of marital fertility thus focused an unprecedented amount of attention on the place of women in society, serving to assign responsibility for the decline even as it was numerically described. This became a common technique of political writers on the subject of depopulation. For example, Senator Edme Piot's *La Question de la dépopulation en France* discussed one by one the possible causes for the diminished rate of population growth in France—increase in emigration, decrease in marriages, increase in deaths, and so on—and he concluded that these factors were all insignificant. Finally, he arrived at marital fertility. As in Bertillon's example cited above, Piot's language transformed the index into a cause of decline in itself, placing the blame squarely at the feet of French wives: "If French wives had the fertility of German women, we would gain 500,000 children per year."[40]

The fertility index, as Duncan, Bertillon, and subsequent writers defined it, created a need for new information about women: their number, their fecundity, their marital status, their age, their age at the birth of their first child and subsequent children, the number of children they had, the age and sex of their children. Significantly, this need for more specific data became the occasion for extended meditations in the demographic literature concerning the ratio of women to men in society and the proportion of children born of either sex. L.-A. Bertillon devoted over a quarter of his article "Natalité" to these questions, revealing a preoccupation with the lines of sexual differentiation as they were drawn through the social order, a preoccupation evidently shared by other writers on the subject.[41]

The primacy accorded to the question of sexual differentiation in the population can be attributed on the one hand to what Mary Poovey and

40. Piot, *La Question de la dépopulation en France*, p. 14. Other writers who focused attention on marital fertility in this fashion include Paul Leroy-Beaulieu, "La Question de la population en France," *Journal de la Société de statistique de Paris* 21 (1880): 118; Arsène Dumont, *Natalité et démocratie* (Paris, 1898), p. 62. Marital fertility had become a part of the Statistique Générale's census in 1856, where it was given as the ratio of legitimate births per marriage (*Statistique de la France, mouvement de la population en 1851, 1852, et 1853*, [Strasbourg, 1856], p. xviii).
41. Statisticians had noted the constant excess of male births relative to female births—a ratio of about thirteen to twelve—quite early. Ian Hacking has called it the first "statistical law," citing John Arbuthnot's work of 1710, which claimed that the constant ratio was evidence of divine Providence. See Hacking, *Taming of Chance*, pp. 21, 41. Pierre Simon de Laplace mentioned the regu-

Thomas Laqueur have called the "incommensurability" of the sexes in nineteenth-century biological thinking.[42] In the context of the fertility debate, such definitions of incommensurability served to delineate the separate spheres that biology called upon men and women to occupy in the social order. Given the historical tendency of scientific writers to think in these terms, it is not surprising that when demographic data indicated regular differences in the number of males and females born, such data would be enlisted to demonstrate the power of a biologically reinforced division of sexual roles in society. In turn, this linkage between the question of sex ratios in the population to the matter of fertility and population decline is evidence of a concern on the part of writers such as Bertillon with the possibility of fixing gender differences in a scientific discourse that was profoundly structured by contemporary social mores.[43] Explanations for the preponderance of males based on the relative age of the parents or their relative constitutional vitality often reflected thinly disguised preconceptions of the ideal heterosexual coupling and perpetuated the familialist ideology that was so widespread in France during this period.

By the 1890s, the demographic literature on fertility and depopulation had come to play a profound role in focusing public attention on the female population in France. The technical advances of Duncan and

---

larity in male and female births in his *Essai philosophique sur les probabilités* of 1795. And in 1835, Adolphe Quetelet wrote about it at length, dismissing older explanations such as that which held that colder climates favored males and warmer climates females. Quetelet mentioned another theory, offered by Prevost, that the general preference for male offspring caused people to stop having children once a male heir was produced, thus skewing the ratio enough to account for the disparity. Nevertheless, Quetelet and his contemporary, the hygienist Michel Levy, concurred that the only measurably intervening factor in the determination of the sex of the newborn was the "relative age of the parents." See Quetelet, *Sur l'homme*, 1:48–49, 51–58; also Levy, *Traité d'hygiène publique et privée*, 2:489. Finally, the editors of the Statistique Générale de la France took care to point out the consistently larger number of males born in the first half of the nineteenth century in its publication of 1856, claiming that the ratio was consistently close to seventeen to sixteen. See *Statistique de la France, mouvement de la population en 1851, 1852, et 1853*, p. xxii.

42. Laqueur, *Making Sex*, pp. 20–21, 149–92; Poovey, *Uneven Developments*, p. 6. In her discussion of nineteenth-century Britain, Poovey described the function of this incommensurability: "The model of binary opposition between the sexes, which was socially realized in separate but supposedly equal 'spheres,' underwrote an entire system of institutional practices and conventions at mid-century, ranging from a sexual division of labor to a sexual division of economic and political rights" (*Uneven Developments*, pp. 8–9).

43. In addition to L.-A. Bertillon's article "Natalité," the following works, in chronological order, treat the matter of sex ratios at birth in relation to fertility, although not always drawing the same conclusions: Lacassagne, "La Natalité à Lyon"; Gustave Lagneau, "Etude démographique de la diminution ou de l'accroissement des familles," *Bulletin de l'académie de médecine* ser. 3, 20 (1888): 498–514; André Sanson, *L'Hérédité normale et pathologique* (Paris, 1893); Arsène Dumont, "Natalité et masculinité," *Revue scientifique* ser. 4, 1 (1894): 752–56; Maurel, *De la dépopulation de la France*.

Bertillon, combined with the rejection of Malthusian analyses of over-population, created a new vocabulary for describing the social obligations of motherhood. The fertility index, a simple numerical ratio designed to allow for the comparison of birthrates among populations of different sizes and age structures, became the occasion for extended meditations on the proper relationship of women to their reproductive capacity and their respective duties toward the French nation. In Jules Simon's terms, the demographic literature set the stage for a debate that cast the majority of French women in the role of "bad wives," even as the "good mother" was extolled and praised.

THE POLITICS OF DEPOPULATION

The demographic definitions of fertility and fecundity were based on assumed connections between a woman's biological capacity to bear children and the nation's need for new members. Natalist writers used these definitions to demonstrate that the decline in the French birthrate was caused by women who placed their own economic and sexual pleasure before the needs of the country. This view gained wide acceptance in the years before World War I and crossed the wide ideological divides that separated republican politicians from Catholic moralists, socialists from liberals, progressives from conservatives. A small but vocal group of neo-Malthusian activists opposed this view. Believing that the emancipation of sexuality from reproduction would liberate the individual and, above all, the individual woman, from the constraints of an oppressive society, these militants sought to distribute information on contraception and sexual hygiene to the French population.[44]

The fertility debate thus became the latest chapter in an unresolved conflict at the heart of French political culture in the nineteenth century, a conflict that sought to define the respective obligations binding the individual to the national community. In governing republican circles, this controversy was addressed in the 1890s by the new doctrine of solidarism, which allowed both republican natalists and moderate feminists to find common cause in supporting motherhood as a moral and social good.[45]

44. The main methods of contraception in use in France were abstinence, withdrawal, and various mechanical devices such as condoms, sponges, and pessaries, often supplemented by douching. Condoms were expensive and not readily available until the mass production of rubber in the late nineteenth century. See McLaren, *Sexuality and Social Order*, pp. 12, 18–25. See also Jean-Pierre Bardet and Jacques Dupâquier, "Contraception: Les Français les premiers, mais pourquoi?" *Communications* 44 (1986): 3–33.
45. Offen, "Depopulation, Nationalism, and Feminism," pp. 664–66.

But whereas republican political theory had usually been content to treat individuals as neutral abstractions, the fertility debate revealed that some individuals, namely women, were more problematic than others.

To understand how the fertility debate resonated in a wider cultural context, one must juxtapose the natalists with their opponents: the neo-Malthusian supporters of birth control. The French birth control movement was founded by Paul Robin, a *lycée* teacher who had become active in radical politics during the Second Empire. After his arrest in 1870 and subsequent exile, Robin had been nominated by Karl Marx to the executive committee of the International Working Men's Association. Because of quarrels with both Marx and Mikhail Bakunin, however, Robin was expelled from the International in 1871. During his exile in London he met Charles and Alice Drysdale, the founders of the British Malthusian League, who convinced him of the necessity of incorporating a program for sexual emancipation into his political platform.[46] He published his first important work, *La Question sexuelle*, in 1878, and soon after he returned to France. The newly ascendant republican administration decided to overlook his political past, and he was appointed director of an orphanage at Cempuis, probably because his secular beliefs accorded well with the anticlerical bent of the government. In the meantime, he quietly worked to distribute information on birth control and in 1896 founded the Ligue de régénération humaine, dedicated to countering the increasingly natalist tone of politics in the Third Republic. Members and associates of his league included the anarchist Eugène Humbert, the feminist organizer Nelly Roussel, the doctor and radical feminist Madeleine Pelletier, and Alfred Naquet, the former senator who had sponsored the divorce law of 1884.[47]

Although the handful of neo-Malthusians never succeeded in estab-

46. On the Drysdales and the Malthusian League in Britain, see Richard Allen Soloway, *Birth Control and the Population Question in England, 1877–1930* (Chapel Hil, 1982), pp. 55–69.

47. McLaren, *Sexuality and Social Order*, pp. 93–95; André Armengaud, "Mouvement ouvrier et néo-malthusianisme au début du XXe siècle," *Annales de démographie historique* (1966): 7–9. On the French neo-Malthusians, see also Francis Ronsin, *La Grève des ventres: Propagande néo-malthusienne et baisse de la natalité en France 19e-20e siècles* (Paris, 1980), esp. pp. 42–50, 55–63; Elinor Accampo, "The Rhetoric of Reproduction and the Reconfiguration of Womanhood in the French Birth Control Movement, 1890–1920," *Journal of Family History* 21 (1996): 351–71; Roger-Henri Guerrand and Francis Ronsin, *Le Sexe apprivoisé: Jeanne Humbert et la lutte pour le contrôle des naissances* (Paris, 1990); and Michelle Perrot, "Malthusianisme and Socialism," in *Malthus Past and Present*, ed. Jacques Dupâquier and A. Fauve-Chamoux (London, 1983), pp. 257–74. On Madeleine Pelletier, see Felicia Gordon, *The Integral Feminist—Madeleine Pelletier, 1874–1939: Feminism, Socialism, and Medicine* (Minneapolis, 1990); Scott, *Only Paradoxes to Offer*, chap. 5; C. Sowerwine, "Madeleine Pelletier (1874–1939): Femme, médecin, militant," *L'Information psychiatrique* 9 (1988): 1183–93; and Marilyn Boxer, "When Radical and Socialist Feminism Were Joined: The Extraordinary Failure of Madeleine Pelletier," in *European Women on the Left: Socialism, Feminism, and the Problems Faced by Political Women, 1880 to the Present*, ed. Jane Slaughter and Robert Kern (Westport, Conn., 1981), pp. 51–73.

lishing the mass movement envisioned by Robin, their work, published in pamphlet form and in a succession of journals—*Régénération, Génération consciente*, and *Le Malthusien*—derived much of its significance from the appropriation of a scientific language that up to that point had been primarily mobilized by the state and its natalist supporters. By linking the language of hygiene and eugenics to a movement for social emancipation and implying that the oppression of the working classes originated in the lack of control which working women had over their reproductive lives, the neo-Malthusians confronted the natalist assumptions of the majority with an alternative vision of the social lessons to be learned from advances in evolutionary biology.[48] Unlike the natalists, however, the neo-Malthusians asserted that the different roles played by men and women in the process of reproduction had no necessary implications for the roles that male and female individuals should occupy in the social order.

This aspect of neo-Malthusian thought found its clearest expression in the writings of Madeleine Pelletier, a doctor who had been the first woman psychiatric intern in a Paris hospital. Pelletier explicitly referred to the importance of gender in understanding the progress of the human species. "Motherhood," she wrote, "is a heavy charge for a woman, and it is above all to her that the dilemma of the species and the individual presents itself."[49] Furthermore, she claimed, the evolution of the collective has always weighed more heavily on individual women than on men.

> As one ascends the animal hierarchy, one sees the individual increase in value at the expense of the species, which declines accordingly. . . . This same antagonism can be found within [the history of] humanity. Among savage and barbarian peoples, individual lives are short and reproduction is intense. Women become fertile at very young ages, and are constantly pregnant or nursing infants, often one after the other. At thirty, they are already old.[50]

Given this history of biological suffering, Pelletier asserted that the decline in fertility could not be regarded as a sign of national degeneration.

48. Michelle Perrot has summarized the importance of this aspect of neo-Malthusian thought: "Science and hygiene replace God and morality, and birth control is supported both as a movement for the liberation of the individual and as a lever for social revolution. Neo-Malthusianism is opposed to traditional morality and subversive of the existing social order by giving the disinherited masses the supreme weapon, control over their reproduction" ("Malthusianism and Socialism," p. 263).
49. Madeleine Pelletier, *L'Emancipation sexuelle de la femme* (Paris, 1911), p. 82. I have chosen to emphasize Pelletier here, but there are other equally compelling examples in the neo-Malthusian movement. See Elinor Accampo's discussion of Nelly Roussel, in "Rhetoric of Reproduction," pp. 356–60.
50. Pelletier, "L'Emancipation sexuelle de la femme," p. 63.

On the contrary, depopulation was "an essential good, a corollary of the general evolution of humanity [*des êtres*], it [was] the expression of the victory of the individual over the species."[51]

Other supporters of Robin's movement made similar evolutionist arguments, although the focus on gender distinctions was not always as explicit as in Pelletier's work. Alfred Naquet, the former senator and neo-Malthusian publicist, asked, "Has not Darwinian law, by elevating . . . the intellectual and moral level of humanity, given us the means to find . . . in hygiene, well-being, and increased morality the elements of our own future perfection? Or are we, like plants or animals, condemned to an organic fatalism?"[52] Even Maria Deraismes, a leader of the moderate feminist Société pour l'amélioration du sort de la femme et la revindication de ses droits, wrote that progress in the social sciences—"the science of human relations in their collectivity"—would allow the French to transcend their current crisis:

> This science is based on the profound understanding of man and the correlation which exists between his anatomical constitution [and] the milieu in which he is formed. . . . It is here and not elsewhere that one must search for the determining factors of his behavior. Thus, one is led to the knowledge that it is possible to exercise a salutary action on the physical and moral attributes of the individual during the period of his formation. . . . Do not doubt it, we are living the last moments of the current civilization, we are at the end of a social era [*une forme social.*].[53]

Despite the curiously masculine language of Deraismes's statement, her message is clear: the problematic individual in French society was feminine, and it was a woman's biology that would be transcended in the new social order. This became the central tenet of neo-Malthusian thinking, made most explicit in Madeleine Pelletier's words: "It is obvious that women are not anatomically identical to men, but that is the individual's concern and has nothing to do with society."[54]

By appropriating the terminology of the population sciences, the neo-Malthusians and their feminist allies unhinged the scientific language of the population sciences from its origins in the bureaucratic state and

51. Ibid., p. 61.
52. Alfred Naquet, *Temps futurs; socialisme—anarchie* (Paris, 1900), p. 197.
53. Maria Deraismes, "De la dépopulation," *Bulletin de la Société de l'allaitement maternel* 8 (1893): 4. For a discussion of Deraismes and the Société d'amélioration, see Steven C. Hause and Ann R. Kenney, *Women's Suffrage and Social Politics in the French Third Republic* (Princeton, 1984), pp. 8, 46, 56–57.
54. Madeleine Pelletier, *La Femme en lutte pour ses droits* (Paris, 1908), p. 42.

made it available to other political visions.[55] Most important, their discussion of fertility refused to recognize the slippage between the circumstances of an individual woman's decision to bear children and the collective "responsibility" of the "nubile population" to provide the nation with a new generation of workers and soldiers. This move made them doubly subversive in the eyes of the authorities, however, and figures such as Robin and Pelletier became objects of police surveillance. A 1907 police report on the Ligue de régénération humaine emphasized only its connection to the militant left and claimed that the hidden goal of Robin's organization was to profit from the sale of contraceptives so that the proceeds could then be used to further its revolutionary aims.[56] The police assumption that the neo-Malthusians were acting out of self-interest reflected a larger conservative tendency to see the movement as a symptom of an excessive individualism that had taken hold in France at the expense of a properly self-effacing commitment to the nation.

The emergence of the neo-Malthusians took place against the backdrop of an enormous escalation of interest in the problem of declining fertility. Until the 1890s, the study of "depopulation" had remained primarily the provenance of doctors, demographers, and economists. This situation changed, however, when the census revealed that in 1890, 1891, 1892, and 1895 there had actually been an excess of deaths over births.[57] These figures created a new sense of urgency among the members of the scientific and political establishment. Most notably, Jacques Bertillon, the son of Louis-Adolphe Bertillon and a prominent demographer and natalist in his own right, founded the Alliance nationale pour l'accroissement de la population française in 1896.[58] Bertillon's public pronounce-

---

55. Typical of this aspect of neo-Malthusian thought was the work of Dr. Justin Sicard de Plauzoles, who later became influential in the social hygiene movement of the interwar period. He wrote, "The goal of neo-Malthusianism is the amelioration of the species, its regeneration, by a process of scientific selection, or rational procreation, whose principle is the value of children rather than their number, and their limitation according to individual resources and social needs; it desires to apply the positive facts of the biological and social sciences such that later generations will no longer be the fruit of blind passion and chance, but on the contrary the results of conscious decisions [*la volonté réfléchie*] made by healthy parents" (*La Fonction sexuelle au point de vue de l'ethique et de l'hygiène sociale* [Paris, 1908], p. 300). On Sicard de Plauzoles's neo-Lamarckian influences, see William Schneider, "Toward the Improvement of the Human Race: The History of Eugenics in France," *Journal of Modern History* 54 (1982): 273.

56. AN: F7 13955, documents pertaining to police surveillance of neo-Malthusianism newspaper *Regénération* and the Ligue de la regénération humaine.

57. Alain Becchia, "Les Milieux parlementaires et la dépopulation de 1900 à 1914," *Communications* 44 (1986): 201.

58. Jacques Bertillon's works on declining fertility included *Le Problème de la dépopulation*; *Des Causes de l'abaissement de la natalité en France et des remèdes à y apporter* (Paris, 1910); and, most important, *La Dépopulation de la France—ses conséquences—ses causes—mesures à prendre pour la combattre* (Paris, 1911).

ments were openly alarmist and focused above all on the allegedly catastrophic effects of egoism. "Between the violent causes of devastation and
Malthusianism," he wrote, "there is one difference—the latter calamity,
even as it slowly destroys the country, makes none of its inhabitants suffer. How true it is that the interests of individuals can be entirely opposed
to those of the collectivity." [59]

The goal of Bertillon's Alliance was to lobby in parliament for policies
that would encourage families to have more children and to act as a forum for the discussion of legislative remedies to the declining birthrate. [60]
On 25 February 1897, the newspaper *L'Eclair* published a debate between
Robin and Bertillon, making their respective organizations known to a
wide public. In 1902, at the urging of Bertillon's Alliance, Interior Minister René Waldeck-Rousseau convened an extraparliamentary commission to discuss the problem of depopulation. The list of the commission's
members contained many of the most respected demographers and statisticians in France at the time, including Emile Levasseur, author of the
monumental study *La Population française* (1889), Lucien March, the director of the Statistique Générale de la France, and Arsène Dumont, an
idiosyncratic social theorist and demographer whose theory of "social
capillarity" had a profound influence on Zola's *Fécondité*. Other members of the parliamentary commission included the economists Yves
Guyot and Charles Gide, Léon Mirman of the Bureau de l'assistance et
d'hygiène publique, and Arthur Fontaine, the author of many reports on
population for the National Assembly. [61] The historian Alain Becchia's description of the commission's composition could be applied to the fertility debate itself: "[It was born] under the triple sign of politics, the bureaucracy, and science." [62]

59. Bertillon, *Le Problème de la dépopulation*, p. 12.
60. McLaren, *Sexuality and Social Order*, pp. 177–78. The stated goal of the Alliance nationale was
"to attract the attention of all to the danger which depopulation brings to the French nation, and
to demand measures, fiscal or other, which would increase the birthrate" (*Alliance Nationale pour
l'accroissement de la population française, programme, statuts, et compte-rendu des travaux* [Paris,
1897], p. 3). The Alliance published a monthly bulletin containing a summary of its efforts, including articles on depopulation and commentaries on the debates in the assembly that dealt with
the measures it proposed. Among the many issues it pursued, aside from statistical reminders of
declining fertility, were aid to pregnant women, assistance for children of working women, prizes
to be awarded the parents of *familles nombreuses*, and privileges for such families, including special
consideration from schools, reductions of military service, and tax breaks. Its members also discussed the feasibility of a tax on the unmarried and reforms of the laws of succession. Although pre-
dominantly secular in tone, it also published the work of Catholic writers, such as George Fonse-
grive's article "Un péril national," which claimed that the simple adhesion to the Christian faith
would bring about an increased birthrate. See *Bulletin de l'alliance nationale pour l'accroissement de
la population française* (15 July 1901): 267–72.
61. Becchia, "Les Milieux parlementaires," 202–5. For a complete list of the commission's members, see Becchia's Annexe 2, pp. 243–45.
62. Ibid., p. 202.

This apparent sense of purpose on the part of the political and scientific establishment did not translate into a uniform consensus on the causes of declining fertility, and there was much disagreement as to the remedies available to the state. Moreover, despite a flurry of parliamentary debate devoted to the reform of military conscription (to grant fathers exemptions), maternity leaves, assistance to *familles nombreuses*, and encouragement in the bureaucracy to allow fathers with more than three children avenues to quicker promotions, remarkably little was passed into law.[63] To be sure, many pieces of protective legislation that focused on the family had been passed in the 1870s and 1880s.[64] Nevertheless, the fact remains that the increased discussion of depopulation did not in itself lead to the passage of any significant legislation aimed specifically at stimulating the birthrate until the eve of the war.[65]

The failure of the natalists to see their proposals enacted into law did not mean that declining birthrates failed to galvanize public opinion during the two decades before the war. The amount of ink spilled and the vitriolic nature of the debate attest to its importance. If anything, the paralysis of the assembly in the face of a crisis many of its members believed to be an immanent threat to the nation's future suggests that the significance of the debate lay outside the world of practical politics and instead involved a crisis of larger proportions permeating the culture as a whole. The discussion of depopulation in the French parliament was only one arena among many in which the relationship between a woman's reproductive capacity and the nation were examined and discussed; only an extremely narrow definition of political significance could justify minimizing the importance of this debate.

The extremely wide range of theories invoked to explain the causes of declining fertility in the decades before World War I attests to the scope of the cultural crisis. One current of thought sought to attribute the decline in births to physiological or evolutionary causes, claiming, as did Gaetan Delaunay, that "inferior species are more fertile than the superior [species], and fertility diminishes as one moves upward through the steps

63. See Becchia's useful summary of the various proposals put forth in the assembly during these years, ibid., 223–30; see also Mary Lynn Stewart's account of the delay in France in enacting maternity leaves for pregnant women in *Women, Work, and the French State*, pp. 169–90. A law mandating maternity leaves was not enacted in France until 1913, despite great success in linking the issue to repopulation.
64. Stewart cited the Roussel Law of 1874 (which regulated wet-nursing), the divorce law of 1884, and the laws on abandoned children of 1889 and 1904 (*Women, Work, and the French State*, p. 69). See also Schafer, *Children in Moral Danger*.
65. After the trauma of World War I, however, the natalist rhetoric reached a fever pitch. For a discussion, see especially Mary Louise Roberts, *Civilization without Sexes: Reconstructing Gender in Postwar France, 1917–1927* (Chicago, 1994), esp. chap. 4 on the law of July 1920, which aimed at eliminating the dissemination of information about contraception and abortion.

of evolution."[66] Likewise, Dr. E. Maurel, in his work *De la dépopulation de la France* attributed the diminished growth to the spread of what he termed *"l'hérédo-arthritisme,"* a hereditary deficiency that led to an excess of female children, birth defects, and infertility.[67] As the economic historian Joseph Spengler has noted, however, the vast majority of writers rejected the search for physiological causes, supporting instead various arguments that found fault with French society and with the cultural practices surrounding reproduction.[68] Among the members of Waldeck-Rousseau's extraparliamentary commission, arguments that sought to enumerate the social and cultural causes of depopulation carried considerable weight, presumably because political intervention would have been considered futile against the forces of nature.[69]

Above all, the writers who sought to trace the social causes of depopulation focused on volitional causes. This explanation accorded well with the assumption that it was individual selfishness that was to blame for the decline in the birthrate. An 1897 article in the newspaper *L'Eclair* asked, "What will become of France if one abandons the birthrate to individual egoism?"[70] The sociologist Frédéric Le Play and his followers at the journal *La Réforme sociale* blamed French inheritance laws and the degradation of paternal authority in the French legal code.[71] Jacques Bertillon cited "the ambition of the father for his child" as the primary cause of declining fertility.[72] Emile Cheysson, the engineer and social economist, faulted French women for their excessive "egoism" and their "fear of being discomforted" by the "pains of motherhood [and] the cares of edu-

---

66. Gaetan Delaunay, "La Fécondité," *Revue scientifique* ser. 3, 10 (1885): 434. An associate of Delaunay's, Dr. Paul Jacoby, developed this idea by comparing the relative fertility of French departments in accordance with his gauges of civilization: population density and the number of "important people" [*personnages remarquables*] who originated in them. See Jacoby, *Etudes sur la sélection chez l'homme* (Paris, 1904), pp. 535–39.

67. Maurel, *De la dépopulation de la France*, pp. 60, 85–98. Reflecting the influence of Lamarckian notions of acquired characteristics in France, Maurel attributed the spread of this hereditary condition to a French propensity to overeating. For a discussion of the importance of Lamarckian heredity for French population thinking, see William Schneider, *Quality and Quantity: The Quest for Biological Regneration in Twentieth-Century France* (Cambridge, 1990), pp. 6–9, 70–73, 87–88.

68. Spengler, *France Faces Depopulation*, p. 136. Spengler summarizes the explanations given for declining fertility, dividing them into three categories: various descriptions of involuntary sterility, those whose Malthusian influence led them to blame an inability of the French economy to support an increasing population; and those that ascribed the decline to volitional causes with social or cultural origins. Spengler noted that the first category had few supporters, while most writers supported some combination of the latter two.

69. Becchia, "Les Milieux parlementaires," p. 222.

70. *L'Eclair*, 29 January 1897, p. 1.

71. See the discussion of Le Play in Zeldin, *France*, pp. 189–95.

72. Bertillon, *Le Problème de la dépopulation*, p. 23.

cation."[73] A conservative Catholic author, D. M. Couturier, wrote: "Depopulation is the most infamous death of a nation because it is a desired and premeditated suicide. . . . It is egoism substituting for divine will."[74] At the opposite end of the political spectrum, the socialist Robert Hertz incorporated these arguments into his own critique of the bourgeois family, "sterilized" by its preoccupation with material goods.[75] Finally, the economist Paul Leroy-Beaulieu blamed the civilizing process of modernity itself, within which he included "the development of education, personal and familial ambition, democratic ideas, competition in diverse professions, the taste for luxury, of an easier life [de sans-gêne], an excess of saving [prévoyance]."[76] Of course, the remedies proposed by these writers differed according to their various political persuasions. The Catholics desired the reestablishment of their religion and an end to the anticlerical policies of the Republic. Le Play attacked the meddling interference of the state in the patriarchal family. Bertillon, Cheysson, and Hertz called for the national implementation of social assistance programs to lift the burden of child rearing from the working classes. Nevertheless, their emphasis on the excesses of individualism in French society had a common target: the growing movement to establish the grounds for the equal participation of women in public life.

The natalist attack on individualism did not necessarily lead to an explicit confrontation with feminists such as Pelletier, but gender often worked its way into natalist arguments in a heavily coded fashion. Arsène Dumont, whose curious blend of socialist politics and positivist science made him one of the most interesting natalist writers, even appeared to agree with Pelletier on the necessity of distinguishing between biological functions of the individual and social obligations to the collective. Dumont criticized Malthus for having pictured men and women as beings who were entirely motivated by desire. "Man has the generative instinct in common with animals," argued Dumont, "but when he accumulates possessions [épargne] and labors, this instinct leads to other results that are different from what animals accomplish with their fertility."[77] Like Pelletier, then, Dumont held that biology was not necessarily destiny, and

73. Cheysson, "L'Affaiblissement de la natalité française."
74. D. M. Couturier, Demain: La Dépopulation de la France, craintes et espérances (Paris, 1901), p. x.
75. Hertz, Socialisme et dépopulation, p. 25.
76. Leroy-Beaulieu, La Question de la population, p. 220. For similar arguments, see Charles Raisin, La Dépopulation de la France et le Code Civil, ou Influence du régime successoral sur le mouvement de la natalité française (Bourg-en Bresse, 1900), p. 177; and Turquan, Contribution à l'étude sur la dépopulation de la France, p. 8.
77. Arsène Dumont, Dépopulation et civilisation (Paris, 1890), p. 41.

he pointed to the fertility decline as the primary evidence that humans were capable of transcending the dictates of their nature.

Unlike Pelletier, however, Dumont could not accept the fertility decline as a positive good. Instead, he developed the critique of modernity found in the work of Beaulieu and others into an all-embracing theory of "social capillarity." Dumont attributed the declining birthrate to a widespread selfish desire for social advancement that made people "regard their children as rivals for their own happiness."[78] Dumont described the action of social capillarity in his influential work *Dépopulation et civilisation*, published in 1890. "All men tend to rise from the inferior levels of society to those which are immediately above . . . ," he wrote. "Guided by an infallible and fatal instinct, each social molecule throws itself with all the energy available . . . into the task of unceasingly rising towards a luminous ideal which seduces and attracts it, as oil rises in the wick of a lamp. The more [this ideal] is ardent and brilliant, the more active and devouring is this action of social capillarity."[79] This powerful image of the seductive attractions of material and social advancement was the basis for his "new population principle": the birthrate exists in inverse proportion to the magnetic appeal of individual social improvement. Accordingly, he reasoned, the progress of the race was inversely related to the "development of the individual in value and personal pleasure."[80] Dumont found "social capillarity" to be most powerful in a liberal democracy such as France because the establishment of equality in theory but not in fact acted as a continual stimulation to personal ambition. A socialist society, in contrast, by establishing real equality "would destroy social capillarity, and bring about an infinite multiplication of births."[81] Unfortunately for Dumont's own career prospects, his socialist convictions prevented his ideas from being wholeheartedly adopted by the natalist mainstream and he committed suicide after being denied a professorship at the Ecole d'anthropologie.[82]

Nevertheless, Dumont's critique of excessive individualism found a wide audience among later writers, and it is in their work that one can find anxious evocations of the role played by women in stimulating a wasteful and debilitating attention to the goals of personal advancement and satisfaction. Georges Deherme defined the decadence of fin-de-siècle French bourgeois society, citing Dumont in the same discussion:

78. Ibid., p. 106.
79. Ibid.
80. Ibid., p. 130.
81. Ibid., p. 127.
82. McLaren, *Sexuality and Social Order*, p. 173.

Our overheated and incoherent life is unhealthy and absurd. The social scene [*le "monde"*], the visits, the receptions, the representations, the excessive luxury, the sumptuous feminine toilettes, the endless search for "relations": to marry young daughters and find connections for young men. These are the imbecile, vulgar crimes of a degenerated class that is incapable of understanding the obligations of its rank. . . . The woman who wears a hat costing thirty louis and who surrounds her neck with jewelry costing 100,000 francs is a monster who is all the more dangerous because all women envy her and attempt to imitate her.[83]

Deherme's careful selection of examples made his message all the more clear: women were particularly susceptible to the egoism that was the ruin of bourgeois society. Women were more likely to be corrupted by the decadent examples of others, and they were more likely to be seduced by a taste for luxury. They were responsible for the ruin of their families and, by extension, the nation.[84]

The anxiety about excessive female individualism, so explicit in the work of Deherme, can also be detected among other natalist writers, although in somewhat more coded language. Couturier, the Catholic moralist, wrote:

The enemy is not outside, it is in our walls, seated at the hearth of our fatherland. It is installed in the cottages of the poor, in the lodgings of workers, and in the mansions and castles of the rich and powerful. It is everywhere and everywhere it brings with it a voluntary death, the extinction of the race and the ruin of the nation, each hour tearing another piece of flesh from France. . . . The enemy is the voluntary sterility of the French race.[85]

Nowhere in his description of the "enemy" did Couturier mention women, but his evocative choice of imagery, which called to mind the intensely private and gendered interior space of the family, left no doubt as

83. Deherme, *Les Classes moyennes*, p. 302. Deherme's citation of Dumont is from the latter's *Dépopulation et civilisation*, p. 300.

84. The danger of female individualism was a continual theme in Deherme's work, and he argued for a strict imposition of separate spheres for men and women in the social order: "Is woman inferior to man? Not at all. Woman cannot be separated from man. The individual is only an abstraction. There is the family, the fatherland, and humanity. These are the real beings [*êtres réels*]. They are each composed of men and women . . . and each attains his [or her] greatest social utility and value in perfecting themselves as such. Above all the woman. Agitation, instability, deviation, changes in social class, and bovarysm [*sic*] are more harmful for women than men" (*Les Classes moyennes*, pp. 198–99).

85. Couturier, *Demain*, pp. 2–3, 7.

to whose decisions were most to blame for this "voluntary sterility." Who else "sat at the hearth" but the wife and mother? Who else was "sterile" but French wives? Couturier's language, which cannot be seen as accidental, revealed the contours of a powerful consensus: the problematic individual in French society was female.

The idea that feminist claims for the right to control fertility constituted a misinterpretation of the liberal ideals of equality and individualism found a wide public in fin-de-siècle France. Anna Lampière, an advocate of woman's education, published a series of articles in the newspaper Le Temps in the 1890s, claiming that feminism "offered to a superficial liberalism the advantage of being an application of the 'principles of 89,' a manifestation of that individualism which is ignorant of all solidarity."[86] Lampière called for the "rational use of feminine activities," in accordance with "biological and sociological laws," such that the "harmonious organization of individual life and social life" might be preserved.[87] Paul Leroy-Beaulieu made a similar argument, warning that legislators concerned with allowing women to earn their own living should beware the "assimilation of woman into men, and avoid the suppression of all legal manifestations of the natural functions of the sexes."[88] He added that

> one must not hide the fact that "the feminist movement" . . . constitutes . . . a serious peril for civilization. By rendering the household less desirable, and making motherhood more feared and incommodious, the masculinization of woman must gradually affect the birthrate, which has already shown only too great a tendency to weaken in the majority of civilized countries.[89]

The curious slippage that occurs in Leroy-Beaulieu's argument, between the supposed immutability of biological definitions of gender and the capacity of social behavior to threaten this only apparent immutability captures the tension and anxiety that pervaded the work of social scientists in this period. Leroy-Beaulieu remained trapped in a double bind of his

---

86. Anna Lampière, Le Rôle social de la femme, devoirs, droits, éducation (Paris, 1898), p. 3. This work is a collection of the articles published in Le Temps.
87. Ibid., pp. 2–3. Dumont, too, claimed that "the toxic principle [is] this individual idealism, the insufficient sense of solidarity" (Natalité et démocratie, p. 165).
88. Leroy-Beaulieu, La Question de la population, p. 273.
89. Ibid. Leroy-Beaulieu concluded by asserting that "a population which remains stationary finishes by languishing, becoming effeminate; and in small families, with only two or three offspring, the children are raised with an overly pusillanimous tenderness, they are surrounded with a softening affection which diminishes their strength of character and mind" (ibid., p. 291).

own creation, between the desire to invoke a natural law that could dictate the separate spheres of men and women in society and the necessity of finding a human law that could protect the natural order threatened by modern civilization.[90]

Caught at opposite ends of the same irreconcilable divisions—between the biological and the social, on the one hand, and the individual and the collective, on the other—the natalists and the neo-Malthusians continued to talk past one another. The natalist critique of French society was primarily an auto-critique of the bourgeoisie, performed on itself by its own self-appointed political and scientific guardians. The neo-Malthusian position on fertility, on the other hand, had a very different audience, aimed not at the middle classes, who were already limiting their births to a large degree, but at the working populations of French cities. In this sense, the fertility debate was not a debate at all, in the dialogic sense of the term. Rather, it was a confrontation between ideological opponents whose respective vocabularies were embedded in a contradictory set of schematic relationships between nature and society, individual and nation.

In the Malthusian paradigm that held sway throughout much of the century, sexuality was to the individual as reproduction was to society. In each case the first term provided the motivating energy that drove the second. Neither term nor case was given priority over the other, and the equation was imbued with fatalist implications because of the assumption that the sexual motor would necessarily drive the social body beyond its capacity to support itself. The natalist assumption, that sexuality was to reproduction as the individual was to society, lent priority to the second term in each case, transforming both sexuality and the individual into functional vehicles for the realization of a society that was congruent with the physiological demands of nature. The neo-Malthusians, in an optimistic corollary of the Malthusian assumption and a reversal of the natalist belief, held that the emancipation of sexuality from reproduction would free the individual from the constraints of an oppressive society.

90. Other writers found themselves caught in the same dilemma, forced to invoke the external power of social institutions in order to meet the threat to the family brought about by the emancipation of women. Deherme, for example, wrote, "The state can only substitute for the family to the extent that it disassociates it—and it is above all through the progress of feminism that this is accomplished" (Les Classes moyennes, p. 196). The socialist Dumont came to the same conclusion, finding the only cure for excessive individualism in the subordination of the individual to the state: "The individual . . . takes himself as the goal, and considers himself to be the primary purpose [la cause finale] of the State and the race. In reality, he must be subordinated to the State, as the State itself must be subordinated to the goal that reason assigns to it in each circumstance" (Dépopulation et civilisation, p. 380).

The play of gender in these formulations followed their implicit values. Just as demography made its measure of fertility the population of "nubile" women, so too did natalist propaganda make its measure of national health the extent to which this population was protected and inscribed with the role of motherhood. The neo-Malthusian feminists, on the other hand, attempted to dismantle the social significance of a woman's biological functions, asserting the necessary right of a woman to control her reproductive life.

Despite the tremendous amount of attention paid to depopulation between 1871 and 1914, no substantial changes in social policy were made until after World War I. During the first half of the Third Republic, the natalist lobby was unable to muster enough support in the assembly to pass any legislation providing incentives for larger families in France. But this failure should not be taken as a sign that the issue had not reached its full significance in these years; on the contrary, the depopulation debate served an important ideological function: the attention paid to reproduction provided moralists and reformers with a vehicle for announcing the special obligations which biology entailed for women in French society. Although nationalist fears of a more populous Germany certainly added to the sense of urgency felt by the French in confronting their own restricted birthrate, "depopulation" remained inextricably linked to an attempt by legislators and social scientists to define the social and political boundaries of women's participation both in the private realm and in public life.

The demographic literature that brought the issue of a declining birthrate to national attention in the 1870s and 1880s contributed a great deal to this focus on the female population. The technical innovations that lay behind the definitions of *fertilité* and *fécondité* reinforced a general tendency to see the problem as an abdication of motherhood by French women for the sake of individual fulfillment and gave this view the full weight of empirical science. Just as Zola's Dr. Boutan was able to move effortlessly from an individual women's decision to use contraception to an apocalyptic vision of nature's revenge on the human species, so too did the demographic literature lay the blame for national decline squarely at the feet of France's excessively "egotistical" wives.

Paradoxically, however, identifying motherhood as the natural destination of all women could only increase the level of anxiety that the French felt in the face of declining fertility. The birth statistics, interpreted in this light, could only reveal a "natural" state that could not take care of itself. And if "nature" was not self-regulating, how useful was the concept as the foundation of social policy? The inability of natalist politicians and demographers to address this contradiction at the heart of their enterprise attests to the power of their preconceptions and points to a persistent blindness at the center of late nineteenth-century French population research.

That the neo-Malthusians were able to appropriate the language of biological regeneration in the service of their own quite different political agenda, however, indicates that the language used to describe these obligations was not inescapably linked to official measures to restrain the reproductive freedom of individual women and men. The neo-Malthusians' critical and rhetorical engagement with the discourse of the population sciences had implications far beyond their actual material accomplishments as propagandists and supporters of family planning because it set up the possibility of a feminist politics that did not retreat into an essentialist vision of gender roles. Rather, it sought to dismantle the connection between social behavior and sex, making it a matter of individual choice rather than biological necessity.

CONCLUSION

The discovery of "population" between the 1770s and the 1830s transformed the relationship between the French state and the French people in several ways. First, the study of population allowed researchers and government offices simultaneously to combine and subdivide groups of subjects or citizens into new social aggregates whose collective bodies shared some essential characteristic. These aggregates were perpetually in motion, but their size and vitality at any given moment could be quantitatively fixed through enumeration. Second, the study of these aggregates made it possible for officials to make new generalizations about collective interests—of the state, of the nation, or even of the population itself—and to make claims about the respective obligations that individuals owed to the whole. Finally, in studying the relations between these aggregate groups, their effects on one another, and their vulnerability to external factors such as disease or the environment, population researchers revealed new lines of causality at work within the population. Once captured and tabulated in statistical tables, this understanding of social cause and effect invited calls for government intervention to defend the newly conceived collective interests against both harmful external effects and unwanted behaviors in the population.

The successes of this new knowledge of "population" were both exciting and disturbing. The apparently random flux of individual lives could now be represented as a universe of unsuspected order and precision; the ebb and flow of humanity could be accurately charted and made transparent by use of numbers. But the very clarity of this vision challenged well-entrenched notions of individual autonomy by implying that social processes that worked at the aggregate level of population had more influence on people's lives than their own decisions and will. In the revolutionary decades of the 1830s and 1840s this epistemological unease was compounded by very real fears of social violence and political unrest. This peculiar combination of methodological uncertainty and social anxiety drove the proponents of statistics to find ways of presenting their research in ways that did not appear either politically permissive or philosophically unorthodox.

To do so, they sought to attach their work on population to moral themes that would not arouse either political or epistemological fears. Beginning in the 1840s and 1850s and increasingly thereafter, population researchers found such themes in work on the family and the special social obligations borne by women as wives and mothers. By structuring their investigations of population in ways that confirmed and reinforced a gendered division of labor in both the household and the economy, population researchers preserved a privileged realm of autonomy for male individuals, while simultaneously making women collectively responsible for preserving the bonds that held society together. Of course, the special obligations that women owed to their families and to the nation were not new ideas—precedents for many of these ideas could be found, for example, in the eighteenth-century works of Jean-Jacques Rousseau. In the second half of the nineteenth century, however, statistical work on women's labor, infant mortality, and fertility established these obligations as an integral part of the very structure of social knowledge about women and men. The woman worker, the working mother, the wet-nurse, the mother of the single child each became an identifiable type, whose lives had no significance for the social observer outside the network of connections set up by the category itself. The power of large numbers thus not only allowed population researchers to make new generalizations based on multiple observations of individuals, it allowed them both to recast and to restrict the meaning of these individuals' lives.

In doing so, the population research that has been the subject of this book lay the groundwork for the development of natalist welfare state policies in the twentieth century.[1] Many of the proposals originally made

1. For work on these issues in the twentieth century, see Roberts, *Civilization without Sexes*; Maria Sophia Quine, *Population Politics in Twentieth-Century Europe: Fascist Dictatorships and Liberal Democracies* (New York, 1996); Andrés Horacio Reggiani, "Procreating France: The Politics of Demography, 1919–1945," *French Historical Studies* 19 (1996): 725–54; Cheryl A. Koos, "Gender, Anti-individualism, and Nationalism: The Alliance Nationale and the Pronatalist Backlash against the Femme moderne, 1933–1940," *French Historical Studies* 19 (1996): 699–723; Jean Elisabeth Pedersen, "Regulating Abortion and Birth Control: Gender, Medicine, and Republican Politics in France, 1870–1920," *French Historical Studies* 19 (1996): 673–98; Susan Pedersen, *Family, Dependence, and the Origins of the Welfare State: Britain and France, 1914–1945* (Cambridge, 1993); Alisa Klaus, *Every Child a Lion: The Origins of Maternal and Infant Health Policy in the United States and France, 1890–1920* (Ithaca, 1993); and the essays in Seth Koven and Sonya Michel, eds., *Mothers of a New World: Maternalist Politics and the Origins of the Welfare States* (New York, 1993), and Gisela

by Jacques Bertillon's Alliance nationale pour l'accroissement de la population were taken up by the government after World War I, and in 1920 the National Assembly passed a new law on contraception and abortion. The law greatly increased the likelihood of conviction both for doctors who practiced abortion and for their patients. The 1920 law also provided severe penalties for those who advertised contraceptive materials.[2] Along with this success, pronatalists convinced the postwar government to establish the Conseil supérieur de natalité, an official body to coordinate government efforts to reverse the fertility decline and provide incentives for large families. The effects of this advisory body were soon felt. In the late 1920s, the assembly passed a series of laws that expanded the scope of social insurance in France and contained many provisions for families, including coverage for childbirth expenses for all insured families. In 1932, the Family Allowance Act called upon all employers to participate in the system of child allowances that had up to then been purely voluntary, and in 1935 payments began to women who nursed their own children. In 1938, Edouard Daladier's government took this encouragement an important step further, providing for an *allocation de la mère au foyer*, directly financing this family allowance system from state funds and simultaneously extending coverage to agricultural laborers and independently employed workers. In July 1939, the republican government passed the so-called Family Code, which provided a birth premium to those couples who had a child within two years of getting married and increased further the penalties for abortion.[3] All of these policies provided firm precedents for the aggressively nationalist and racist pronatalist programs undertaken by the wartime Vichy regime, which made abortion a crime against the state and executed a woman accused of performing them in July 1943.[4]

This terrible event stands as a sobering reminder of the power and flexibility of the many political arguments that harnessed gendered obligations to a politics of national renewal and collective definitions of wellbeing. This book has already shown how the attention to gender could work both ways. In the 1840s and 1850s, as Chapter 4 demonstrated, political economists turned their attention to the family and the situation of female laborers to counter a worrying tendency to divide the popula-

Bock and Pat Thane, eds., *Maternity and Gender Policies: Women and the Rise of the European Welfare States, 1880–1950s* (New York, 1991).
2. Roberts, *Civilization without Sexes*, esp. pp. 120–47.
3. These measures are discussed by Reggiani, "Procreating France," pp. 731–34; and Quine, *Population Politics*, pp. 76–83.
4. See Miranda Pollard, *Reign of Virtue: Mobilizing Gender in Vichy France* (Chicago, 1998).

tion along class lines. In so doing, they promoted an individualist vision of the market economy that sought to portray male individuals as independent agents working for the benefit of their dependent families. By the end of the century, however, when both conservatives and republicans alike expressed anxiety about the selfish egoism in the middle classes, they could again focus on the family, claiming that the problem was women who sought to express their own individuality while refusing to conform to the dependent condition that was their lot and obligation. Whether the problem was too little autonomy for individuals or too much, the answer always lay in the proper definition of one social aggregate: women.

Perhaps inevitably, the close link that pronatalists established between the health of the population and the obligation of women to be good mothers also influenced the claims made by French feminists in the late nineteenth and early twentieth centuries.[5] Female activists who sought to make the government more responsive to women's needs could have no formal influence over the political process because of their lack of citizenship rights—they could not vote or hold office. Finding few other avenues for gaining public support, many feminists endorsed the pronatalist message in the hope that women could benefit from government measures to protect maternity and that women's status in society would be raised as a result. In the decades leading up to World War I, writers and activists as diverse as the republican-solidarist Louise Koppe, the socialist Léonie Rouzade, the well-known journalist Marguerite Durand, and the suffrage militant Hubertine Auclert campaigned in support of maternalist policies and for public recognition of the contributions mothers made to the nation.[6] In the interwar period, similar claims were made by an equally diverse group of feminists, including the social Catholic Andrée Butillard, the socialist Madeleine Vernet, and the neo-Malthusian Nelly Roussel.[7] These feminists, whose political beliefs were otherwise very different, all attempted to use the pronatalists' valorization of motherhood and family to further the cause of women's rights.

It would be perverse and unfair to suggest that these feminists were operating from the same logic that the Vichy regime used to execute a suspected abortionist, but in one important respect the misogyny of the Vichy regime and the ideology of maternalist feminism overlapped: in their claim that the social aggregate known as "women" achieved its fullest significance for the collective body of the population in motherhood.

5. Cova, "French Feminism and Maternity," pp. 119–37; and Offen, "Body Politics," pp. 139–59.
6. Cova, "French Feminism and Maternity," pp. 119–24.
7. Offen, "Body Politics," pp. 146–48.

For Vichy this made abortion tantamount to treason; for maternalist feminism this same assumption was grounds for granting women the full rights of citizenship as individuals. To the extent that both positions were about resolving difficult decisions about individual rights through a set of gendered generalizations about aggregate truths, both Vichy and maternalist feminism remained trapped in the confines of nineteenth-century population thinking.

Joan Scott pointed to the difficulty faced by many French feminists as they sought to make claims for female citizenship during the last two centuries. Scott wrote that "in the age of democratic revolutions, 'women' came into being as political outsiders through the discourse of sexual difference. . . . To the extent that it acted for 'women,' feminism produced the 'sexual difference' that it sought to eliminate. This paradox—the need both to accept *and* to refuse 'sexual difference'—was the constitutive condition of feminism as a political movement throughout its long history." [8] My intent in this book has been to show the workings of a similar and related paradox, faced by an empirical science that sought to render scientific truths about the aggregate interests of population and the nation, even while defending a rhetorical space for individual autonomy. Population researchers, government administrators, and public moralists of diverse political backgrounds had trouble maintaining the compatibility between these two ideals without invoking entrenched ideas about sexual difference to paper over the contradictions in their enterprise. The difficulty that French feminists faced as they attempted to counter the workings of this slippery logic is not theirs alone; it is the difficulty faced by anyone in a society such as our own, which cannot conceive of the autonomous individual citizen without projecting "him" onto the background of a complex web of social and gendered obligations that fall most heavily on "her."

8. Scott, *Only Paradoxes to Offer*, p. 5.

BIBLIOGRAPHY

ARCHIVAL SOURCES

Archives Nationales (AN)

Series F7 Police

F7 13955. Mélanges—Dossiers sur des journaux des hommes politiques (1907–35). [Documents pertaining to the surveillance of neo-Malthusian organizations and publications.]

Series F20 Statistique

F20 1. Correspondance: Copies et enrégistrements de lettres. An IX–an II.

F20 5. Reseignements fournis par les préfets sur la rédaction des grands mémoires de statistique et indication d'ouvrages et d'articles concernant la statistique. An X–1807.

F20 22–26. Population de la République française par départements et par communes. Vendémiaire à pluviose an VII.

F20 27. Tableaux de population de divers communes avec proportion entre la population, les naissances, mariages et décès (an VIII–an XI). En tête, circulaire adressée a ce sujet aux préfets de 30 départments (30 fructidor an X).

F20 103. Bureau de statistique. Pièces relatives à la Statistique Générale de la France. Etat des travaux du Bureau de statistique. 1787–1829.

F20 105. Etats et rapports au ministre au sujet de la population et de l'état civil des citoyens.

F20 106–127. Correspondance relative à la statistique et tableaux de statistique, par départements. 1793–1832.

F20 132. Documents rélatifs à la longévité. Instructions et rapports sur les états de population (an II–an X). Divers états de population. Classement des villes à raison de leur population active. Correspondance au sujet de la statistuqe (an II–an XI). Lettres de préfets au Minstre de l'Intérieur sur la statistique (ans IX et X). 1802–7.

F20 440, n. 2–4. Tableaux de statistique de la mortalité.

F20 440, n. 5. Tableaux de statistique de la mortalité (1841–50). Tableaux de décès par categories d'age (1841–46). Tableaux des naissances légitimes (1846–47). Tableaux des mariages (1836–50). Décès dans la population rurale (1853).

F20 440, n. 8. Relevé statistique des décès dans la ville de Paris fourni par la Préfecture de Police. 1830–49.

F20 441. Divers états de population de quelques provinces du royaume. 1750–86.

F20 442, n. 1. Divers états de population de quelques provinces du royaume. 1750–86.

F20 442, n. 2. Population de la généralité de Paris en 1699. Notes et calculs sur la population de la France. Etat générale des villes du ci-devant royaume, divisé en cinq classes, d'après La Michaudière [sic]. Fin du XVIII siècle.

F20 547, n. 14. Nomenclature des causes de décès. Tableaux C. 1861–63.

Series H

H1 1444. Mémoires sur la population de la France et sur les rapports de la population avec l'impôt, XVIIIe siècle.

Archives de Paris (AdP)

Series VD4 Fond des Mairies

VD4 0001. Etat civil. Inspection de la vérification des décès.

VD4 0002. Population. Recensements.

VD4 0011. Santé publique et Conseils d'hygiene.

Series VD6 Fonds des Mairies

VD6 0015, n. 2. Prefecture du Département de la Seine. Instruction sur la vérification des décès dans la ville de Paris, 1844.

VD6 1388. Société protectrice de l'enfance.

VD6 1503. Correspondances des mairies.

VD6 1575. Protection des enfants en nourrice.

VD6 1575, n. 4. Protection et surveillance médicale des enfants du premier âge, 1870–86.

Archives de la Préfecture de Police (APP)

Series Vbis Q7 Placement des enfants en nourrice

DA 121. Projet de création d'un Service de statistique générale.

DB 61. Enfants du première âge. Organisation du service.

DB 62. Enfants du première âge. Renseignements divers, presse.

DB 63–4. Enfants du première âge. Documents parlementaires.

DB 65. Protection des enfants du première âge. Rapports annuels, 1874–92.

DB 66. Protection des enfants du première âge. Rapports annuels, 1893–1905.

DB 67. Protection des enfants du première âge. Rapports annuels, 1906–15.

DB 70. Note sur le service de la protection des enfants du première âge dans le département de la Seine. 1899.

DB 426. Familles nombreuses.

Archives de l'Assistance Publique (AAP)

Series Fossoyeux, Liasse 709, n. 1. Instruction sur le service des préposés à la surveillance des enfans placés dans les départements par l'intermédiaire de la direction des nourrices (1823).

PERIODICALS

Annales de démographie internationale
Annales des sciences naturelles
Annales d'hygiène publique et de médecine légale
Assistance
L'Aurore
Bulletin de l'Académie de médecine
Bulletin de l'Académie impériale de médecine
Bulletin de l'Académie royale de médecine
Bulletin de l'Alliance nationale pour l'acroissement de la population française
Bulletin de la Société de l'allaitement maternal
Bulletin de la Société d'anthropologie de Lyon
Comptes-rendus des séances de l'Académie des sciences
Les Droits de l'homme
L'Eclair
L'Evénement
La Fronde
Journal de la Société de statistique de Paris
Journal des économistes
Mémoires de l'Académie royale de médecine
Le Petit journal
La Petite république
La Philosophie positive
Le Rappel
La Réforme sociale
Registres de l'Académie royale des sciences
La République française
Revue d'économie politique
Revue des deux mondes
Revue encyclopédique
Revue scientifique
Séances et travaux de l'Académie des sciences morales et politiques
Le Siècle

Le Temps
Transactions of the Royal Society of Edinburgh
Union médicale

PUBLISHED PRIMARY SOURCES: ANONYMOUS

"L'Actualité, l'interdiction du mariage à certain malades." *L'Eclair*, 3 March 1897, p. 1.

Alliance nationale pour l'acroissement de la population française: Programme, statuts, et compte-rendu des travaux. Paris: E. Camping, 1897.

Chambre de commerce de Paris. *Statistique de l'industrie á Paris, 1847–48.* Paris: 1851.

Collection compléte des lois, decrèts, ordonnances, réglements et avis du Conseil d'etat, Vol. 74, edited by J. B. Duvergier. Paris: Charles Noblet, 1874.

Commission de statistique municipale, procès-verbaux. Paris: Imprimerie Nationale, 1881.

Commission spéciale de statistique municipale. Paris: Imprimerie Nationale, 1880.

Compte-rendu générale du Congrès international de statistique dans ses séances tenus à Bruxelles, 1853, Paris, 1855, Vienne, 1857, et Londres, 1860. Berlin: R. Decker, 1863.

Conseil de salubrité. *Rapports généraux des travaux du Conseil de salubrité pendant les années 1840 à 1845 inclusivement.* Paris: Boucquin, 1847.

Documents statistiques sur la France, publiés par le Ministre du Commerce. Paris: Imprimerie Royale, 1835.

Encyclopédie internationale d'assistance, prévoyance, hygiène sociale et dèmographie. Paris: Giard & Brière, 1909.

"Faites des enfants." *L'Eclair*, 29 January 1897, p. 1.

"L'Hégire de M. Robin." *La République française*, 13 May 1898, p. 2.

"Impots et patentes." *L'Eclair*, 7 February 1897, p. 1.

"Mémoire sur la population de la ville de Paris depuis la fin du XVIIe siècle." *Recherches statistiques sur la ville de Paris et le département de la Seine*, pp. xiii–xxviii. Paris: Imprimerie Royale, 1823.

"Neo-malthusianisme et repopulation ou quantité et qualité." *L'Eclair*, 25 February 1897, p. 1.

"Population." In *Grand dictionnaire universel du XIXe siècle*, edited by Pierre Larousse, vol. 12, part 2, pp. 1423–28. Reprint. 17 vols. Geneva: Slatkine, 1865–90.

"Prospectus." *Annales d'hygiène publique et de médecine légale* 1 (1829).

Rapport sur la marche et les effets du choléra morbus dans Paris et les communes rurales du département de la Seine. Paris: Imprimerie Royale, 1834.

Recherches statistiques sur la ville de Paris et le département de la Seine. Paris: Imprimerie Royale, 1823.

Recherches statistiques sur la ville de Paris et le département de la Seine. Paris: Imprimerie Royale, 1826.

Recherches statistiques sur la ville de Paris et le département de la Seine. Paris: Imprimerie Royale, 1829.

Recherches statistiques sur la ville de Paris et le département de la Seine. Paris: Imprimerie Royale, 1844.

Recherches statistiques sur la ville de Paris et le département de la Seine, année 1821.
Paris: Imprimerie Royale, 1833.

Statistique de la France, mouvement de la population en 1851, 1852, et 1853. Strasbourg: Imprimerie Administrative de Veuve Berger-Levrault, 1856.

Statistique de la France, mouvement de la population pendant l'année 1854. Strasbourg: Imprimerie Administrative de Veuve Berger-Levrault, 1857.

Statistique de la France. Résultats généraux du dénombrement de 1872. Nancy: Imprimerie Administrative de Berger-Levrault, 1874.

Statistique de la France. Territoire, population. Paris: Imprimerie Royale, 1837.

"Travaux de la Société." *Journal de la Société de statistique de Paris* 1 (1860): 1–13.

PUBLISHED PRIMARY SOURCES BY AUTHOR

Allart, Hortense. *La Femme et la démocratie de nos temps.* Paris: Delaunay, 1836.

d'Amador, Risueño. "Mémoire sur le calcul des probabilités appliqué à la médecine." *Bulletin de l'Académie royale de médecine* 1 (1837): 622–80.

d'Amilaville, Etienne-Noël. "Population." *Encyclopédie, ou Dictionnaire raisonné des sciences, des arts et des métiers,* vol. 13. Neufchâtel: Samuel Faulche, 1765.

d'Angeville, Adolphe. *Essai sur la statistique de la population française.* Bourg: Renard, 1836.

Armand-Blanc, May. "La Femme dans l'oeuvre d'Emile Zola." *La Fronde,* 1 October 1931.

Aubert, C. "Les Livres." *L'Aurore,* 23 October 1899, p. 3.

Barbery, Bernard. *Le Fils unique.* Paris: Eugène Figuière, 1914.

Beaujon, A. "La Fécondité des mariages aux Pays-Bas et les causes de ses variations." *Journal de la Société de Statistique de Paris* 29 (1888): 296–310.

Benoiston de Chateauneuf, L.-F. "De la durée de la vie chez le riche et le pauvre." *Annales d'hygiène publique et de médecine légale* 3 (1830): 5–15.

——. "Notice sur l'intensité de la fécondité en Europe au commencement du XIXe siècle." *Annales des sciences naturelles* 9 (1826): 431–50.

——. *Recherches sur les consommations de tout genre de la ville de Paris.* Paris: Martinet, 1821.

Béquet, Léon, Emile Morlot, and Trigant de Beaumont. *Régime et législation de l'assistance publique en France.* Paris: Paul Dupont, 1885.

Bernouilli, Jakob. *Die Werke von Jacob Bernouilli.* 3 vols. Basel: Birkhauser, 1969, 1975, 1989.

Bertillon, Jacques. *Cours élémentaire de statistique—élaboration des statistiques—organisation des bureaux de statistique—éléments de démographie.* Paris: Société d'éditions scientifiques, 1895.

——. *De la fréquence des principales causes de décès à Paris pendant la seconde moitié du XIXeme siècle et notamment pendant la période 1886–1905.* Paris: Imprimerie municipale, 1906.

——. "De la morbidité et de la mortalité par profession." *Journal de la Société de statistique de Paris* 33 (1892): 341–87.

——. *La Dépopulation de la France—ses conséquences—ses causes—mesures à prendre pour la combattre.* Paris: Alcan, 1911.

——. *Eléments de démographie*. Paris: Société d'editions scientifiques, 1896.

——. *Les Naissances illégitimes en France et dans quelques pays d'Europe*. Vienna: Organisations Commission des Congresses, 1887.

——. *Le Problème de la dépopulation*. Paris: Colin, 1897.

——. *La Statistique humaine de la France*. Paris: Baillière, 1880.

——. *La Vie et les oeuvres du Docteur L.-A. Bertillon*. Paris: Masson, 1883.

Bertillon, Louis-Adolphe. *Conclusions statistiques contre les détracteurs de la vaccine, précédés d'un essai sur la méthode statistique appliquée à l'étude de l'homme*. Paris: Masson, 1857.

——. *Congrès internationale de statistique*. Paris: L. Martinet, 1855.

——. "De la méthode statistique dans l'anthropologie." *Annales de démographie internationale* 6 (1882): 69–100.

——. "De la mortalité parisienne, croissante selon les morts, décroissante selon les ministres." *La Philosophie positive* 4 (1869): 445–57.

——. "Démographie, démologie." *Dictionnaire enyclopédique des sciences médicales*, ser. 2, 26: 650–61. Paris: Masson, 1882.

——. *La Démographie figurée de la France*. Paris: G. Masson, 1874.

——. "De quelques éléments de l'hygiène dans leur rapport avec la durée de la vie." Thesis, Ecole de Médecine, 1852.

——. "Des diverses maniéres de mesurer la durée de la vie humaine." *Journal de la Société de statistique de Paris* 7 (1866): 45–64.

——. "Détermination de la mortalité." *Journal de la Société de statistique de Paris* 10 (1869): 29–40, 57–65.

——. "Etude statistique sur les nouveau-nés." *Annales de démographie internationale* 7 (1883): 169–78.

——. "Mortalité." *Dictionnaire enyclopédique des sciences médicales*, ser. 2, 9: 725–91. Paris: Masson, 1875.

——. "Natalité." *Dictionnaire enyclopédique des sciences médicales*, ser. 2, 11: 444–92. Paris: Masson, 1876.

——. "La Place de la démographie dans les sciences anthropologiques." *Annales de démographie internationale* 1 (1877): 517–39.

——. "Rapport au nom de la Sous-commission de démographie á la Commission spéciale de statistique municipale." *Commission spéciale de statistique municipale, rapports*. Paris: Imprimerie Mouillot, 1880.

——. "Statistique des causes de décès." *Union médicale* 10 (1856): 1.

Blanqui, Adolphe. *Histoire de l'économie politique en Europe depuis les anciens jusqu'à nos jours*. Paris: Guillaumin, 1837.

Block, Maurice. *Statistique de la France, comparée avec les autres états de l'Europe*. Paris: Amyot, 1860.

——. *Traité théorique et pratique de statistique*. Paris: Guillaumin, 1878.

Bodio, Louis. "Louis-Adolphe Bertillon et la science démographique d'après l'école française." *Annales de démographie internationale* 7 (1883): 47–58.

Boiteau, Paul. "Curiosité de la statistique parisienne." *Journal de la Société de statistique de Paris* 15 (1874): 231–46.

Bonzon, Jacques. *La Législation de l'enfance*. Paris: Guillaumin, 1899.

Bouchardat, M. *Instruction sur l'essai et l'analyse du lait*. Paris: Bouchard-Huzard, Germer-Bailliére, 1857.

Bouchut, E. *Hygiène de la première enfance, guide des mères pour l'allaitement et le sevrage et le choix de la nourrice*. Paris: Baillière, 1879.

Boudet, Félix. *Discussion sur la mortalité des jeunes enfants*. Paris: Baillière, 1870.

Boudin, Jean. "Des races humaines, considérées au point de vue de l'acclimatement et de la mortalité dans les divers climats." *Journal de la Société de statistique de Paris* 1 (1860): 29–50.

———. "Etudes statistiques sur les moyens de diminuer la mortalité des Européens dans les pays chauds." *Journal de la Société de statistique de Paris* 1 (1860): 121–31.

———. "Lois pathologiques de la mortalité, influence de la densité des populations sur leur état sanitaire." *Annales d'hygiène publique et de médecine légale* 39 (1848): 364–80.

Broca, Paul. "Rapport sur les travaux de statistique de M. le docteur Bertillon." *Bulletin de l'Académie de médecine* ser. 2, 4 (1876): 97–111.

Brochard, André. *De l'allaitement maternel étudié aux points de vue de la mère, de l'enfant et de la société*. Paris: Maillet & Baillière, 1868.

———. *De la mortalité des nourrissons en France*. Paris: Baillière, 1866.

———. *De l'industrie des nourrices dans la ville de Bordeaux*. Bordeaux: Féret, 1867.

———. *Des causes de la dépopulation en France et des moyens d'y rémédier*. Lyon: Librairie Médicale de J.-P. Mégret, 1873.

Broussais, Casimir. *De la statistique appliquée á la thérapeutique*. Paris: Baillière, 1840.

———. *Hygiène morale, ou application de la physiologe à la morale et à l'éducation*. Paris: Baillière, 1837.

Brulat, Paul. "Fécondité." *Les Droits de l'homme*, 22 October 1899.

Cabet, Etienne. *Etat de la question sociale en Angleterre, en Ecosse, en Irland et en France*. Paris: Populaire, 1843.

———. *L'Ouvrier; ses misères actuelles, leur cause et leur remède; son futur bonheur dans la communauté; moyens de l'établir*. Paris: Populaire, 1844.

Casper, Dr. "De l'influence du mariage sur la durée de la vie humaine." *Annales d'hygiène publique et de médecine légale* 14 (1835): 227–39.

Cauderlier, G. *Les Causes de la dépopulation de la France*. Paris: Guillaumin, 1901.

Chervin, Arthur. "Louis-Adolphe Bertillon, 1821–1883." *Journal de la Société de statistique de Paris* 24 (1883): 133–42.

Cheysson, Emile. "L'Affaiblissement de la natalité française—ses causes—ses remèdes." *La Réforme sociale*, 1 June 1891.

Coirard, Louis. *La Famille dans le Code Civil*. Aix: Makaire, 1907.

Condorcet, Marie-Jean-Antoine-Nicolas, Pierre Simon de Laplace, and Achille-Pierre Dionis du Séjour. "Essai pour connoître la population du royaume et le nombre des habitants de la campagne, en adaptant sur chacune des cartes de M. Cassini, l'année commune des naissances, tant des villes des bourgs et des villages dont il est fait mention sur chaque carte, presenté à l'Académie." In *Histoire de l'Académie royale des sciences avec les mémoires de mathématique et de physique tirés des registres de cette Académie*, 703–18 (1786); 577–92 (1787); 601–89 (1788); 703–17 (1789); 601–10 (1790). Paris: Imprimerie Royale, 1786–91.

Cousin, Victor. *Justice et charité*. Paris: Pagnerre, Paulin, Firmin, Didot Frères, 1848.

Couturier, D. M. *Demain: La Dépopulation de la France, craintes et espérances.* Paris: Maison de la bonne presse, 1901.

Dalloz, M. D. *Répertoire méthodique et alphabétique de législation de doctrine et de jurisprudence en matière de droit civil, commercial, criminel, administratif, de droit des gens et de droit public.* 2 vols. Paris: Bureau de la jurisprudence générale, 1845.

Debury, Roger. *Un Pays de célibataires et de fils uniques.* Paris: Dentu, 1897.

Deghilage, Pierre. *La Dépopulation des campagnes, les causes, les effets, les remèdes.* Paris: F. Nathan, 1970.

Deherme, Georges. *Les Classes moyennes: Etude sur le parasitisme social.* Paris: Perrin, 1912.

Delaunay, Gaetan. "La Fécondité." *Revue scientifique* ser. 3, 10 (1885): 433–37, 466–70.

Delisle, A. *Protection des enfants de premier âge: Tableau synoptique concernant les lois, decrèts, et instructions.* Chartres: Imprimerie l'Anglois, 1882.

Démar, Claire. "Appel d'une femme au peuple sur l'affranchissement de la femme." In *Textes sur l'affranchissement des femmes,* edited by Valentin Pelosse, pp. 11–22. Paris: Payot, 1976.

Déparcieux, Antoine. *Essai sur les probabilités de la durée de la vie humaine.* Paris: Guérin Frères, 1746.

Deschamps, Gaston. "Contre la dépopulation." *Le Temps,* 22 October 1899.

Desfossé, Edmond. *Décroissance de la population en France—causes—remède.* Paris: Le Chevalier, 1869.

Despaulx-Ader, Pierre-Auguste. *De l'allaitement maternel au point de vue de la mère, de l'enfant, de la société.* Paris: Félix Malteste, 1868.

———. *De l'influence de l'hygiène sur le développement physique, moral et intellectuel de la première enfance.* Paris: Jouast, 1866.

Droz, Joseph. *Economie politique, ou Principes de la science des richesses.* Paris: Renouard, 1846.

———. *Essai sur l'art d'être heureux.* Paris: Renouard, 1806.

Du Camp, Maxime. "L'Etat civil à Paris." *Revue des deux mondes,* 18 March 1874, pp. 341–71.

Duchâtel, M.-T. *De la charité dans ses rapports avec l'état moral et le bien-être des classes inférieures de la société.* Paris: Mesnier, 1829.

Dufau, P. A. *Traité de statistique, ou Théorie de l'étude des lois d'après lesquelles se développent les faits sociaux.* Paris: Delloye, 1840.

Dumont, Arsène. *Dépopulation et civilisation.* Paris: Lecrosnier et Babé, 1890.

———. *La Morale basée sur la démographie.* Paris: Schleicher Frères, 1901.

———. *Natalité et démocratie.* Paris: Schleicher Frères, 1898.

———. "Natalité et masculinité." *Revue scientifique* ser. 4, 1, no. 24 (1894): 752–56.

Duncan, J. Matthews. *Fecundity, Fertility, Sterility, and Allied Topics.* Edinburgh: Adam and Charles Block, 1868.

———. "On a Lower Limit to the Power Executed in the Function of Parturition." *Transactions of the Royal Society of Edinburgh* 24 (1867): 639–51.

———. "On Some Laws of the Sterility of Women." *Transactions of the Royal Society of Edinburgh* 24 (1867): 313–25.

——. "On the Laws of the Fertility of Women." *Transactions of the Royal Society of Edinburgh* 24 (1867): 287–314.

——. "On the Variations of the Fertility and Fecundity of Women according to Age." *Transactions of the Royal Society of Edinburgh* 23 (1864): 475–90.

Dunoyer, Charles. *L'Industrie et la morale considerées dans leurs rapports avec la liberté*. Paris: A. Sautelet, 1825.

Dupin, Charles. *Bien-être et concorde des classes du peuple français*. Paris: Didot Frères, 1840.

——. *Des forces productives et commerciales de la France*. Paris: Bachelier, 1827.

Duval, Georges. "Variations sur un thème." *L'Evénement*, 27 October 1899, p. 1.

Duvillard, Emmanuel. "Mémoire sur le travail du Bureau de la statistique," *Etudes et documents. Comité pour l'histoire économique et financière de la France* 1 (1989): 425–32.

d'Espine, Marc. "Essai statistique sur la mortalité du canton de Genève pendant l'année 1838." *Annales d'hygiène publique et de médecine légale* 23 (1840): 5–130.

——. "Influence de l'aisance et de la misère sur la mortalité." *Annales d'hygiène publique et de médecine légale* 37 (1847): 322–57, 38 (1847): 5–32.

Expilly, Jean-Joseph. *Dictionnaire géographique, historique et politique des gaules et de la France*. 5 vols. Amsterdam: Desaint et Saillant, 1762–70.

——. *Tableau de la population de la France*. Paris, 1780.

Fourier, Jean-Baptiste. "Mémoire sur les résultats moyens déduits d'un grand nombre d'observations." In *Oeuvres de Fourier*, vol. 2, edited by Gaston Darboux, pp. 523–45. Paris: Gauthier-Villars, 1890.

——. "Rapport sur la proposition de fonder un prix annuel de statistique." In *Registres de l'Académie royale des sciences*. Paris: F. Didot, n.d.

——. "Second mémoire sur les résultats moyens et sur les erreurs des mesures." *Oeuvres de Fourier*, vol. 2, edited by Gaston Darboux, pp. 547–90. Paris: Gauthier-Villars, 1890.

de Foville, A. "La Statistique et ses ennemis." *Journal de la Société de statistique de Paris* 26 (1885): 448–54.

Frégier, H.-A. *Des classes dangereuses de la population dans les grandes villes et des moyens de les rendre meilleurs*. 2 vols. Paris: Baillière, 1840.

Garnier, Joseph. *Du principe de population*. Paris: Guillaumin, 1857.

——. "Population." *Dictionnaire de l'économie politique*, 2:382–420. Paris: Guillaumin, 1873.

——. "Tableau des causes de la misère et des remèdes qu'on peut y apporter." *Journal des économistes* ser. 2, 14 (1857): 340–50.

Gasté, L.-F. *Du calcul appliqué à la médecine comme complément de la théorie, des faits, et des raisonnements*. Paris: Bailliére, 1838.

Gavarret, Jules. *Principes généreux de statistique médicale*. Paris: Bechet jeune & Labé, 1840.

Geffroy, Gustave. "La Nourrice." *L'Aurore*, 24 October 1899, p. 1.

Giffard, Pierre. "Un Impot sur les familles nombreuses." *Le Petit Journal*, 20 June 1896, p. 1.

de Gramont, Louis. "Les Médecins du mariage." *L'Eclair*, 4 March 1897, p. 1.

——. "La Question vitale." *L'Eclair*, 4 February 1897, p. 1.

Guérard, Jacques Alphonse. "Rapport de M. Guérard sur les statistiques des causes de décès." *Bulletin de l'Académie impériale de médecine* 23 (1857–58).

Guillard, Achille. "Démographie (lois de population)." *Journal de la Société de statistique de Paris* 1 (1860): 277–88.

——. *Elements de statistique humaine.* Paris: Guillaumin, 1855.

Guyot, Ludovic. *Hygiène et protection des enfants du premier âge.* Paris: Baillière, 1878.

Guyot, Yves. "Zola et son dernier livre." *Le Siècle,* 13 October 1899, p. 1.

de Haussonville, Othenin. "L'Enfance à Paris." *Revue des deux mondes* 17 (1876): 481–511.

Herbin de Halle, P. *Statistique générale et particulière de la France et de ses colonies, avec une nouvelle déscription topographique, physique, agricole, politique, industrielle et commerciale de cet état.* 7 vols. Paris: F. Buisson, 1803–4.

Hertz, Robert. *Socialisme et dépopulation.* Paris: Librairie du Parti socialiste, 1910.

Husson, Armand. *Les Consommations de Paris.* Paris: Guillaumin, 1856.

——. *Discours sur la mortalité des jeunes enfants.* Paris: Baillière, 1866.

——. *Note sur la mortalité des enfants du premier âge, nés dans la ville de Paris.* Paris: Baillière, 1870.

d'Ivernois, Francis. "Sur les centenaires et sur les conséquences à tirer de leur nombre plus ou moins grand." *Annales d'hygiène publique et de médecine légale* 15 (1836): 276–93.

Jacoby, Paul. *Etudes sur la sélection chez l'homme.* Paris: Alcan, 1904.

Körösi, Joseph. "De la mesure et des lois de la fécondité conjugale." *Revue d'économie politique* 9 (1895): 1–10.

Lacassagne, Alexandre. "La Natalité à Lyon." *Bulletin de la Société d'anthropologie de Lyon* 6 (1887): 52–58.

de La Farelle, F. F. *Du progrès social au profit des classes populaires et non-indigentes.* Paris: Guillaumin, 1847.

Lagneau, Gustave. "Etude démographique de la diminution ou de l'accroissement des familles." *Bulletin de l'Académie de médecine* ser. 3, 20 (1888): 498–514.

Lamouroux, Alfred. "Rapport présenté par M. Lamouroux sur la réorganisation de la statistique municipale de Paris." *Conseil municipale de Paris, rapports et documents,* no. 12 (1877).

Lampière, Anna. *Le Role social de la femme, devoirs, droits, éducation.* Paris: Alcan, 1898.

Laplace, Pierre Simon de. *A Philosophical Essay on Probabilities.* Translated by Frederick Wilson Truscott and Frederick Lincoln Emery. New York: Dover, 1951.

——. "Sur les naissances, les mariages et les morts à Paris, depuis 1771 jusqu'en 1784; et dans toute l'étendue de la France, pendant les années 1781 et 1782." In *Histoire de l'Académie royale des sciences avec les mémoires de mathématique et de physique tirés des registres de cette Académie,* pp. 693–702. Paris: Imprimerie Royale, 1786.

de Lavergne, Léonce. "L'Agriculture et la population." *Revue des deux mondes* 8 (1857): 481–501.

——. "Les Animaux reproducteurs." *Revue des deux mondes* 11 (1855): 179–212.

——. "Du principe de population." *Séances et travaux de l'Académie des sciences morales et politiques* ser. 3, 23 (1858): 365–72.

——. "Rapport verbal sur un ouvrage de M. Doubleday intitulé: Véritable loi de la population." *Séances et travaux de l'Académie des sciences morales et politiques* 43 (1858): 93–98.

Lédé, F. "Résultats de l'application de la loi du 23 décembre, 1874 concernant la protection des enfants placés en nourrice." *Assistance* 5 (1895): 225–34, 241–48, 276–81, 291–99.

Lefort, Léon. "La Mortalité des nouveau-nés et l'industrie des nourrices en France." *Revue des deux mondes* 86 (1870): 362–91.

Legouvé, Ernest. *Histoire morale des femmes*. Paris: Sandré, 1849.

Legoyt, Alfred. "Les Accidents en Europe." *Journal de la Société de statistique de Paris* 6 (1865).

——. "De la mortalité á Paris, á Londres, á Vienne, et á New York en 1865." *Journal de la Société de statistique de Paris* 8 (1867): 158–61.

——. "De la mortalité en France de 1800 à 1860." *Journal de la Société de statistique de Paris* 4 (1863): 212–22, 241–47.

——. "De quelques particularités du mouvement de la population en France en 1853." *Journal des économistes* ser. 2, 13 (1857): 200–224.

——. "Du mouvement de la population en France d'aprés les dénombrements." *Journal des économistes* ser. 2, 13 (1857): 321–35.

——. "Du mouvement de la population en France, du XVIIe au XIXe siècle." *Journal de la Société de statistique de Paris* 1 (1860): 131–43, 149–57.

——. *La France statistique*. Paris: Curmer, 1843.

——. "L'Infécondité de la France." *Revue scientifique* ser. 2, 19 (1880): 218–27, 278–83.

Le Play, Fréderic. *La Réforme sociale en France*. Paris: Dentu, 1878.

Le Roux, Henri. "Les Travaux de la Commission de statistique municipale de Paris." *Journal de la Société de statistique de Paris* 21 (1880): 228–31.

Leroy-Beaulieu, Paul. *La Question de la population*. Paris: Alcan, 1913.

——. "La Question de la population en France." *Journal de la Société de statistique de Paris* 21 (1880): 117–21.

——. "La Question de la population et la civilisation démocratique." *Revue des deux mondes* 143 (1897): 851–89.

Leuret, François. "Notice sur les indigens de la ville de Paris." *Annales d'hygiène publique et de médecine légale* 15 (1836): 294–355.

Levasseur, Emile. "France." In *25ème anniversaire de la Société statistique de Paris*, pp. 145–204. Paris: Berger-Levrault, 1886.

——. "Histoire de la natalité française." In *25ème anniversaire de la Société statistique de Paris*. Paris: Berger-Levrault, 1886.

——. "Note sur la situation faite à la France parmi les grandes puissances." *Annales de démographie internationale* 3 (1879): 309–14.

——. "L'Organisation, les travaux et les publications de la statistique officielle en France." *Journal de la Société de statistique de Paris* 26 (1885): 1–59.

——. *La Population française*. 3 vols. Paris: A. Rousseau, 1889.

Levy, Michel. *Traité de hygiène publique et privée*. 2 vols. Paris: Baillière, 1844.

Loir, Joseph-Napoléon. *De l'état civil des nouveau-nés au point de vue de l'hygiène et de la loi.* Paris: Cotillon, 1854.

———. *De l'exécution de l'article 55 du Code Civil relatif à la constatation des naissances.* Paris: Joubert, 1846.

———. *Des sexes en matières d'etat civil, comment prévenir les erreurs résultant de leurs anomalies.* Paris: Cotillon, 1854.

———. *Du service des actes de naissance en France et à l'étranger, nécéssité d'améliorer ce service.* Paris: d'Amyot, 1845.

Lombard, H. C. "De l'influence des professions sur la durée de la vie." *Annales d'hygiène publique et de médecine légale* 14 (1835): 88–131.

Loua, Toussaint. *Atlas statistique de la population de Paris.* Paris: J. Dejey, 1873.

———. "De la mortalité de Paris dans ses rapports avec la transformation de la ville." *Journal de la Société de statistique de Paris* 6 (1865): 46–52.

Loudon, Charles. *Solution du problème de la population et de la subsistance.* Paris: Girard, 1842.

Louis, Pierre. *Recherches sur les effets de la saignée dans quelques maladies inflammatoires et sur l'action émétique et des vésicatoires dans la pneumonie.* Paris: Baillière, 1835.

Mallet, Edouard. "Recherches historiques et statistiques sur la population de Genève, son mouvement annuel et sa longévité, depuis le XVIe siècle jusqu'à nos jours (1549–1833)." *Annales d'hygiène publique et de médecine légale* 17 (1837): 5–172.

Malthus, Thomas. *Essai sur le principe de population ou Exposé des effets passés et présents de l'action de cette cause sur le bonheur du genre humain; suivi de quelques recherches relative á l'espèrence de guérir ou d'adoucir les maux qu'elle entraîne.* Geneva and Paris: Paschoud, 1809.

———. *An Essay on the Principle of Population* (1803 ed.). Cambridge: Cambridge University Press, 1992.

———. *An Essay on the Principle of Population* (1798 ed.). New York: Norton, 1976.

———. *Principles of Political Economy.* London: William Pickering, 1836.

Marc, Charles. "Examen médico-légal des causes de la mort de S. A. R. le prince de Condé." *Annales d'hygiène publique et de médecine légale* 5 (1831): 156–224.

March, Lucien. "La Société de statistique de Paris, 1860–1910." In *Notes sur Paris, la Société de statistique de Paris.* Paris: Berger-Levrault, 1909.

Martin, Georges. "Frais de publication d'un bulletin hebdomadaire et mensuel de statistique, et fourniture d'imprimés pour travaux de statistique." *Conseil municipal de Paris, rapports et documents,* no. 132 (1880).

Maurel, E. *De la dépopulation de la France, étude sur la natalité.* Paris: O. Doin, 1896.

Mayer, Alexandre. *De la création d'une société protectrice de l'enfance pour l'amélioration de l'espèce humaine par l'éducation du premier âge.* Paris: Librairie des sciences sociales, 1865.

———. *De la mortalité excessive du premier âge considérée comme cause de dépopulation et des moyens d'y remédier.* Paris: Baillière, 1873.

———. *Des rapports conjugaux considérés sous le triple point de vue de la population, de la santé, et de la morale publique.* 4th ed. Paris: Baillière, 1860.

Messance, Louis. *Nouvelles recherches sur la population de la France.* Lyon, 1788.

———. *Recherches sur la population des généralités d'Auvergne, de Lyon, de Rouen, et de quelques provinces et villes du royaume.* Paris: Durand, 1766.

Millaud, Edouard. "Rapport addressé au ministère du commerce, au nom de la commission du Conseil supérieure de statistique." *Journal de la Société de statistique de Paris* 24 (1885): 151–62.

Mirabeau, Octave. "Fécondité." *L'Aurore,* 29 November 1899, p. 1.

Mirabeau, Victor de Riqueti, marquis de. *L'Ami des hommes ou Traité de la population.* 1756. Reprint. Darmstadt, 1970.

Moheau, Jean-Baptiste. *Recherches et considérations sur la population de la France.* Paris: Institut national d'études démographiques, 1994.

———. *Recherches et considérations sur la population de la France.* Paris: Moutard, 1778.

Monot, Charles. *De l'industrie des nourrices et de la mortalité des petits enfants.* Paris: A. Faure, 1867.

———. *De la mortalité excessive des enfants pendant la première année de leur existence, ses causes, et des moyens de la restreindre.* Paris: Baillière, 1872.

Montesquieu, Charles Louis de Secondat. *De l'esprit des lois.* Paris: Garnier Frères, 1973.

———. *Persian Letters.* Translated by J. C. Betts. New York: Penguin, 1973.

———. *The Spirit of the Laws.* Cambridge: Cambridge University Press, 1989.

Montorgeuil, George. "Fin de race." *L'Eclair,* 28 February 1997, p. 1.

Moreau de Jonnès, Alexandre. "La Patrie, ou Statistique sommaire de la France." *Séances et travaux de l'Académie des sciences morales et politiques* 16 (1849): 35–47.

———. "Population de la France comparée à celle des autres etats de l'Europe." *Journal des économistes* 1 (1842): 161–72.

Morel de Vindé, Charles. *Sur la théorie de la population ou Observations sur le système professé par M. Malthus et ses disciples.* Paris: Huzard, 1829.

Naquet, Alfred. *Temps futurs; socialisme—anarchie.* Paris: P.-V. Stock, 1900.

Parent-Duchâtelet, Alexandre. *De la prostitution dans la ville de Paris, considérée sous le rapport de l'hygiène publique, de la morale et de l'administration.* Paris: Baillière, 1836.

———. *Hygiène publique, ou Mémoires sur les questions les plus importantes de l'hygiène appliquée aux professions et aux travaux d'utilité publique.* Paris: Baillière, 1836.

Passy, Hippolyte. *Des causes de l'inégalité des richesses.* Paris: Pagnerre, Paulin, Didot Frères, 1848.

Pelletier, Madeleine. *L'Emancipation sexuelle de la femme.* Paris: Giard & Brière, 1911.

———. *La Femme en lutte pour ses droits.* Paris: Giard & Brière, 1908.

Peuchet, Jacques. *Statistique élémentaire de la France.* Paris: Gilbert, 1805.

Pinel, Philippe. "Analyse." *Dictionnaire des sciences médicales,* 2:19–30. Paris: Panckoucke, 1819.

———. "Observation." *Dictionnaire des sciences médicales,* 37:29–48. Paris: Panckoucke, 1819.

Piot, Edmé-Georges. *La Dépopulation, enquête personelle sur la dépopulation en France.* Paris: P. Mouillot, 1902.

———. *La Question de la dépopulation en France, le mal—ses causes—ses remèdes*. Paris: P. Mouillot, 1900.

des Pommelles, M. le chevalier. *Tableau de la population de toutes les provinces de France et de la proportion, sous tous les rapports, des naissances, des morts & des mariages depuis dix ans, d'après les registres de chaque généralité, accompagné des notes & observations*. Paris: n.p., 1789.

Pouchet, F.-A. *Théorie positive de l'ovulation spontanée et de la fécondation des mammifères et de l'espèce humaine*. Paris: Baillière, 1847.

Pouillet, Claude. "Sur les lois générales de la population." *Comptes-rendus des séances de l'Académie des sciences* (1842).

Prunelle, C. G. *De l'action de la médecine sur la population des états*. Paris: Feugueray, 1818.

———. *De la médecine politique en général et de son objet; de la médecine-légale en particulier, de son origine, de ses progrès, et des secours qu'elle fournit au magistrat dans l'exercice de ses fonctions*. Montpellier: Martel ainè, 1814.

Quetelet, Adolphe. *Congrès internationale de statistique*. Brussels: Hayez, 1873.

———. *Recherches statistiques*. Brussels: Hayez, 1844.

———. *Sur l'homme et le développement de ses facultés ou Essai de physique sociale*. 2 vols. Paris: Bachelier, 1835.

Quevenne, T.-A. *Du lait en général, des laits de femme, d'ânnesse, de chèvre, de brebis, de vache en particulier*. Paris: Bouchard-Huzard, Germer-Baillière, 1857.

Raisin, Charles. *La Dépopulation de la France et le code civil, ou Influence du régime successoral sur le mouvement de la natalité française*. Bourg-en-Bresse: Imprimerie du "Courrier de l'Ain," 1900.

Raudot, C. M. *De la décadence de la France*. Paris: Amyot, 1850.

Robin, Paul. *Libre amour, libre maternité*. Paris: Editions du Groupe Fresnes-Antony, 1981.

Roulliet, Antony. "Les Présidents de la Société de statistique de Paris." In *25ème anniversaire de la Société de Statistique de Paris, 1860–1885*, pp. 25–37. Paris: Berger-Levrault, 1886.

Rousseau, Jean-Jacques. *Oeuvres complètes*. Paris: Gallimard, 1964.

Roussel, Théophile. "Proposition de loi ayant pour objet la protection des enfants du premier âge et en particulier des nourrissons." *Assemblé nationale*, no. 1707 (1873).

———. "Rapport au nom de la commission chargée d'examiner la proposition de loi de M. Théophile Roussel relative à la protection des enfants du premier âge, et en particulier des nourrissons." *Assemblé nationale*, annex no. 2446 (1874).

Sadler, Michael Thomas. *The Law of Population: A Treatise in Six Books; in Disproof of the Superfecundity of Human Beings, and Developing the Real Principle of Their Increase*. London: John Murray, 1830.

Sanson, André. *L'Hérédité normale et pathologique*. Paris: Asselin & Houzeau, 1893.

Saugrain, Charles. *Dénombrement du royaume par généralitez, élections, paroisses et feux*. 2 vols. Paris: Saugrain, 1709.

Savary, Auguste-Charles. "Analogie." *Dictionnaire des sciences médicales*, 2:18. 60 vols. Paris: Panckoucke, 1812–22.

Say, Jean-Baptiste. *Cours complet d'économie politique pratique.* Paris: Guillaumin, 1840.

———. "De l'objet et de l'utilité des statistique." *Revue encyclopédique* 35 (1827): 1–27.

———. *Lettres à M. Malthus sur différens sujets d'économie politique.* Paris: Bossange, 1820.

———. *Traité d'économie politique.* 1841. Reprint. Osnabrück: Otto Zeller, 1966.

Say, Léon. "La Statistique internationale." *Journal de la Société de statistique de Paris* 26 (1885): 438–47.

Serrurier, J. B. T. "Sémiotique." *Dictionnaire des sciences médicales,* 50:556–69. Paris: Panckoucke, 1820.

Sicard de Plauzoles, Justin. *La Fonction sexuelle au point de vue de l'éthique et de l'hygiène sociale.* Paris: Giard & Brière, 1908.

Simon, Jules. *La Femme du vingtième siècle.* Paris: Calman Lévy, 1892.

de Sismondi, J.-C. L. Simonde. *Nouveaux principes d'économie politique ou de la richesse dans ses rapports avec la population.* 2 vols. Paris: Delaunay, 1819.

Smith, S. "De l'influence des conditions physiques et morales sur la longévité." *Annales d'hygiène publique et de médecine légale* 15 (1836): 87–114.

Strauss, Paul. *Dépopulation et puériculture.* Paris: Fasquelle, 1901.

Tailhade, Laurent. "Vénus Victrix." *La Petite République,* 25 October 1899, p. 1.

de Tocqueville, Alexis. *The Old Regime and the French Revolution.* Translated by Stuart Gilbert. New York: Anchor, 1955.

Trébuchet, Adolphe. "Statistique des décès dans la ville de Paris." *Annales d'hygiène publique et de médecine légale* 45–46 (1851): 336–86, 5–39.

Turquan, Victor. *Contribution à l'étude de la population et de la dépopulation.* Lyon: H. Georg, 1902.

———. "Contribution à l'étude sur la dépopulation de la France." *Bulletin de la Société d'anthropologie de Lyon* 21 (1902): 1–170.

Vacher, Dr. "La Mortalité à Paris en 1872." *Journal de la Société de statistique de Paris* 15 (1874): 99–105.

Victor-Meunier, Lucien. "Fécondité." *Le Rappel,* 16 October 1899, p. 1.

de Villeneuve, Alban. *De l'influence des passions sur l'ordre économique des sociétés.* Paris: Panckoucke, 1846.

Villermé, Louis-René. "De la mortalité dans les divers quartiers de la ville de Paris, et des causes qui la rendent très différente dans plusieurs d'entre eux, ainsi que dans les divers quartiers de beaucoup de grandes villes." *Annales d'hygiène publique et de médecine légale* 3 (1830): 294–331.

———. "De la mortalité des enfants trouvés considérée dans ses rapports avec le mode d'allaitement, et sur l'accroissement de leur nombre en France." *Annales d'hygiène publique et de médecine légale* 19 (1838): 39–78.

———. "Des épidémies sous les rapports de l'hygiène publique, de la statistique médicale, et de l'économie politique." *Annales d'hygiène publique et de médecine légale* 9 (1833): 5–58.

———. "Mémoire sur la distribution de la population française, par sexe et par état civil, et sur la nécéssité de perfectionner nos tableaux et de mortalité." *Annales d'hygiène publique et de médecine légale* 17 (1837): 245–80.

——. "Mémoire sur la durée moyenne des maladies aux différentes âges, et sur l'application de la loi de cette durée et de la loi de la mortalité à l'organisation des sociétés mutuels." *Annales d'hygiène publique et de médecine légale* 2 (1829): 242–66.

——. "Mémoire sur la mortalité en France dans la classe aisée et dans la classe indigente." *Mémoires de l'Académie royale de médecine* 1 (1828): 51–98.

——. "Rapport fait par M. Villermé et lu à l'Académie royale de médecine, au nom de la Commission de statistique sur une série de tableaux relatifs au mouvement de la population dans les douze arrondissements municipaux de la ville de Paris pendant les cinq années 1817, 1818, 1819, 1820, et 1821." *Archives générales de médecine* 10 (1826): 216–47.

——. *Tableau de l'état physique et moral des ouvriers employés dans les manufactures de coton, de laine et de soie.* 2 vols. Paris: Renouard, 1840.

Zola, Emile. *Fécondité.* 1899. Reprint. Paris: Bernouard, 1927.

SECONDARY SOURCES

Accampo, Elinor. *Industrialization, Family Life, and Class Relations: Saint Chamond, 1815–1914.* Berkeley: University of California Press, 1989.

——. "The Rhetoric of Reproduction and the Reconfiguration of Womanhood in the French Birth Control Movement, 1890–1920." *Journal of Family History* 21 (1996): 351–71.

Accampo, Elinor, Rachel Fuchs, and Mary Lynn Stewart, eds. *Gender and the Politics of Social Reform in France, 1870–1914.* Baltimore: Johns Hopkins University Press, 1995.

Ackerknecht, E. A. *Medicine at the Paris Hospital, 1794–1848.* Baltimore: Johns Hopkins University Press, 1967.

——. "Villermé and Quetelet." *Bulletin of the History of Medicine* 26 (1952): 317–29.

Anderson, Benedict. *Imagined Communities: Reflections on the Origin and Spread of Nationalism.* London: Verso, 1991.

Anderson, Margo. *The American Census: A Social History.* New Haven: Yale University Press, 1988.

Ariès, Philippe. *Centuries of Childhood.* New York: Vintage, 1962.

Armengaud, André. "L'Attitude de la société à l'égard de l'enfant au XIXe siècle." *Annales de démographie historique* (1973): 303–12.

——. *Démographie et sociétés.* Paris: Editions Stock, 1966.

——. *Les Français et Malthus.* Paris: Presses Universitaires de France, 1975.

——. "Mouvement ouvrier et néo-malthusianisme au début du XXe siècle." *Annales de démographie historique* (1966): 7–19.

——. "Les Nourrices du Morvan au XIXe siècle." *Etudes et chronique de démographie historique* 1 (1964): 131–39.

——. *La Population française au XIXe siècle.* Paris: Presses Universitaires de France, 1971.

——. "Population in Europe, 1700–1914." In *The Fontana Economic History of*

Europe: The Industrial Revolution, edited by Carlo Cipolla. London: Collins, 1975.

Baker, Keith. *Condorcet: From Natural Philosophy to Social Mathematics*. Chicago: University of Chicago Press, 1975.

————. "The Early History of the Term, 'Social Science.'" *Annals of Science* 20 (1964): 211–26.

————. *Inventing the French Revolution*. Cambridge: Cambridge University Press, 1990.

Bardet, Jean-Pierre. "Aux origines du Bureau de la statistique, Duvillard de Durand, 1755–1832." *Population et société* 4 (1980): 154–64.

————. "La Chute de la fécondité: Le constat." In *Histoire de la population française*, edited by Jacques Dupâquier, 3:351–64. Paris: Presses Universitaires de France, 1988.

————. "La Chute de la fécondité: Les incertitudes de l'explication." In *Histoire de la population française*, edited by Jacques Dupâquier, 3:364–78. Paris: Presses Universitaires de France, 1988.

Bardet, Jean-Pierre, and Jacques Dupâquier. "Contraception: Les Français les premiers, mais pourquoi?" *Communications* 44 (1986): 3–33.

Barrows, Susanna. *Distorting Mirrors: Visions of the Crowd in Late Nineteenth-Century France*. New Haven: Yale University Press, 1981.

Beaver, M. W. "Population, Infant Mortality and Milk." *Population Studies* 27 (1973): 243–54.

Becchia, Alain. "Les Milieux parlementaires et la dépopulation de 1900 à 1914." *Communications* 44 (1986): 201–41.

Bergues, Hélène. *La Prévention des naissances dans la famille*. Paris: Institut national des études démographiques, 1960.

Bideau, Alain, Jacques Dupâquier, and Jean-Noël Biraben. "La Mortalité de 1800 à 1914." In *Histoire de la population française*, edited by Jacques Dupâquier, 3:279–98. Paris: Presses Universitaires de France, 1988.

Biraben, Jean-Noël. "La Statistique de population sous le Consulat et sous l'Empire." *Revue d'histoire moderne et contemporaine* 17 (1970): 359–72.

Biraben, Jean-Noël, and Jacques Léonard. "Les Maladies et la médecine." In *Histoire de la population française*, edited by Jacques Dupâquier, 3:299–321. Paris: Presses Universitaires de France, 1988.

Bock, Gisela, and Pat Thane, eds. *Maternity and Gender Policies: Women and the Rise of the European Welfare States, 1880–1950s*. New York: Routledge, 1991.

Bogue, Donald J. *Principles of Demography*. New York: Wiley, 1969.

Bonar, James. *Theories of Population from Raleigh to Arthur Young*. London: Allen & Unwin, 1931.

Bosher, J. F. *French Finances, 1775–1795: From Business to Bureaucracy*. Cambridge: Cambridge University Press, 1970.

Bourgeois-Pichat, J. "The General Development of the Population of France Since the Eighteenth Century." In *Population in History*, edited by D. V. Glass and D. E. C. Eversley, pp. 474–93. Chicago: Aldine, 1965.

Bourguet, Marie-Noëlle. *Déchiffrer la France: La statistique départementale à l'époque Napoléonienne*. Paris: Editions des archives contemporaines, 1988.

———. "Décrire, Compter, Calculer: The Debate over Statistics during the Napoleonic Period." In *The Probabilistic Revolution*, edited by Lorenz Krüger, Lorraine J. Daston, and Michael Heidelberger, 1:305–16. Cambridge, Mass.: MIT Press, 1987.

Boxer, Marilyn. "When Radical and Socialist Feminism Were Joined: The Extraordinary Failure of Madeleine Pelletier." In *European Women on the Left: Socialism, Feminism, and the Problems Faced by Political Women, 1880 to the Present*, edited by Jane Slaughter and Robert Kern, pp. 51–73. Westport, Conn.: Greenwood Press, 1981.

Brian, Eric. *La Mesure de l'etat: Administrateurs et géomètres au XVIIIe siècle*. Paris: Albin Michel, 1994.

———. "Le Prix Montyon de statistique à l'Académie royale des sciences pendant la Restauration." *Revue de synthèse* ser. 4, no. 2 (1991): 207–36.

Canguilhem, Georges. *The Normal and the Pathological*. New York: Zone Books, 1989.

Charbit, Yves. "Les Economistes libéraux et la population (1840–1870)." In *Histoire de la population française*, edited by Jacques Dupâquier, 3:467–81. Paris: Presses Universitaires de France, 1988.

———. *Du malthusianisme au populationisme*. Paris: Presses Universitaires de France, 1981.

———. "The Fate of Malthus's Work: History and Ideology." In *Malthus Past and Present*, edited by Jacques Dupâquier and A. Fauve-Chamoux, pp. 17–30. London: Academic Press, 1983.

Chevalier, Louis. *Laboring Classes and Dangerous Classes in Paris during the First Half of the Nineteenth Century*. Princeton: Princeton University Press, 1973.

———. "La Statistique et la déscription sociale de Paris." *Population* 11, no. 4 (1956): 621–52.

Coale, Ansley J., and Susan Cotts Watkins. *The Decline of Fertility in Europe*. Princeton: Princeton University Press, 1986.

Cole, Joshua. "The Chaos of Particular Facts: Statistics, Medicine and the Social Body in Early 19th-Century France." *History of the Human Sciences* 7 (1994): 1–27.

———. "'A Sudden and Terrible Revelation': Motherhood and Infant Mortality in France, 1858–1874." *Journal of Family History* 21 (October 1996): 419–45.

———. "'There Are Only Good Mothers': The Ideological Work of Women's Fertility in France before World War I." *French Historical Studies* 19 (Spring 1996): 639–72.

Coleman, William. *Death Is a Social Disease: Public Health and Political Economy in Early Industrial France*. Madison: University of Wisconsin Press, 1982.

Comiti, Vincent-Pierre. "Elements historique de l'utilisation de la méthode statistique en médecine." *Histoire des sciences médicales* 13, no. 2 (1979): 121–30.

Corbin, Alain. *Les Filles de noce*. Paris: Aubier Montaigne, 1978.

Cova, Anne. "French Feminism and Maternity: Theories and Policies, 1890–1918." In *Maternity and Gender Policies: Women and the Rise of the European Welfare States, 1880–1950s*, edited by Gisela Bock and Pat Thane, pp. 119–38. New York: Routledge, 1991.

Daston, Lorraine. *Classical Probability in the Enlightenment.* Princeton: Princeton University Press, 1988.
——. "The Ideal and Reality of the Republic of Letters in the Enlightenment." *Science in Context* 4 (1991): 367–86.
Davidoff, Leonore, and Catherine Hall. *Family Fortunes: Men and Women of the English Middle Class.* Chicago: University of Chicago Press, 1987.
Dean, Mitchell. *The Constitution of Poverty: Toward a Genealogy of Liberal Governance.* London: Routledge, 1991.
Desrosières, Alain. "Comment faire des choses qui tiennent: Histoire sociale et statistique." *Histoire & mesure* 4 (1989): 225–42.
——. "Histoire de formes: Statistiques et sciences sociales avant 1940." *Revue français de sociologie* 26 (1985): 277–310.
——. "Masses, individus, moyennes: La statistique sociale au XIXième siècle." *Hermes* 2 (1988): 41–66.
——. *La Politique des grands nombres, histoire de la raison statistique.* Paris: Editions la Découverte, 1993.
Donzelot, Jacques. *L'Invention du social, essai sur le déclin des passions politiques.* Paris: Fayard, 1984.
——. *The Policing of Families.* New York: Pantheon, 1979.
Dupâquier, Jacques, ed. *Histoire de la population française.* Vol. 2,. *De la Renaissance à 1789.* Paris: Presses Universitaires de France, 1988.
——. *Histoire de la population française.* Vol. 3, *De 1789 à 1914.* Paris: Presses Universitaires de France, 1988.
Dupâquier, Jacques, and Michel Dupâquier. *Histoire de la démographie.* Paris: Perrin, 1985.
Dupâquier, Jacques, and A. Fauve-Chamoux, eds. *Malthus Past and Present.* New York: Academy Press, 1983.
Dupâquier, Jacques, and René Le Mée. "La Connaissance des faits démographiques de 1789 à 1914." In *Histoire de la population française*, 3: 15–61, edited by Jacques Dupâquier. Paris: Presses Universitaires de France, 1988.
Dupâquier, Michel. "La Famille Bertillon et la naissance d'une nouvelle science sociale, la démographie." *Annales de démographie historique* (1983): 293–311.
Duroselle, Jean-Baptiste. *Les Débuts du catholicisme social en France, 1822–1870.* Paris: Presses Universitaires de France, 1951.
Esmonin, Edmond. *Etudes sur la France des XVIIIe et XVIIIe siècles.* Paris: Presses Universitaires de France, 1964.
Eversley, D. E. C. "Population, Economy, and Society." In *Population in History*, edited by D. V. Glass and D. E. C. Eversley, pp. 23–69. Chicago: Aldine, 1965.
——. *Social Theories of Fertility and the Malthusian Debate.* Oxford: Oxford University Press, 1959.
Ewald, François. *L'Etat providence.* Paris: Grasset, 1986.
Eyler, John M. *Victorian Social Medicine: The Ideas and Methods of William Farr.* Baltimore: Johns Hopkins University Press, 1979.
Fine-Sauriac, A. "Mortalité infantile et allaitement dans le sud-ouest de la France au XIXe siècle." *Annales de démographie historique* (1978): 81–103.
Foucault, Michel. *The Birth of the Clinic.* New York: Vintage, 1973.

———. *Discipline and Punish.* New York: Vintage, 1979.

———. *The History of Sexuality.* Vol. 1, *An Introduction.* New York: Vintage, 1980.

———. "Omnes et Singulatum: Towards a Criticism of 'Political Reason.'" In *The Tanner Lectures on Human Values,* edited by Sterling M. McMurrin, 2:223–54. Salt Lake City: University of Utah Press, 1981.

Fuchs, Rachel. *Abandoned Children: Foundlings and Child Welfare in Nineteenth-Century France.* Albany: SUNY Press, 1984.

———. *Poor and Pregnant in Paris: Strategies for Survival in the Nineteenth Century.* New Brunswick: Rutgers University Press, 1992.

Furet, François, ed. *Livre et société dans la France du XVIIIe siècle.* Vol. 1. Paris: Mouton, 1965.

Gaillard, Jeanne. "La Formation d'une élite: Les médecins parisiens sous le Second Empire." *Bulletin du Centre de l'histoire de la France contemporaine* 4 (1983): 51–63.

Gallagher, Catherine. "The Body versus the Social Body in the Works of Thomas Malthus and Henry Mayhew." *Representations* 14 (1986): 83–106.

Galliano, Paul. "La Mortalité infantile dans la banlieue sud de Paris à la fin du XVIIIe siècle (1774–1794)." *Annales de démographie historique* (1966): 139–77.

Geiss, Imanuel. *Geschichte des Rassismus.* Frankfurt/Main: Suhrkamp, 1988.

Gelfand, Toby. *Professionalizing Modern Medicine: Paris Surgeons, Medical Science, and Institutions in the 18th Century.* Westport, Conn.: Greenwood Press, 1980.

Gigerenzer, Gerd, Zeno Switjink, Theodore Porter, Lorraine Daston, John Beatty, and Lorenz Krüger. *The Empire of Chance: How Probability Changed Science and Everyday Life.* Cambridge: Cambridge University Press, 1989.

Gille, Bertrand. *Les Sources statistiques de l'histoire de France, les enquêtes du 17e siècle à 1870.* Paris: Minard, 1964.

Gillispie, Charles. "Probability and Politics: Laplace, Condorcet, and Turgot." *Proceedings of the American Philosophical Society* 116 (1972): 1–20.

Girard, Louis. *Les Libéraux français, 1814–1875.* Paris: Aubier, 1985.

Glass, D. V. *Population Policies and Movements in Europe.* New York: Augustus Kelley, 1968.

Goldstein, Jan. *Console and Classify: The French Psychiatric Profession in the Nineteenth Century.* Cambridge: Cambridge University Press, 1987.

Gonnard, René. *Histoire des doctrines de la population.* Paris: Nouvelle Librairie Internationale, 1923.

Gordon, Felicia. *The Integral Feminist—Madeleine Pelletier, 1874–1939: Feminism, Socialism, and Medicine.* Minneapolis: University of Minnesota Press, 1990.

Gossiaux, P. "Anthropologie des Lumières (Culture "naturelle"et racisme rituel)." In *L'Homme des lumières et la dècouverte de l'autre,* edited by D. Droixhe and P.-P. Gossiaux, pp. 49–69. Brussels: Editions de l'Université de Bruxelles, 1985.

Goubert, P. "Recent Theories and Research in French Population between 1500 and 1700." In *Population and History,* edited by D. V. Glass and D. E. C. Eversley. Chicago: Aldine, 1965.

Grattan-Guiness, Ivor. *Joseph Fourier, 1768–1830.* Cambridge, Mass.: MIT Press, 1972.

de Grazia, Victoria, with Ellen Furlough, eds. *The Sex of Things: Gender and Consumption in Historical Perspective.* Berkeley: University of California Press, 1996.

Guegan, Isabelle. *Inventaire des enquêtes administratives et statistiques, 1789–1795.* Paris: Editions du C. T. H. S., 1991.

Guerrand, Roger-Henri, and Francis Ronsin. *Le Sexe apprivoisé: Jeanne Humbert et la lutte pour le contrôle des naissances.* Paris: Editions de la Découverte, 1990.

Hacking, Ian. "Biopower and the Avalanche of Printed Numbers." *Humanities in Society* 5 (Summer–Fall 1982): 279–95.

——. *The Emergence of Probability.* Cambridge: Cambridge University Press, 1975.

——. "How Should We Do the History of Statistics?" *Ideology and Consciousness* 8 (1981): 15–26.

——. *The Taming of Chance.* Cambridge: Cambridge University Press, 1990.

Halbwachs, Maurice. *La Théorie de l'homme moyen: Essai sur Quetelet et la statistique morale.* Paris: Alcan, 1912.

Hankins, Frank H. *Adolphe Quetelet as Statistician.* New York: Columbia University Press, 1908.

Haraway, Donna. "The Biopolitics of Postmodern Bodies." *Differences* 1 (1989): 3–43.

Harris, Marvin, and Eric B. Ross. *Death, Sex, and Fertility: Population Regulation in Preindustrial and Developing Societies.* New York: Columbia University Press, 1987.

Harris, Robert D. *Necker: Reform Statesman of the Ancien Régime.* Berkeley: University of California Press, 1979.

Hartmann, Heidi. "The Family as the Locus of Gender, Class, and Political Struggle: The Example of Housework." *Signs* 6 (Spring 1981): 366–94.

Hause, Steven C., and Anne R. Kenney. *Women's Suffrage and Social Politics in the French Third Republic.* Princeton: Princeton University Press, 1984.

Hecht, Jacqueline. "French Utopian Socialists and the Population Question: 'Seeking the Future City.'" In *Population and Resources in Western Intellectual Traditions,* edited by Michael Teitelbaum and Jay Winter, pp. 49–73. Cambridge: Cambridge University Press, 1989.

Henry, Louis. "The Population of France in the Eighteenth Century." In *Population in History,* edited by D. V. Glass and D. E. C. Eversley, pp. 434–56. Chicago: Aldine, 1965.

Herbert, Christopher. *Culture and Anomie: Ethnographic Imagination in the Nineteenth Century.* Chicago: University of Chicago Press, 1991.

Heywood, Colin. *Childhood in Nineteenth-Century France: Work, Health, and Education among the "Classes Populaires."* Cambridge: Cambridge University Press, 1988.

Hilts, Victor L. "Statistics and Social Science." In *Foundations of Scientific Method: The Nineteenth Century,* edited by Ronald N. Giere and Richard S. Westfall. Bloomington: Indiana University Press, 1973.

Horvath, R. "La Quantification et les débuts de la science statistique et sociologique." *Population* 33 (1978): 85–98.

Hunter, John C. "The Problem of the French Birth Rate on the Eve of World War I." *French Historical Studies* 11 (1962): 490–503.

Isambert, F. A. "Les Recherches statistiques d'Ange-Michel Guerry." *Cahiers internationaux de sociologie* 16, no. 2 (1969): 35–44.

James, Patricia. *Population Malthus: His Life and Times*. London: Routledge & Kegan Paul, 1979.

Kang, Zheng. "Lieu de savoir social: La Société de statistique de Paris au XIXe siècle (1860–1910)." Ph.D. dissertation, Ecole des hautes études en sciences sociales, Paris, 1989.

Kanipe, Esther. "The Family, Private Property and the State in France, 1870–1914." Ph.D. dissertation, University of Wisconsin, Madison, 1976.

Keyfitz, N. "The Evolution of Malthus's Thought: Malthus as a Demographer." In *Malthus Past and Present*, edited by Jacques Dupâquier and A. Fauve-Chamoux, pp. 3–16. London: Academic Press, 1983.

Klaus, Alisa. "Depopulation and Race Suicide: Maternalism and Pronatalist Ideologies in France and the United States." In *Mothers of a New World: Maternalist Politics and the Origins of Welfare States*, edited by Seth Koven and Sonya Michel, pp. 188–212. London: Routledge, 1993.

———. *Every Child a Lion: The Origins of Maternal and Infant Health Policy in the United States and France, 1890–1920*. Ithaca: Cornell University Press, 1993.

Koos, Cheryl A. "Gender, Anti-individualism, and Nationalism: The Alliance Nationale and the Pronatalist Backlash against the *Femme moderne*, 1933–1940." *French Historical Studies* 19 (1996): 699–723.

Koven, Seth, and Sonya Michel, eds. *Mothers of a New World: Maternalist Politics and the Origins of the Welfare States*. New York: Routledge, 1993.

Krüger, Lorenz, Lorrain Dastone, and Michael Heidelberger, eds. *The Probabilistic Revolution*. Cambridge, Mass: MIT Press, 1987.

Kselman, Claudia S. "The Modernization of Family Law: The Politics and Ideology of Family Reform in Third Republic France." Ph.D. dissertation, University of Michigan, 1980.

Kudlick, Catherine. *Cholera in Post-Revolutionary Paris: A Cultural History*. Berkeley: University of California Press, 1996.

La Berge, Ann F. *Mission and Method: The Early Nineteenth-Century French Public Health Movement*. Cambridge: Cambridge University Press, 1992.

Laqueur, Thomas. *Making Sex: Body and Gender from the Greeks to Freud*. Cambridge, Mass.: Harvard University Press, 1990.

Leavitt, Judith Walzer. "Medicine in Context: A Review Essay of the History of Medicine." *American Historical Review* 95 (1990): 1471–84.

Le Bras, Hervé. "La Chute de la fécondité: Géographie de la fécondité française au XIXe siècle." In *Histoire de la population française*, edited by Jacques Dupâquier, 3:378–96. Paris: Presses Universitaires de France, 1988.

———. "Malthus and the Two Mortalities." In *Malthus Past and Present*, edited by Jacques Dupâquier and A. Fauve-Chamoux, pp. 31–42. London: Academic Press, 1983.

———. *Marianne et les lapins*. Paris: Olivier Orban, 1991.

———. "La Statistique Générale de la France." In *Les Lieux de mémoire*, vol. 2, *La Nation*, edited by Pierre Nora, pp. 317–53. Paris: Gallimard, 1986.

———. "Le Vrai nature du taux de natalité." *Population* 34, no. 1 (1979): 91–107.

Lécuyer, Bernard-Pierre. "Démographie, statistique et hygiène publique sous la monarchie censitaire." *Annales de démographie historique* (1977): 215–45.

Lécuyer, Bernard-Pierre, and Jean-Noël Biraben. "L'Hygiène publique et la révolution pastorienne." In *Histoire de la population française*, edited by Jacques Dupâquier, 3:321–43. Paris: Presses Universitaires de France, 1988.

Le Mée, René. "Introduction." In Jean-Baptiste Moheau, *Recherches et considérations sur la population de la France*, edited by Eric Vilquin. Paris: Institut national d'études démographiques, 1994.

———. "La Statistique démographique officielle de 1815 à 1870 en France." *Annales de démographie historique* (1975): 251–78.

Léonard, Jacques. *La Médecine entre les pouvoirs et les savoirs*. Paris: Aubier, 1981.

Lottin, Joseph. *Quetelet, statisticien et sociologue*. Paris: Alcan, 1912.

Lyotard, Jean-François. *The Postmodern Condition: A Report on Knowledge*. Minneapolis: University of Minnesota Press, 1984.

Lynch, Katherine. *Family, Class, and Ideology in Early Industrial France*. Madison: University of Wisconsin Press, 1988.

Mailly, Nicolas Emile. "Essai sur la vie et les ouvrages de Lambert-Adolphe-Jacques Quetelet." *Annuaire de l'Académie royale des sciences, des lettres et des beaux-arts de Belgiques* 41 (1875): 109–297.

Marec, Yannick, and Evelyne Barbin. "Les Recherches sur la probabilité des jugements de Simon-Denis Poisson." *Histoire de la mesure* 2 (1987): 39–58.

McDougall, Mary Lynn. "Protecting Infants: The French Campaign for Maternity Leaves, 1890s–1913." *French Historical Studies* 13 (1983): 79–105.

McLaren, Angus. "Abortion in France: Women and the Regulation of Family Size, 1800–1914." *French Historical Studies* 10 (1978): 461–85.

———. "Sex and Socialism: The Opposition of the French Left to Birth Control in the Nineteenth Century." *Journal of the History of Ideas* 27 (1976): 475–92.

———. *Sexuality and Social Order: The Debate over the Fertility of Women and Workers in France, 1770–1920*. New York: Holmes & Meier, 1983.

———. "Some Secular Attitudes toward Sexual Behavior in France." *French Historical Studies* 8 (1974): 604–25.

Mentré, F. *Cournot et la renaissance du probabalisme au XIXe siècle*. Paris: Marcel Riviére, 1908.

Miller, Richard. *Fact and Method: Explanation, Confirmation and Reality in the Natural and the Social Sciences*. Princeton: Princeton University Press, 1987.

Mitchell, Allan. *The Divided Path: The German Influence on Social Reform in France after 1870*. Chapel Hill: University of North Carolina Press, 1991.

Mitchell, Brian. *European Historical Statistics*. New York: Facts on File, 1978.

Morel, M. F. "Théories et pratiques de l'allaitement en France au XVIIIe siècle." *Annales de démographie historique* (1976): 393–426.

Moricourt, C. "Bibliographie analytique des oeuvres de la famille Bertillon." Unpublished manuscript. Paris: Institut national des études démographiques.

Moses, Claire Goldberg. *French Feminism in the 19th Century*. Albany: State University of New York Press, 1984.

Mosse, George. *Toward the Final Solution: A History of European Racism*. Toronto: J. M. Dent, 1978.

Murphy, Terence. "The French Medical Profession's Perception of Its Social Function, 1776–1830." *Medical History* 23 (1979): 229–78.

———. "Medical Knowledge and Statistical Methods in Early Nineteenth-Century France." *Medical History* 25 (1981): 301–19.

Myrdal, Gunnar. *Population: A Problem for Democracy.* Gloucester, Mass.: Peter Smith, 1962.

Nye, Robert. *Crime, Madness, and Politics in Modern France: The Medical Concept of National Decline.* Princeton: Princeton University Press, 1984.

———. "Honor, Impotence, and Male Sexuality in Nineteenth-Century French Medicine." *French Historical Studies* 16 (1989): 48–71.

———. *Masculinity and Male Codes of Honor in Modern France.* New York: Oxford University Press, 1993.

Offen, Karen. "Body Politics: Women, Work and the Politics of Motherhood in France, 1920–1950." In *Maternity and Gender Policies: Women and the Rise of the European Welfare States, 1880–1950s*, edited by Gisela Bock and Pat Thane, pp. 138–59. London: Routledge, 1991.

———. "Depopulation, Nationalism, and Feminism in Fin-De-Siècle France." *American Historical Review* 89 (1984): 648–76.

Pedersen, Jean Elisabeth. "Regulating Abortion and Birth Control: Gender, Medicine, and Republican Politics in France, 1870–1920." *French Historical Studies* 19 (1996): 673–98.

Pedersen, Susan. *Family, Dependence, and the Origins of the Welfare State: Britain and France, 1914–1945.* Cambridge: Cambridge University Press, 1993.

Perrot, Jean-Claude. "Les Economistes, les philosophes et la population," In *Histoire de la population française*, edited by J. Dupâquier, 2:499–551. Paris: Presses Universitaires de France, 1988.

———. *Une Histoire intellectuelle de l'économie politique (XVIIe-XVIIIe siècle).* Paris: Ecole des hautes études en sciences sociales, 1992.

Perrot, Jean-Claude, and Stuart Woolf. *State and Statistics in France, 1789–1815.* New York: Harwood Academic Publishers, 1984.

Perrot, Michelle. *Enquêtes sur la condition ouvrière en France au XIXe siècle.* Paris: Hachette, 1972.

———. "Malthusianism and Socialism." In *Malthus Past and Present*, edited by Jacques Dupâquier and A. Fauve-Chamoux, pp. 257–74. London: Academic Press, 1983.

———. "Premières mesures des faits sociaux: Les debuts de la statistique criminelle en France, 1780–1830." In *Pour une histoire de la statistique*, vol. 1. Paris: Institut national de la statistique et des études économiques, 1977.

Petchesky, Rosalind Pollack. *Abortion and Women's Choice: The State, Sexuality, and Reproductive Freedom.* New York: Longman, 1984.

Petersen, William. *Malthus.* Cambridge, Mass.: Harvard University Press, 1979.

Pollard, Miranda. *Reign of Virtue: Mobilizing Gender in Vichy France.* Chicago: University of Chicago Press, 1998.

Poovey, Mary. *Making a Social Body: British Cultural Formation, 1830–1864.* Chicago: University of Chicago Press, 1995.

———. *Uneven Developments: The Ideological Work of Gender in Mid-Victorian England.* Chicago: University of Chicago Press, 1988.

Porter, Theodore. *The Rise of Statistical Thinking, 1820–1900.* Princeton: Princeton University Press, 1986.

——. *Trust in Numbers: The Pursuit of Objectivity in Science and Public Life.* Princeton: Princeton University Press, 1995.

Pour une histoire de la statistique. Paris: Institut national de la statistique et des études économiques, 1977.

Procacci, Giovanna. *Gouverner la misère: La question sociale en France.* Paris: Seuil, 1993.

——. "Social Economy and the Government of Poverty." In *The Foucault Effect: Studies in Governmentality,* edited by Graham Burchell, Colin Gordon, and Peter Miller, pp. 151–68. London: Harvester Wheatsleaf, 1991.

Quine, Maria Sophia. *Population Politics and Twentieth-Century Europe: Fascist Dictatorships and Liberal Democracies.* New York: Routledge, 1996.

Rabinow, Paul. *French Modern: Norms and Forms of the Social Environment.* Cambridge, Mass.: MIT Press, 1989.

Ramsey, Matthew. *Professional and Popular Medicine in France, 1770–1830: The Social World of Medical Practice.* Cambridge: Cambridge University Press, 1988.

Reddy, William. *The Rise of Market Culture: The Textile Trade and French Society, 1750–1900.* Cambridge: Cambridge University Press, 1984.

Reggiani, Andrés Horacio. "Procreating France: The Politics of Demography, 1919–1945." *French Historical Studies* 19 (1996): 725–54.

Rigaudias-Weiss, H. *Les Enquêtes ouvrières en France entre 1830 et 1848.* Paris: Presses Universitaires de France, 1936.

Riley, Denise. *Am I That Name? Feminism and the Category of 'Women' in History.* London: Macmillan, 1988.

Roberts, Mary-Louise. *Civilization without Sexes: Reconstructing Gender in Postwar France, 1917–1927.* Chicago: University of Chicago Press, 1994.

Rollet-Echalier, Catherine. *La Politique à l'égard de la petite enfance sous la IIIe République.* Paris: Presses Universitaires de France, 1990.

Ronsin, Francis. *La Grève des ventres: Propagande néo-malthusienne et baisse de la natalité en France 19e–20e siècles.* Paris: Aubier Montaigne, 1980.

——. "Liberté, natalité: Réaction et répression anti-malthusiennes avant 1900." *Recherche* 29 (1977): 365–93.

Rosanvallon, Pierre. *L'Etat en France de 1789 à nos jours.* Paris: Seuil, 1990.

Rosen, George. "The Philosophy of Ideology and the Emergence of Modern Medicine in France." *Bulletin of the History of Medicine* 20 (1946): 328–39.

Ryder, Norman B. "The Character of Modern Fertility." *Annals of the American Academy of Political and Social Science* 369 (1967): 26–36.

Schafer, Sylvia. *Children in Moral Danger and the Problem of Government in Third Republic France.* Princeton: Princeton University Press, 1997.

Schiebinger, Londa. *Nature's Body: Gender in the Making of Modern Science.* Boston: Beacon, 1993.

Schneider, William. *Quality and Quantity: The Quest for Biological Regeneration in Twentieth-Century France.* Cambridge: Cambridge University Press, 1990.

——. "Toward the Improvement of the Human Race: The History of Eugenics in France." *Journal of Modern History* 54 (1982): 268–91.

Schor, Naomi. *Breaking the Chain: Women, Theory, and French Realist Fiction.* New York: Columbia University Press, 1985.

Schweber, Libby. "The Assertion of Disciplinary Claims in Demography and

Vital Statistics: France and England, 1830–1885." Ph.D. dissertation, Princeton University, 1996.

Scott, Joan. *Only Paradoxes to Offer: French Feminism and the Rights of Man*. Cambridge, Mass.: Harvard University Press, 1996.

——. "'L'ouvrière! Mot impie, sordide': Women Workers in the Discourse of French Political Economy." In Joan Scott, *Gender and the Politics of History*, pp. 139–63. New York: Columbia University Press, 1988.

——. "A Statistical Representation of Work: 'Le Statistique de L'Industrie à Paris, 1847–48.'" In Joan Scott, *Gender and the Politics of History*, pp. 113–38. New York: Columbia University Press, 1988.

Scott, Joan, and Louise Tilly. *Women, Work, and Family*. New York: Holt, Rinehart, and Winston, 1978.

Shorter, Edward. *The Making of the Modern Family*. New York: Basic Books, 1975.

Smith, Bonnie. *Ladies of the Leisure Class*. Princeton: Princeton University Press, 1981.

Smith, Jay. *The Culture of Merit: Nobility, Royal Service, and the Making of the Absolute Monarchy in France, 1600–1789*. Ann Arbor: University of Michigan Press, 1996).

Smith, Kenneth. *The Malthusian Controversy*. New York: Octagon, 1978.

Soloway, Richard Allen. *Birth Control and the Population Question in England, 1877–1930*. Chapel Hill: University of North Carolina Press, 1982.

Sowerwine, C. "Madeleine Pelletier (1874–1939): Femme, médicin, militante." *L'Information psychiatrique* 9 (1988): 1183–93.

Spengler, Joseph J. *France Faces Depopulation*. Durham: Duke University Press, 1979.

——. *French Predecessors of Malthus*. Durham: Duke University Press, 1942.

Spiegel, Henry William. *The Growth of Economic Thought*. Durham: Duke University Press, 1991.

Staum, Martin. *Cabanis: Enlightenment and Medical Philosophy in the French Revolution*. Princeton: Princeton University Press, 1980.

Steinmetz, George. *Regulating the Social: The Welfare State and Local Politics in Imperial Germany*. Princeton: Princeton University Press, 1993.

Stewart, Mary Lynn. *Women, Work, and the French State*. Montreal: McGill-Queen's University Press, 1989.

Stigler, Stephen. *The History of Statistics*. Cambridge, Mass: Belknap Press of Harvard University Press, 1986.

Sussman, George. *Selling Mother's Milk: The Wet Nursing Business in France, 1715–1914*. Urbana: University of Illinois Press, 1982.

Szreter, Simon. *Fertility, Class and Gender in Britain, 1860–1940*. Cambridge: Cambridge University Press, 1996.

Talmy, Robert. *Histoire du mouvement familial en France, 1896–1939*. Paris: Union national des caisses d'allocations familiales, 1962.

Teitelbaum, Michael, and J. M. Winter, eds. *The Fear of Population Decline*. Orlando: Academic Press, 1985.

——. *Population and Resources in Western Intellectual Traditions*. Cambridge: Cambridge University Press, 1988.

Tilly, Louise. "Individual Lives and Family Strategies in the French Proletariat." In *Family and Sexuality in French History*, edited by Robert Wheaton and Tamara K. Hareven. Philadelphia: University of Pennsylvania Press, 1980.

Todorov, Tzvetan. *On Human Diversity: Racism, Nationalism, and Exoticism in French Thought.* Cambridge, Mass.: Harvard University Press, 1993.

Tomaselli, Sylvana. "Moral Philosophy and Population Questions in Eighteenth-Century Europe." In *Population and Resources in Western Intellectual Traditions*, edited by Michael Teitelbaum and Jay Winter. Cambridge: Cambridge University Press, 1988.

Tomlinson, Richard. "The Disappearance of France, 1896–1940: French Politics and the Birthrate." *Historical Journal* 28 (1985): 405–15.

Tomlinson, Richard, Marie-Monique Huss, and Philip E. Ogden. "France in Peril: The French Fear of Dénatalité." *History Today* 35 (April 1985): 24–31.

Van de Walle, Etienne. "La Fécondité française au XIXe siècle." *Communications* 44 (1986): 35–45.

Vedrenne-Villeneuve, Edmonde. "L'Inégalité sociale devant la mort dans la première moitié du XIXe siècle." *Population* 16 (1961): 665–99.

Walkowitz, Judith. *Prostitution and Victorian Society: Women, Class, and the State.* Cambridge: Cambridge University Press, 1980.

Weeks, Jeffrey. "Foucault for Historians." *History Workshop* 14 (1983): 106–19.

———. *Sex, Politics, and Society: The Regulation of Sexuality since 1800.* New York: Longman, 1989.

Weiner, D. B. "Public Health under Napoleon: The Conseil de salubrité de Paris, 1802–1815." *Clio Medica* 9 (1974): 271–84.

Weisz, George. "The Politics of Medical Professionalization in France, 1845–48." *Journal of Social History* 12 (1978): 3–30.

Weissbach, Lee Shai. *Child Labor Reform in Nineteenth-Century France: Assuring the Future Harvest.* Baton Rouge: Louisiana State University Press, 1989.

White, Hayden. *Metahistory: The Historical Imagination in Nineteenth-Century Europe.* Baltimore: Johns Hopkins University Press, 1973.

Winch, Donald. *Riches and Poverty: An Intellectual History of Political Economy in Britain, 1750–1834.* Cambridge: Cambridge University Press, 1996.

Woolf, Stuart. "Towards the History of the Origins of Statistics: France, 1789–1815." In *State and Statistics in France, 1789–1815*, edited by Jean-Claude Perrot and Stuart Woolf. New York: Harwood Academic Publishers, 1984.

Wrigley, E. A. "The Fall of Marital Fertility in Nineteenth-Century France." *European Journal of Population* (1985): 31–60, 141–77.

———. "Introduction: What Was the Industrial Revolution?" In *Population, Cities and Wealth, The Transformation of Traditional Society*, edited by E. A. Wrigley, pp. 1–17. Oxford: Basil Blackwell, 1987.

Wrigley, E. A., R. S. Davies, J. E. Oeppen, and R. S. Schofield. *English Population History from Family Reconstitution, 1580–1837.* Cambridge: Cambridge University Press, 1997.

Zeldin, Theodore. *France, 1848–1945: Anxiety and Influence.* Oxford: Oxford University Press, 1981.

INDEX